lass

Jenifer Roberts has been fascinated by the Lyne Stephens fortune since childhood. After family papers came into her possession, she began to research the story and soon learnt that the dramatic *cause célèbre* which held England in thrall for almost a century had vanished from public consciousness. And as her research into the early years of the fortune took her to Portugal, she realised that an even more extraordinary story lay buried in the archives of Lisbon and Marinha Grande.

In addition to her historical work, the author is well-known in photographic circles. A book of her black and white landscape photographs, *Spirit of the Place*, was published by Creative Monochrome in 1992. She is a Fellow of the Royal Photographic Society and has held several one-woman exhibitions in major galleries in London and the provinces.

Glass

The Strange History of the Lyne Stephens Fortune

JENIFER ROBERTS

TEMPLETON PRESS

First published in 2003
by Templeton Press

A CIP catalogue record for this book
is available from the British Library.

ISBN 0 9545589 0 1

Typeset by Tradespools, Frome
Printed and bound in Great Britain by
Antony Rowe Ltd, Chippenham

Templeton Press
42 The Common, Langley Burrell
Chippenham SN15 4LQ

To the memory of my mother,
who introduced me to the story

Contents

CONTENTS

Illustrations

Author's Note

When I was a child, my mother told me of a great fortune in the family. Her grandfather, a lawyer in Cornwall, was one of the beneficiaries but he invested unwisely in tin mines and sold his interest in 1861 to pay off his debts. Over the years, I met a number of distant cousins who also remembered a family fortune, some of them with boxes tucked away in lofts and garages containing papers proving their lineage.

Details had been lost down the generations. We knew only that the wealth was acquired by relatives in Portugal and, when their second cousin (my great-grandfather's great-uncle) inherited the fortune in 1826, he added their name to his. Curious to know more, I began to research the family in English records and then, by chance, I met the cultural counsellor of the Portuguese Embassy. She offered her help, gave me a list of contacts in Portugal, and soon I was learning of the Stephens brothers and the vast fortune they made in a glass factory in Marinha Grande.

MONETARY VALUES AND CURRENCY: There were several periods of inflation and deflation during the course of this story. One pound sterling in 1750 would be worth £81 today. The value dropped to £71 in 1760, to £60 in 1780, and to £31 by 1800. It recovered after 1815, reached a high of £52 in 1822, then declined to £39 in 1825. During the next sixty years, it ranged between £38 and £56. It began to increase in the mid-1880s, rising to a maximum of £59 in 1893, then declined to around £54 in the first years of the new century. By 1908, it had fallen to £52.[1]

The significance of historical values in present-day terms is also affected by the size of the economy. In the past, the owner of a million pounds in today's values owned proportionally more of the economy – and was far wealthier – than a millionaire today. I have not taken this into account when making calculations of present-day values, which should therefore be viewed as understatements.

The Portuguese currency of the eighteenth and early nineteenth centuries was based on a decimal system. There were many different coins in circulation, but the basic unit was the *real* which had an insignificant value. One thousand *reis* (the plural of *real*) formed a *milreis*, in which accounts were maintained and payments made, and one thousand *milreis* formed a *conto* of *reis* (a million *reis*). The *milreis* was worth about 5s. 7d. in English money, a little over three and a half *milreis* to the pound sterling. One *conto* of *reis* was worth around £286.

Varying values of the pound sterling are not a reliable indicator of present-day values of the Portuguese *milreis*, but I have sometimes used such calculations to give an idea of scale.

THE CALENDAR: The Gregorian calendar was introduced into most European countries, including Portugal, in the late sixteenth century but not adopted in England until September 1752. The difference in time between the Gregorian and the old Julian calendar was eleven days. For example, 1 January in the Julian calendar (Old Style) became 12 January in the Gregorian (New Style). Therefore, during the first years of this story, dates in England were eleven days behind dates in Portugal.

The New Year started on 25 March in the Julian calendar but, in September 1752, it was brought forward to 1 January. As a result, January, February and most of March changed from being the last months of the old year to the first months of the new. Although the convention for transcribing such dates is to use both Old and New Style (1 January 1750/1), only New Style is used in the text to date events prior to 1752.

ACKNOWLEDGEMENTS: I should like to thank everyone who assisted me in my research, particularly Professor José Pedro Barosa, without whose enthusiasm, help and encouragement this book could never have been written. Over a period of several years, Professor Barosa responded with courtesy and generosity to my constant requests for information about the glass industry in Portugal in the eighteenth and nineteenth centuries, a subject on which he is the acknowledged authority. He guided my research, provided material, read the manuscript with a careful eye, and made many helpful suggestions.

Luís de Abreu e Sousa looked after me in Marinha Grande, collected information, and talked about the history of his home town. Graça Rodrigues, cultural counsellor at the Portuguese Embassy in London, offered invaluable help at an early stage of my research. The mayor of Câmara Municipal da Marinha Grande granted access to several thousand letters in his care, and Paula Maia, archivist at Marinha Grande, undertook the lengthy task of reading the letters and sending me a précis of their contents. Ana Margarida Magalhães carried out research in Lisbon; Clive Gilbert of the British Historical Society of Portugal was generous with his time; and Yvonne Cova and Christine Robinson spent many hours helping with translations.

I am grateful to the late Carlos Vitorino da Silva Barros, who transcribed a large number of original documents in his book, *Real Fábrica de Vidros da Marinha Grande, II Centenário 1769–1969* (Lisbon, 1969), and to Emília Margarida Marques, who transcribed further documents in her study, *O Período Stephens: na Real Fábrica de Vidros da Marinha Grande* (Santos Barosa, Estudos e Documentos no. 11 March 1999). These publications give a comprehensive picture of the factories in Alcântara and Marinha Grande during the period of my story.

In England, Henry and Mary Bedingfeld provided access to many historical papers and entertained me with generous hospitality. Sir Jonathan Backhouse provided information on the Claremont family; Ivor Guest shared his research into the dancing years of Yolande Duvernay; and Philip Wilkins showed me around the church of Our Lady and the English Martyrs in Cambridge. Joanna Mattingly provided information on sailing dates of Lisbon packets; Jenny Allsop gave me a tour of Melton Mowbray; David Hamilton sent information on chancery fraud; and Monica Jenks in New Zealand provided copies of family letters.

I have also received help from Sarah Millard, archivist at the Bank of England; Roger Ward, historian of Chicksands Priory; Jane Read, archivist at Froebel College; and Sister Mary Coke, archivist at the Convent of the Sacred Heart in Roehampton.

Thanks are due to the staff of the British Library; Cornish Studies Library; Courtney Library (Royal Institution of Cornwall); Greater London Archives; Guildhall Library (Corporation of London); Hammersmith and Fulham Archives; Public Record Office; Wandsworth Local History Library; the library of the British Historical Society of Portugal (Lisbon branch); and the Record Offices of Bedfordshire, Cornwall, Devon, North Devon, and Norfolk. Their knowledge and kindness greatly simplified my work.

Finally, I am deeply grateful to my husband, Paul Beck, for his patience over the years, his company and help on most of my travels, and his tolerance as I worked long hours on the manuscript. I owe him far more than these words can express.

PERMISSIONS: Permission to quote from original material has been granted by Christ's Hospital Museum and Archive and the Governors of Christ's Hospital; the Banks Project at the Natural History Museum; Froebel Archives for Childhood Studies, Froebel College; Câmara Municipal da Marinha Grande; and the British Historical Society of Portugal, Lisbon branch.

I am grateful to Henry Bedingfeld, Charles Lyne, Douglas Lyne, John Lyne, Monica Jenks and Phyllida Warner for permission to quote from letters and documents in their possession; to John Pym for permission to quote from his essay on Horace Pym (published in *Sentimental Journey* by Francis Pym, 1998); to Mrs Timothy Mitchell Ellis for permission to quote from the Portugal diary of William Julius Mickle (published in *The Visit to Portugal in 1779–80 of William Julius Mickle* by S George West, 1972); and to Ivor Guest for permission to use his translations of original French material.

I am also grateful to Donald D Horward for permission to quote from his book, *The French Campaign in Portugal 1810–1811* by Jean-Jacques Pelet (University of Minnesota Press, 1973); and to Oxford University Press for permission to use c.132 words from *Journals of a Residence in Portugal 1800–1801* by Robert Southey (edited by Adolfo Cabral, Clarendon Press, 1960).

Every effort has been made to contact copyright holders. The publisher would be interested to hear from any copyright holders not here acknowledged.

ILLUSTRATIONS: Many of the illustrations have come from a private collection and are reproduced by kind permission of the owner. Permissions for the other pictures are as follows: Arquivo Fotográfico, Câmara Municipal de Lisboa (no. 1); Mr Henry Bedingfeld (no. 11); Câmara Municipal da Marinha Grande (nos. 5, 6, 7, 8, 9, 14); Friends of Chicksands Priory (no. 19); reproduced by permission of the Governors of Christ's Hospital (no. 15); P J Loobey (nos. 29, 30); Mr John Lyne (nos. 18, 28); Museu Nacional de Arte Antiga, Lisbon, photographed by José Pessoa, Divisão de Documentação Fotográfica, Instituto Português de Museus (no. 4); National Maritime Museum Cornwall (nos. 2, 3); by courtesy of the National Portrait Gallery, London (no. 24); with the permission of the parish archive, Church of Our Lady and the English Martyrs, Cambridge (no. 37); Mr David Rose (no. 40); Royal Institution of Cornwall (no. 16); V&A Picture Library (no. 21).

August 2003

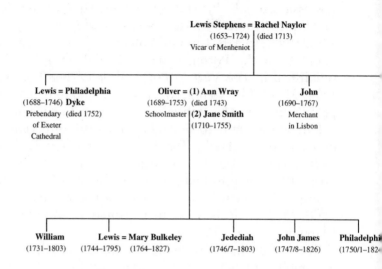

Lewis Stephens = Rachel Naylor
(1653–1724) | (died 1713)
Vicar of Menheniot

Lewis = Philadelphia
(1688–1746) **Dyke**
Prebendary (died 1752)
of Exeter
Cathedral

Oliver = (1) Ann Wray
(1689–1753) (died 1743)
Schoolmaster | (2) Jane Smith
(1710–1755)

John
(1690–1767)
Merchant
in Lisbon

William
(1731–1803)

Lewis = Mary Bulkeley
(1744–1795) (1764–1827)

Jedediah
(1746/7–1803)

John James
(1747/8–1826)

Philadelphia
(1750/1–1824)

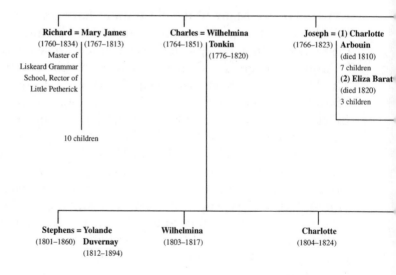

Richard = Mary James
(1760–1834) | (1767–1813)
Master of
Liskeard Grammar
School, Rector of
Little Petherick

10 children

Charles = Wilhelmina
(1764–1851) | **Tonkin**
(1776–1820)

Joseph = (1) Charlotte
(1766–1823) | **Arbouin**
(died 1810)
7 children
(2) Eliza Barat
(died 1820)
3 children

Stephens = Yolande
(1801–1860) **Duvernay**
(1812–1894)

Wilhelmina
(1803–1817)

Charlotte
(1804–1824)

The Stephens and Lyne Families

(only characters mentioned in the text are included)

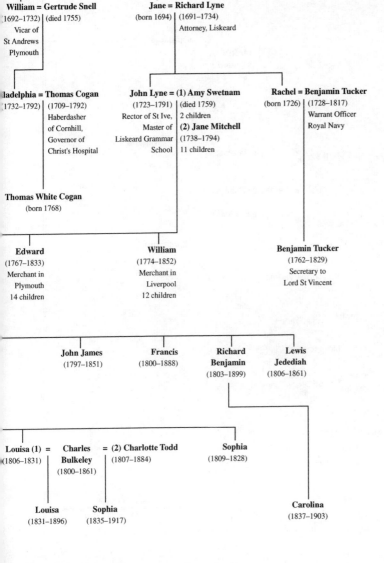

William = Gertrude Snell
(1692–1732) (died 1755)
Vicar of
St Andrews
Plymouth

Jane = Richard Lyne
(born 1694) (1691–1734)
Attorney, Liskeard

ladelphia = Thomas Cogan
(1732–1792) (1709–1792)
Haberdasher
of Cornhill,
Governor of
Christ's Hospital

John Lyne = (1) Amy Swetnam
(1723–1791) (died 1759)
Rector of St Ive, 2 children
Master of **(2) Jane Mitchell**
Liskeard Grammar (1738–1794)
School 11 children

Rachel = Benjamin Tucker
(born 1726) (1728–1817)
Warrant Officer
Royal Navy

Thomas White Cogan
(born 1768)

Edward
(1767–1833)
Merchant in
Plymouth
14 children

William
(1774–1852)
Merchant in
Liverpool
12 children

Benjamin Tucker
(1762–1829)
Secretary to
Lord St Vincent

John James
(1797–1851)

Francis
(1800–1888)

Richard Benjamin
(1803–1899)

Lewis Jedediah
(1806–1861)

Louisa (1) = Charles = (2) Charlotte Todd
(1806–1831) **Bulkeley** (1807–1884)
(1800–1861)

Sophia
(1809–1828)

Louisa
(1831–1896)

Sophia
(1835–1917)

Carolina
(1837–1903)

CENTRAL
PORTUGAL

COIMBRA

Mondego Bay

R. Mondego

Pombal

MARINHA
GRANDE

Leiria

Batalha

Tomar

São Martinho

Alcobaça

R. Tagus

Abrantes

Caldas da Rainha

Rio Maior

Alcoentre

Santarém

Torres Vedras

Mafra

Vila Franca

Montachique

R. Tagus

Cintra

Queluz

LISBON

N

Scale: in miles

0   5   10   15   20   25

xviii

PART ONE

William
The Years of Misfortune

Prelude
England

1730–1746

Five days before his twelfth birthday, William entered the church of St Mary Major in Exeter. He had never visited such a large town before, nor seen anything so imposing as St Peter's cathedral, its west front just a few yards from the cool interior of the parish church. Two days earlier, his mother had collected him from his grandparents' house in Cornwall and, sitting in the coach as it rattled along the roads, explained that she was going to Exeter to marry his father and they would live together in lodgings near the cathedral.

Jane Smith was nineteen years old when William was conceived.[1] Daughter of a yeoman farmer in the Cornish village of Pillaton, she was employed as a servant in the nearby parish of Landulph, working in the big house, Pentillie Castle. It was here that she met Oliver Stephens, who taught the children of the Pentillie estate in a school run by the local churchwarden.[2] Forty years old and trapped in a stale and childless marriage, Oliver was attracted by Jane and she, flattered by the attentions of an older man, soon returned his affections. As the summer of 1730 brought hot sunny days to Landulph, they would meet in the countryside and, one August evening, after their duties were done and they had slipped away separately and unseen, the warm earth of the Pentillie estate was a bed for their lovemaking.

Two months later, when the times for her monthly bleeds had come and gone, Jane returned to her parents in Pillaton.

3

When her belly began to swell, they sent her to relatives in Laneast, a hamlet in the foothills of Bodmin Moor. Here, on 16 May 1731, she gave birth to a son. Four days later, she carried her baby to church; the boy was baptised in the granite font and the curate filled in the register: "May 20, William, ye son of Jane Smith of Landulph, father unknown."[3]

Jane was loyal to Oliver. She refused to name him as father of her child but, twenty miles away in Landulph, her lover felt uneasy. The ecclesiastical court ruled in such matters and, if reported for adultery, he could lose his position as schoolmaster in the diocese. The wisest course was to leave the area and, having given notice to the churchwarden, he and his wife crossed the River Tamar into Devon.

Oliver came from an educated family. His father, Lewis Stephens (Fellow of Exeter College, Oxford, and a noted botanist), had been vicar of Menheniot in Cornwall for almost forty years; his mother was the daughter of Oliver Naylor, prebendary of Exeter cathedral and rector of Tavistock. Two of his brothers had followed their father into the church and his sisters had all married men of good family. Oliver, too, had been destined for Oxford and holy orders until, at the age of eighteen, he shocked his parents by eloping with a family servant.[4] His father refused to support him through university so he had found work as a teacher, but his positions were humble and poorly-paid for all schoolmasters of any standing were men of the church.

He moved to Exeter when his son was born and, with the help of his brother Lewis (a prebendary of the cathedral), obtained a position in a charity school for boys.[5] He found lodgings in Cathedral Close and kept in touch with Jane, who had returned to domestic service while William lived on his grandparents' farm in Pillaton. Oliver had to wait twelve years before he could meet his son and, when the time came, he showed no hesitation. A few days after his wife died in March 1743, he obtained a marriage licence and sent for Jane, who gave notice to her employers, collected William from Pillaton and set out on the journey to Exeter. They were

married in St Mary Major, then Oliver took his wife and son
to their new home in Cathedral Close.[6]

William's uncle (the prebendary) had obtained a place for
him in the Exeter Free Grammar School, which provided a
classical education for middle-class boys, preparing them for
entry to university or the professions. He was older than the
boys with whom he took lessons, for he was untutored in
Latin and had much work to do to catch up with pupils of his
own age. Every morning, he walked along the cobbled Close
to the lane which led to the High Street, then turned his steps
towards the East Gate and the old building of St John's
Hospital, where he spent his days reading Latin primers and
struggling with ancient grammar.

In the spring of 1744, a new headmaster arrived at the
school, fresh from Eton and Cambridge. He brought new
ideas of education and was an excellent teacher. He
emphasised the study of English and introduced arithmetic,
which allowed William to master book-keeping and accoun-
tancy. He taught contemporary culture and the boys
performed plays before the mayor and city dignitaries,
sometimes by classical authors but more often by modern
writers such as Richard Steele.[7] William was inspired by the
new master, speeding ahead with his schoolwork and
developing a love of literature and drama. He was taught
at home too, for Oliver was brought up in a learned
household and studied botany at his father's knee.

Meanwhile, his parents wasted little time in starting a new
family. His first brother was born in November 1744 and his
uncle came to Cathedral Close to baptise the boy with his
own name, Lewis.[8] Eighteen months later, shortly before Jane
became pregnant with another boy (named Jedediah),
William had caught up with his age group at the Grammar
School and was studying the works of Horace, Cicero and
Seneca. With his fifteenth birthday approaching, his studies
were coming to an end; his father could not afford to send
him to university and it was time to find employment.

William was attracted by the idea of a mercantile career. Several of his schoolfriends were sons of merchants, for Exeter had a thriving trade in woollens. Over to France, Holland, Portugal and Spain went the woollen cloth, and back came wine, a lucrative trade which enriched the merchants who congregated on open spaces around the cathedral to discuss the latest business and mercantile news. On his few half-days from school, William watched the merchants from the windows of his lodgings and sometimes he spent time amongst them, eavesdropping on their conversations.

One of Oliver's brothers was a merchant in Lisbon and it was soon arranged that William would be apprenticed to his uncle for seven years, sailing to Portugal on the Post Office packet boat from Falmouth. In the early summer, Oliver took leave from his charity school to accompany his son to Cornwall. He delivered him into the care of the captain, then watched from the shore as the packet slipped its moorings and set sail for the open sea.

1

A Young Merchant

1746–1755

"He who never saw Lisbon never saw a fine thing."
Old Portuguese proverb

*"A great body of his Majesty's trading subjects reside at Lisbon, rich,
opulent, and every day increasing their fortunes... These people can be
said to be under no government but that of their own opinion."*
Lord Tyrawley, April 1752

The packet service used brigantines, the smallest of the
square-rigged sailing ships. Less than a hundred feet long and
twenty-three feet wide, they were tossed about on the rough
waters of the Bay of Biscay and most travellers complained of
sea-sickness. William suffered too, spending the first two
days in a tiny cabin just six feet by three. "Here," wrote
another passenger, "the poor devil is confined in a dark and
dismal hole below the level of the water, with the waves
roaring in his ears. The depression which accompanies the
sickness deprives the mind of all its energy."[1]

William felt better on his third morning at sea. Leaving the
cabin, he spent his days on deck, watching sailors at work
and scanning the horizon, for England was at war with
France and there was danger from enemy vessels. Just a few
weeks earlier, British merchants had complained of the large
number of privateers which preyed on shipping and one of
the Lisbon packets had recently disappeared without trace.[2]
But the voyage passed uneventfully, the days became warmer
and, as the coast of Portugal came into view, William saw its
brown hills fringed with sandy beaches. Soon the ship moved
into a bay lined with palaces and villas, and reached Belém

where the bay narrowed into the River Tagus. All vessels dropped anchor here, and waited for customs and health officials to come aboard and inspect the passengers and their luggage.

William looked around him. The fortified tower of Belém occupied a small island near the shore; behind it stood the monastery of Jerónimos, the vast, exuberant building constructed during the age of discovery, the years when Portugal had been a great maritime power. On the far side of the Tagus lay a range of folded hills and, when the ship set sail again and rounded a bend in the river, he saw the city of Lisbon rising up its seven hills, its domes and towers gleaming in the sunshine.

After landing formalities had been completed and he had met his uncle at the quayside, William began to absorb his new surroundings. Bathed in the bright light of a Portuguese summer, the city rambled over steep slopes, its narrow streets lined with four and five storey houses. Merchants and the upper classes travelled on horseback or in two-wheeled chaises drawn by mules, while the streets and squares were crowded with beggars and negro slaves and thousands of feral dogs which roamed the city at night, scavenging and fighting. Raised in a Cornish village and the sober environment of clerical Exeter, William was astounded by the noise of so many people and animals, by the glare of sunlight on pale stone, by the stench of rubbish piled high in the streets.

During the next few days, he discovered that every large building was a church, monastery or convent, all adorned with statues, gold and silver candlesticks, reliquaries and monstrances studded with precious stones. As he walked through the city, he met processions of priests and friars carrying relics or statues; everyone fell to their knees as they passed and William learnt that he too must kneel to avoid arrest for heresy. And sometimes, at night, the main square was filled with torches and flaming pyres as victims of the Inquisition suffered and died for their convictions.

John Stephens lived above his counting-house near the river and William was put to work as a clerk, copying correspondence, working on invoices and accounts, and learning the lucrative business of Anglo-Portuguese trade. English merchants in Lisbon were laden with privileges. Under several treaties, they were exempt from domestic taxes, from the jurisdiction of Portuguese courts, and from most commercial regulations. Through their activities, Portugal had become reliant on imports, unable to feed or clothe its people from its own resources. It depended on imports of textiles, of wheat, fish and other foodstuffs, which it paid for in gold from the mines of Brazil; and because of the advantages conferred by treaty, it was British merchants who handled the bulk of this highly profitable trade.

A few weeks after William's arrival, the English Factory in Lisbon (a trade organisation for British merchants) arranged a celebration in honour of the Duke of Cumberland and his recent victory over the Scottish rebels at Culloden. "We are preparing so elegant an entertainment," wrote the British envoy on 24 August, "to which the secretary of state, the presidents of the tribunals, and all the grandees in town have been invited."[3] Two pavilions were built in the garden of the envoy's house, the largest in the form of a Roman temple with a portrait of the Duke of Cumberland placed on a gilded throne in the portico. The pavilions were lit by crystal chandeliers, the walls hung with crimson damask, the floors laid with tapestry.[4]

As well as the grandees and aristocrats, most English merchants had been invited and, on a warm autumn evening, dressed in silk clothes and powdered wig, William accompanied his uncle to the envoy's house in the suburb of Buenos Aires. Sixty soldiers stood guard as carriages and chaises clattered into the courtyard, and a military band welcomed the guests as they entered the house for refreshments. At seven o'clock, they crossed an illuminated bridge to the temple pavilion where musicians played and the cream of Lisbon society danced minuets. Dinner was served shortly before midnight, twenty-nine courses accompanied by different wines, then the tables were removed and younger merchants danced until the sun rose in the morning.[5]

William was enchanted; he had never seen anything so elegant, so opulent, so extravagant. He watched the servants move around the pavilion and realised how dramatically his circumstances had changed. Bastard grandchild of a yeoman farmer, he now belonged to the rich, self-confident British community in Lisbon, one of the wealthiest cities in Europe.

For the next four years, William worked long hours in his uncle's counting-house but, despite the advantages conferred by treaty, John's trading house was bankrupted (or "broken" as it was known at the time) in 1750.[6] William was eighteen years old, just halfway through his apprenticeship, and the next few months were an anxious time for him – and for his parents in Exeter to whom he wrote by every packet boat. His prospects improved in 1751 when George Medley, a merchant returning to London, employed William and another young man to act as his agents in Lisbon. They would receive commission on the sale of goods shipped to the Tagus, as well as on products (wine, fruit and salt) sent to England on the return voyage.[7]

Having impressed George Medley with his intelligence and administrative skills, William was not required to complete the final years of his apprenticeship. He and his partner dealt with all aspects of book-keeping and bills of exchange, sent copies of correspondence to their employer in London, and kept him informed of the latest information on trade and diplomatic relations. And in Exeter, Jane and Oliver celebrated their son's good fortune by naming their latest (short-lived) baby, George Medley Stephens.[8]

Meanwhile, a new political regime was taking shape in Portugal. In July 1750, Dom José I succeeded to the throne on the death of his father (João V) and, having no taste or capacity for public affairs, appointed three ministers to run the country for him. One of these, the highly ambitious

Sebastião de Carvalho e Melo, was newly returned from a diplomatic appointment in Vienna where he had married a member of the Austrian aristocracy, a marriage which led him into the favour of João's Austrian-born queen. João himself had never trusted Carvalho, calling him a man with "a hairy heart," but his widow had great influence over her son. "Carvalho may be looked upon as the principal minister," explained the French chargé d'affaires a few weeks after José inherited the throne. "He is indefatigable, active and expeditious. He has won the confidence of the king and, in all political matters, none has it more than he."[9]

Carvalho, known to history as the Marquês de Pombal, was an imposing man, six feet tall, with a long face and handsome features. Before moving to Vienna, he had spent several years as Portuguese envoy in London. He was impressed by the success of the English middle classes, but angry that the government granted no reciprocal privileges to Portuguese merchants (although bound to do so by treaty). He also had many complaints about the treatment of the small Portuguese community; even the sailors suffered as Londoners threw stones at them, telling them to go back to their own country and stop taking bread and beer from the mouths of honest Englishmen.[10]

Such behaviour rankled with a man who was aware that English merchants in Portugal had appropriated a large part of his country's trade and commerce. He nursed his anti-British sentiments during his years in Vienna and, now he was rising to power in his own country, he set out to curb the privileges of the English Factory. "The government is inclined to discourage us in all branches," wrote the merchants a few years later. "They attack us whenever they can and study every artifice to burden and embarrass our commerce. Almost every day produces something new and, though it be in trifles that at first are disregarded, still so many creep upon us that trade must in the end sink under the weight of them."[11]

Most of all, Carvalho wanted power, an ambition that made him as unpopular with the Portuguese as he was with the English Factory. Less than four years after the change of government, the British envoy referred to the minister's "haughty airs." He was, he wrote, "universally disliked, not to give it a harsher name. This he cannot but realise and it makes him jealous of every man, native or foreigner. The queen mother has lost her influence over her son and greatly regrets having saddled him with Monsieur de Carvalho."[12]

As the minister strengthened his position in the court of Dom José, William was proving to be a successful agent and, on 17 July 1752, he was elected a member of the English Factory.[13] Although membership depended mainly on an ability to pay the contributions required, it was a much coveted achievement. Applicants had to prove that they were making money from trade, had paid their dues and tariffs on time, and were earning sufficient profits to pay their contributions.

Factory meetings were rowdy occasions. As Carvalho said to Lord Tyrawley (a British envoy on special mission), "You have many merchants here of worth and prudence, but you also have many young people in the Factory who affect to lead and govern others and whose conduct is by no means prudent."[14] Writing to London eight days before William's election, Tyrawley hoped these younger merchants would "take my advice and act with more caution, though I am far from being the guarantee of either."[15] A few months later, he received a letter from an older merchant, referring to an altercation, "which caused such clamour as I never saw till then. A great deal of foul language and unmannerly reflections were thrown out on various subjects, and many other shocking things, all proceeding from spleen and passion." And there was a postscript: "I beg your Lordship to keep this letter to yourself, being unwilling to bring on my head this nest of wasps."[16]

In October, a new British consul arrived in Lisbon to take the chair at Factory meetings. George Crowle was inexperienced in mercantile affairs and found it difficult to control the merchants. "Since I have been here" he wrote to London on 5 November, "I have received great civility from gentlemen of the Factory, but still a very unpleasant spirit prevaileth and nothing but grievances are talked of. I hope this violent spirit will soon cease, but it will be some time before things are brought into their proper channel."[17]

William attended meetings and signed letters and petitions, but he felt uneasy during the early months of his membership. Merchants in Exeter never behaved so boisterously and his uncle John was an even-tempered man who had learnt his manners in the vicarage at Menheniot. But William was young and enthusiastic, and the next time Carvalho tampered with trading privileges, he was ready to add his voice to the clamour of complaint.

Harvests in the Iberian peninsula had been poor for several years and, by the autumn of 1753, Spain was threatened with famine. Cargoes of British corn arrived regularly in the Tagus but, with higher prices prevailing across the border, Carvalho was concerned that merchants would send their cargoes to Spain, leaving Portugal with insufficient grain. He drew up regulations forbidding the re-exportation of corn and ordered that all grain entering the city should be delivered to a central entrepôt for distribution to Lisbon market traders.

The merchants were alarmed at these orders, which were in breach of privileges granted by treaty (under which English traders could import all types of merchandise and sell it as they pleased without impediment). Grain which they hoped to re-export was sitting in ships in the harbour, in danger of deterioration, while the vessels were unable to be reloaded with produce for England. The British envoy arranged a meeting with Carvalho and, when he explained the situation, the minister's face hardened. "What!" he said, "would you pretend to be entitled to greater privileges than the Portuguese themselves?" Carvalho was aware that English merchants were indeed entitled to greater privileges than the

Portuguese, so the envoy answered, "Yes, Sir," and quoted the words of the treaty.[18]

Meanwhile, George Crowle had refused to sign a petition from Factory members to the secretary of state in London. He considered the wording to be biased and exaggerated (the new regulations being imposed, according to the merchants, "in an unreasonable manner and on the most trifling pretences, to the great prejudice and even peril of ruin to many of his Majesty's subjects").[19] Dated 10 September, the petition was delivered to the envoy after the consul refused to sign it and Crowle, who had suffered abuse on several occasions, chose not to attend the next two meetings of the Factory.[20]

Angered at his absence, the members persuaded him to chair a meeting on 25 September. As the consul restated his opinion that the Factory had no justifiable complaint, shouts of "Sir, that is false" erupted from the members. A few minutes later, when Crowle explained that the wording of a treaty, "should not prevent the king of Portugal from making what laws he pleases to prevent famine in his country," a young merchant jumped to his feet. "If you will sacrifice the rights of the nation," he yelled at the consul, "you will be a traitor to your king and an enemy to your country." Shocked and angry, Crowle muttered to himself, hitched up his breeches, and left the room.[21]

He refused to attend any further meetings and, on 19 October, the merchants wrote a letter of complaint to London. Addressed to the secretary of state, it referred to the "mortification" felt by Factory members at Crowle's "persistent refusal to join with us in measures to procure redress of our many heavy grievances." Previous consuls had always agreed to measures resolved by a majority of members, whereas Crowle "appears activated by so strange a spirit that he sets himself in opposition to all proposals that might have eased ourselves of the calamities we suffer. We find he stands more and more in need of counsel in mercantile matters than anyone remembered by us in that office."[22]

The merchants nursed their anger for another eight months before the new regulations were suspended and they could once more import corn freely into Lisbon. Factory members rejoiced in the reinstatement of their privileges, but George Crowle was less fortunate. He was dismissed from office in June and died from a massive stroke three weeks later, never having recovered from his treatment by the merchants. "Their behaviour to me is without precedent," he had written to London, "and such conduct as obliged me to leave the assembly rather than be insulted. I did everything in my power to conciliate and gain all I could. Perhaps I should have obtained more if their behaviour had been more decent."[23]

William was troubled by the news, aware that he had played a part in the consul's distress. At the same time, he was anxious about his family in Exeter. His father had died in October and Jane was left with five children – the youngest a baby of seven months – and no money to pay the rent or buy food and clothing.[24] Lewis Stephens, the prebendary who had enrolled William in the Free Grammar School, had died several years earlier, so her two older boys were attending the charity school where their father had taught and where they were receiving a limited education.

Grieving for the father he had known for just three years, William sent money to Exeter but, over the following months, he received more worrying news. Jane's baby died and soon Jane herself became ill. In the spring of 1755, when it was clear she was dying, she arranged for her youngest son to be accepted by Christ's Hospital in London, a school for children of good family whose parents were unable to maintain them.[25] Only one child from a family could enter the Hospital and, although John James would not be admitted for at least a year, she knew he would be fed and housed and given a good education. Friends had promised to care for the other children but she asked William to provide for them; she wanted to die with her mind at rest, knowing they would be well looked after and given a proper schooling as their father would have wished.

William was earning generous commission on the sale of goods sent by his employer to Lisbon. As he strolled in the evening along the banks of the Tagus, meeting his Factory colleagues in the central square and walking with them along the marble quay near the custom-house, he considered bringing his brothers and sister to Lisbon. He could afford to employ servants and a tutor and, in time, the boys could be apprenticed to his merchant business.

Interlude

Exeter

1755

Jane died in late September and a letter was sent to Falmouth to await the Lisbon packet.[1] In normal circumstances and with favourable winds, William should have received the news between three and five weeks after the letter was posted.

A month later, during the afternoon of 1 November, the people of Exeter learned that high waves were battering the coast nearby. As the days passed, they heard news from further afield. At Kinsale in County Cork, a mass of water had poured into the harbour, breaking anchor cables and causing fishing boats to "whirl around like so many corks"; at St Ives in Cornwall, the sea had risen between eight and nine feet; at Plymouth, a bore had moved up the harbour, driving ships from their moorings. Then further reports came in. In the Scilly Isles, people had felt a trembling of the earth and rushed out of their houses, the ground had vibrated in Poole, and a gardener in Reading had felt the land move and watched the water oscillating in his fish pond.[2]

These events were the subject of much discussion amongst the people of Exeter, but it was not until three weeks later that they received an explanation.

2

Earthquake

1755–1756

"Our poor Factory, from a very opulent one, is totally ruined. There is hardly one merchant in a hundred that has saved anything, except some little part of their cash which they have been raking for among the ruins."
Abraham Castres, 19 November 1755

The morning of 1 November, All Saints' Day, was unseasonably warm in Lisbon. By half past nine, William was sitting at his desk on the first floor of his house, working on some papers; his partner was taking breakfast in another room.

At twenty to ten, he was disturbed by a noise which sounded like the king's heavy carriage rattling through the street. After a brief pause, the room began to shake and, as William left his desk and ran downstairs, the earth jerked itself upwards in a motion that felt like a wagon being driven violently over rough stones. The captain of a ship in the Tagus watched the buildings of Lisbon rocking to and fro like corn in the wind and, by the time William reached the street, they had begun to collapse in a deafening roar of destruction.[1]

Clouds of dust billowed into the air and William, frozen with terror, stood motionless as houses fell around him. And when the dust began to clear, he saw a swarm of people stumbling among the ruins. "Old, young, male and female, seeking their parents, children, relations and friends, many sick, many maimed from the fall of houses, some dead and most half naked, so dismal a sight as was never seen," wrote a woollens merchant in his pocket book that night. "Neither

18

can thought imagine the scenes of misery: the friars and priests giving absolution, confessing and praying with everyone; the coaches and chaises, horses and mules, buried under the ground; people under the ruins begging for assistance and none able to get near them; old people, hardly able to walk, without shoes and stockings."[2]

William pulled at the stones and the rubble, shouting for his partner, but he was in great danger – houses were still falling around him – and he soon set out for the safety of the river bank. His progress was hampered by piles of shattered stonework, by the distressed and injured people he tried to help, and by three giant waves, twenty feet high, which came speeding up the Tagus. "Turning my eyes towards the river," wrote an English merchant who had reached the low-lying area of São Paulo, "I perceived it heaving and swelling in a most unaccountable manner. In an instant, there appeared a vast body of water, rising like a mountain. It came on foaming and roaring, and rushed towards the shore with such impetuosity that, although we all ran for our lives, many were swept away."[3] Ships were ripped from their anchors and crashed into each other, while the waves tore at buildings on the foreshore and destroyed the marble quay near the custom-house.

Aftershocks continued throughout the morning and, by early afternoon, much of the city was in flames. The fall of curtains and woodwork onto the candles lit for All Saints' Day in every church and chapel in Lisbon led to numerous fires, which joined into one vast conflagration. Survivors fled towards open spaces and William fled too, clambering over the ruins towards the western suburbs. His way was littered with the dead and dying: "In some places lay coaches, with their masters, horses and riders almost crushed in pieces; here mothers with infants in their arms; there ladies richly dressed. Priests, friars, gentlemen, mechanics, some with their backs or thighs broken, others with vast stones on their breasts. Some lay almost buried in the rubbish and, crying out in vain for succour, were left to perish with the rest."[4]

White with dust, William made his way to the outskirts of the city and, as night fell, he found himself among crowds of confused and frightened people. "As it grew dark," wrote one merchant, "the whole city appeared in a blaze so bright I could easily see to read by it. The people were so dejected and terrified. Everyone had their eyes turned towards the flames and stood looking on with silent grief, interrupted by the shrieks of women and children whenever the earth began to tremble, which was so often this night that the tremors did not cease for a quarter of an hour together."[5]

"If you happened to forget yourself with sleep," wrote another, "you were awakened by the tremblings of the earth and the howlings of the people. Yet the moon shone, and the stars, with unusual brightness. Long wished-for day at last appeared and the sun rose with great splendour on the desolated city in the morning."[6]

It was another bright, sunny day and William made his way to a public house in Buenos Aires run by an Englishman, Joseph Morley, whose house had been damaged in the earthquake but whose garden was full of refugees. During the next few days, he searched the suburbs and was delighted to find his uncle and most of his fellow merchants. "It is inconceivable," wrote one of them, "the vast joy it gave us to meet our friends again. Each looked upon the other as risen from the dead and, all having a wonderful escape to relate, all were equally satisfied to have preserved their lives."[7] But despite an exhaustive search, William failed to find his partner and had to presume that his body lay buried in the ruins of their counting-house.[8]

Fanned by a north-east wind, the fires in the city burned for six days, watched by the refugees in the suburbs. And when the flames died down, they returned to Lisbon and moved with difficulty through the rubble. "It is not to be expressed by human tongue," wrote the captain of a ship who ventured ashore, "how dreadful and awful it was to enter the city after the fire was abated. Looking upwards, one was struck with terror in beholding pyramids of ruined fronts, some inclining one way, some another. Then one was struck with horror in beholding dead bodies, six or seven in a heap, crushed to death, half buried and half burnt. And nothing to be met with but people bewailing their misfortunes, wringing their hands and crying the world is at an end."⁹

The area where William lived and worked was the worst affected. "The part of the town near the water," explained the British consul, "where most of the merchants dwelt for the convenience of transacting their business, is so totally destroyed by the earthquake and the fire that it is nothing but a heap of rubbish."¹⁰ Warehouses had been destroyed as well as counting-houses and, as the envoy wrote to London, "Our poor Factory, from a very opulent one, is totally ruined. There is hardly one merchant in a hundred that has saved anything, except some little part of their cash which they have been raking for among the ruins. As to their goods, their houses being burned to ashes, not one of them has been able to save a rag, nor can the Portuguese pay one single shilling of what they owe them."¹¹

Responsible to George Medley for his agency business, William ventured into the city and clambered over the ruins until he found the heaps of blackened stonework that had been his home and counting-house. "Oh, dreadful sight!" wrote one of his friends who searched the ruins in a nearby street. "Dead bodies, some halfway up in the rubbish, standing like statues, and the stench so great it was impossible to stay long."¹² Digging around in the rubble, William may have rescued a metal box or a pile of fused coins. He may also have found the body of his partner but he had to leave it there, lying in the ruins, until a team of workmen threw it on a cart and took it away for dumping at sea.

Sebastião de Carvalho had taken charge of the situation. His house in the upper town remained intact and, as soon as the first panic subsided, he had driven to the king's palace in Belém. "What can be done?" José asked his minister, to which Carvalho replied, "Bury the dead and feed the living."[13] Given full powers to restore order, the minister lived in his carriage for eight days. He wrote more than 200 proclamations, and encouraged people to dig for survivors and provide food and shelter for the homeless. For one period of twenty-four hours, he ate nothing but a bowl of soup brought by his wife, who picked her way over the ruins to his carriage.

He gave orders that looters should be hanged; that corpses be collected in barges, towed out to sea and thrown overboard; that troops converge on the city from the provinces, driving back the refugees required for relief operations. Prices of foodstuffs and building materials were fixed at those prevailing on 31 October. Incoming vessels with shipments of fish, corn and meat were compelled to sell their cargoes; outgoing vessels were searched for stolen treasure. Depots were requisitioned, food centres organised, and camp-kitchens and ovens built. Makeshift shelters were erected in open spaces around the city, latrines dug, and temporary hospitals set up for the wounded and destitute.

Meanwhile, members of the English Factory fretted about their business affairs. As early as 8 November, they drafted a letter to Dom José in which Carvalho had no difficulty in detecting self-interest. They offered their condolences and assured the king of: "their determined resolution to prosecute a commerce which is particularly necessary at this time and always so advantageous to the kingdoms of Great Britain and Portugal. They think it their duty to express the strong reliance they have on your Majesty for making such wise regulations for the security of commerce and the re-establishment of mercantile credit as may fix them on the firmest foundations."[14]

Some of the wealthier merchants were living in tents in the British envoy's garden; others had rented a house in Marvila, a few miles north-east of Lisbon. Ships were arriving in the

Tagus but, with no warehouses, it was impossible to offload the cargoes. The consul had a word with Carvalho. "I represented to him the deplorable condition of the merchants," he wrote to London on 19 November, "and how necessary it was to take steps towards the re-establishment of commerce. His answer was that it could not be yet, that I could see the distressed situation they were in, that the kingdom was threatened with plague and famine." These matters had to be dealt with first, the minister told him, only then would "commerce be taken care of."[15]

In January, Carvalho accepted an offer by Portuguese merchants to pay an additional four percent duty on imports, a contribution towards the cost of rebuilding the city. The English Factory objected (on the grounds that the total tax on British goods was now higher than the maximum percentage agreed by treaty) and the envoy asked Carvalho to suspend the duty on imports from England. The minister refused with some irritation. He would have thought, he told the envoy, "that English merchants, who are so greatly involved with the commerce of Portugal, would be at least as anxious as the Portuguese to see Lisbon restored to its ancient lustre." He had never expected opposition to a scheme aimed at the revival of trade, "even if it were attended with some little inconvenience."[16]

All merchant houses had assets outside Lisbon and, despite their protests, Factory members soon resumed their trading activities. But George Medley chose to retire from business and William was left without income or employment. His parents were dead, his house was destroyed, he had lost his agency and all his possessions, and apart from his uncle who relied on him for sustenance, he was alone in a devastated city. Joseph Morley's garden was now his home and, sleeping outdoors in a makeshift shelter, he shivered in the cold night air and winter rains, while beneath him the earth continued to tremble. Miserable and depressed, he stopped attending Factory meetings and worried about his orphaned siblings, aware that he was powerless to help them.

Interlude

England

1755–1761

News of the earthquake took over a fortnight to reach England and it was a letter from the British ambassador in Madrid that brought the information to London. "A courier dispatched from Lisbon," he wrote, "has brought an account of such desolation as I do not remember to have heard of in any age in these parts of Europe. The whole city is either in ruins by the shock or devoured by the flames which ran from one entrance to the town to the other."[1]

People were stunned by the news. The government sent a convoy of ships with money and provisions, and a royal proclamation declared 6 February 1756 to be a national fast-day, a day for people to confess their sins and pray for repentance. Special prayers were published and Psalm 46 was rewritten as a hymn, "recommended for children to learn by heart, in order to impress on their minds a sense of their creator's omnipotence in the melancholy destruction of Lisbon."[2]

On 6 February, all business stopped for the day as people flocked into churches to hear the clergy pronounce on the significance of the earthquake. In Exeter, the bishop preached a moderate sermon. Men should repent and call upon God for salvation, he proclaimed from the pulpit, but they should not be terrified out of their wits by earthquake-fright.[3] William's youngest brother, eight years old and in the care of a family friend, was taken to the cathedral and, after the sermon, he sang the hymn that he had – as instructed – learnt by heart:

Tho' earth her ancient seat forsake
By pangs convulsive torn,
Tho' her self-balanced fabrick shake,
And ruin'd nature mourn.

Tho' hills be in the ocean lost,
With all their trembling load,
No fear shall e'er disturb the just,
Or shake his trust in God.[4]

Three months later, his temporary guardian signed the petition for him to be admitted into Christ's Hospital, explaining that he had "taken care of a poor child named John James Stephens, whose father and mother are both dead and left him and several more unprovided for, who are assisted by friends."[5] After money for the journey had been received from London, John James was taken to the stage-coach and delivered into the care of the driver. The coach had heavy wagon-type wheels and no springs and, for several days, he sat in the cramped interior as it rattled and jolted along the roads. At night, he ate at the inns, then dossed down to sleep. He tried to imagine the new life ahead of him, but his childhood in the calm of Cathedral Close gave him no clue to his future.

On 17 June, he entered the gates of Christ's Hospital, the school founded two hundred years earlier for the education of free-born children whose parents were unable to provide for them. His two brothers were living with relatives in Cornwall, his sister with a cousin in London who worked for Thomas Cogan, a haberdasher in Cornhill. Cogan was a governor of Christ's Hospital and it was he who arranged for John James to be admitted here.[6]

After enrolment formalities in the counting-house, John James was taken to a room lined with portraits where he had to strip naked for a medical inspection. Then he was clothed in the Tudor-style uniform of the Hospital: ankle-length blue coat with yellow lining, white metal buttons and full gathers for the skirt, yellow worsted stockings, plum-coloured belt, and two white bands at the neck.

That evening, after a meal of bread and cheese in the Great Hall, he was taken to his dormitory where he read aloud the night-time prayers written especially for Christ's Hospital. "Let the rest that we are going to remind us of the hour of death," he whispered with the other boys. "Preserve us from all evil dreams, all affrighting fancies, and the horrors of the night."[7] The children slept two to a bed and, as the candles were blown out, John James lay alongside a stranger in a room with sixty other boys. He was lonely, homesick and apprehensive, but he was to receive little sympathy. "Boy!" said one of the masters to a homesick pupil, "The school is your father! The school is your mother! The school is your brother! The school is your sister! The school is your first cousin, and your second cousin, and all the rest of your relations! Let's have no more crying!"[8]

There were more than 600 boys at Christ's Hospital. They enjoyed no holidays apart from a few days rest after the half-yearly examinations and at Christmas, Easter and Whitsun. No boy was allowed to sleep outside the Hospital precincts; to stay with relatives, even for one night, was a penal offence. And although one of the masters described the diet as "plain and simple, consequently wholesome and good; the children are lively and healthy and but few die,"[9] the food was inadequate for growing boys: dry bread and ale for breakfast, bread and milk at midday (with a small piece of meat every other day), and bread and cheese for supper. No vegetables were served and John James was always hungry, or "cruggy" as the boys called it, and looked forward to the small portion of roast beef which was served once a month for Sunday dinner.

He soon became accustomed to the daily routine. At six o'clock, he was woken by the bell and, after combing his hair and washing his hands and face, he ate his breakfast. He was in the classroom for three hours in the morning and four hours in the afternoon, and went to bed after an early supper in the Great Hall. On Sundays, he attended two services in nearby Christ Church, sitting on a narrow plank in the balcony above the organ, and in the evenings, he learnt the catechism. This was taught by the monitors (boys entrusted with discipline in the dormitories), several of whom were bullies and whipped their charges with a leather thong.

There were three types of education at Christ's Hospital: the Grammar School, where boys of academic ability were prepared for university; the Mathematical School, where boys were trained for apprenticeships in the navy and mercantile marine; and the Writing School, where those not destined for professional life were trained for commerce and trade. The Mathematical was the most prestigious. Its pupils felt superior to other boys and it was a great dishonour for them to be transferred to the Writing School (as several were during John James's schooldays) for being "extremely dull and backward in their learning."[10]

Initially, John James was enrolled in the Lower Grammar School but, in April 1759, he was transferred to the Writing School.[11] "Classical learning," explained his teacher, "is confined to those who have parts, taste and a disposition for it; those who are found incapable of making progress are put to writing and accounts."[12]

For the next three years, John James spent his days in a room where 300 boys sat at long writing boards. One hour a week was allotted to reading; all other hours of study were devoted to writing (copying) and arithmetic. "Boys were discharged able penmen indeed and accurate accountants," wrote a future master, "but so miserably defective in reading and spelling as to be incapable of writing a decent letter, turning a grammatical sentence, or even spelling the most simple words."[13] Pupils in the lower forms cleaned the dormitories and, on Saturday afternoons, when other boys played games in the open spaces, they cleaned the schoolroom, sweeping the floor beneath the boards and benches.[14]

Tedium was relieved by a number of traditional ceremonies. The most important were during Easter week when, with strips of paper marked "He is risen" pinned to their coats, the boys marched through the city to attend the Spital Sermons at St Bride's church. On Easter Tuesday, they were presented to the lord mayor at the Mansion House, given a newly-minted sixpence, and rewarded with buns and wine. And every Sunday evening between Christmas and Easter, distinguished visitors were admitted to "Public Suppings" in the Great Hall, where they watched the pupils eat their simple supper of bread and cheese.

John James behaved well at Christ's Hospital. He learnt his lessons, refused to join in escapades, and caused no trouble. He watched other boys being caned by the masters or deprived of their supper, but he was rarely disciplined himself. Good reports were made to his presenting governor and, at Public Suppings, Thomas Cogan rewarded him by pressing coins into his hand.

3

Alcântara

1756–1762

"A little genius who has a mind to be a great one in a little country is a very uneasy animal."
Sir Benjamin Keene on Sebastião de Carvalho, October 1745

When John James began his schooldays in London, his eldest brother was still living in the shack he had built in Joseph Morley's garden. Provisions were in short supply and aftershocks continued to jolt the city, but William was emerging from the depression that had gripped him since the earthquake and was putting his mind to business opportunities.

Sebastião de Carvalho was now in control of the government. The fact that his house remained intact was, in the king's opinion, a sign of divine guidance, proof that the minister had been sent by God to help him in his hour of need. Carvalho's influence with Dom José was greatly enhanced by this stroke of luck, as well as by his efficient handling of the disaster, and in the spring of 1756, he was appointed the most senior of the triumvirate of ministers. As the British consul wrote to London, "Monsieur de Carvalho is the leading man and is in effect prime minister, for nothing is done without him."[1]

A few weeks after the earthquake, Carvalho had discussed ideas for a modern city to rise from the ruins, a city with wide streets built on a grid system. To enable the work to be carried out quickly and cheaply, the design was a simple one, a style of plain-fronted buildings with wrought iron balconies which became known as Pombaline. As the architects drew up the plans, William realised that there would soon be great demand for building materials. The supply of stone and timber presented few opportunities but large volumes of mortar would be required, so he thought of lime. Limestone was plentiful to the west of the city, but lime kilns were energy-intensive and firewood was in short supply (most available timber had been used to build shelters for the homeless people of Lisbon).

There were a number of Portuguese lime-makers in the area but their output was small, their lime of low quality, and their kilns fuelled by firewood. William had to offer a more advanced technology, so he also thought of coal. A small quantity of coal was imported from England (for use in iron foundries and kitchens) and William investigated the possibility of building coal-fired kilns, using fuel imported from his home country. He ordered books on lime-making and studied plans of the larger, more industrial kilns in operation elsewhere in Europe.[2] These kilns could not use ordinary coal (the lumps did not burn at sufficient heat); instead, they were fuelled by culm, waste powder from the mining of anthracite, a type of coal found mainly in the collieries of south Wales. A cheap and inferior form of coal, culm was an inadequate fuel for other purposes but its great advantage in lime production was an ability to burn at consistently high temperatures.

Having done his research, William was ready to explain his project to Carvalho. As an unknown foreigner, he was not in a position to approach him directly but, with the help of a Portuguese intermediary, he was soon summoned into the minister's presence to describe the operation of coal-fired kilns.[3] This, for Portugal, was new technology and Carvalho was enthusiastic. He intended the reconstruction to start as soon as possible, an undertaking that required large amounts of mortar. Since Portuguese producers were unable to provide sufficient lime for such a massive project, he was convinced of the value of William's proposal.

Details of the lime concession were agreed over the next few days. The kilns would be built in Alcântara, a mile west of Lisbon, the limestone transported from quarries further up the Alcântara valley. Cargoes of imported culm would be exempt from customs duties for a period of fifteen years, and finished lime had to be sold at or below the price fixed by Carvalho at the time of the earthquake.[4]

Dom José signed the concession on 3 November 1756, and William left Joseph Morley's garden and moved to Alcântara, an area populated by refugees from Lisbon who were still living under makeshift shelters in open spaces around the city. With a loan from the government, he rented a house and for the first time in twelve months, slept with a roof over his head.[5] His uncle moved with him to help with the paperwork; money was raised to set up the business, plans were drawn up for the factory complex, and twenty workmen employed to clear the site and construct the buildings.

The existing kilns of the region were simple in construction. Open platforms built above a furnace, they worked intermittently, the furnaces being extinguished while finished lime was removed from the platforms and replaced by piles of freshly quarried stone.[6] William's kilns were more advanced than this ancient method of production. Four batteries of deep cylindrical chambers, each with four furnaces, provided a total of sixteen kilns.[7] Fuel and limestone were loaded in layers and the furnaces burned continuously, new materials being loaded at the top of the kilns and finished lime extracted from the base.

Lime production required at least a third of its volume in fuel, so large quantities of culm were needed for sixteen kilns to operate continuously. William employed an agent in England (Charles Dingley, an old acquaintance who had returned to London after the earthquake) and commissioned a military engineer (William Elsden) to examine the mines in south Wales and select those which provided the best quality culm.[8] Intending to start production as soon as the kilns were completed, he instructed Dingley "to send him any quantity, to charter and load any number of ships with culm,"⁹ but he encountered so many difficulties during the first year of importation that he was brought to the brink of despair.

In April 1757, when the first cargo arrived at the Alcântara quay, he was horrified to discover that Dingley had shipped low-grade coal instead of culm. This was unusable in his furnaces which required coal in powder form (even if he had the technology to pulverise lumps into powder, the coal would still have been inadequate, for only waste from anthracite could be used in the kilns as it burned hotter and more cleanly than waste from softer types of coal).

Four more ships containing low-grade coal arrived during the next few weeks and, after an urgent exchange of letters, William learnt that Dingley had been daunted by the high cost of chartering vessels at the Welsh ports.¹⁰ He had therefore ordered his agent in the north of England "to ship an inferior sort of coals, which he was told would burn lime as well as culm." As Dingley explained, "the sending of these coals has proved a very great loss and disappointment to Mr Stephens, as he cannot burn lime with them and they lay on his hands useless."¹¹ Meanwhile, more than 700 tons of unusable coal was occupying space in William's warehouse (a problem he solved by paying import duties and selling it on to third parties).¹²

As soon as Dingley learnt of his mistake, he did his best to remedy the situation. Between May and July, he loaded nine ships with a total of 2000 tons of culm from the collieries of south Wales, but four of these vessels failed to arrive in Lisbon. One was burnt at sea and, because England was once again at war with France, three were captured by French privateers and sunk. As a result, only 1200 tons had arrived by August 1757, the time when the kilns were ready to enter production.¹³

The three cargoes taken by the French were carried in British craft, so William asked Dingley to charter foreign ships which received less attention from enemy vessels. A few more cargoes arrived in the autumn, but customs officers in Wales were charging such high export duties that it was impossible for William to sell lime at the price fixed by Carvalho. By December, Dingley had paid duties totalling £45,000 in today's values and William was forced to instruct him to send no more culm to Lisbon.[14]

Dingley appealed to the Treasury, explaining that William had ("at very great expense") built kilns to provide lime for the rebuilding of Lisbon, fuelled by culm exported from England. Dom José had agreed to exempt the culm from import duties and promised that William's lime would be used in all rebuilding works in the city – on condition it was sold at the price fixed after the earthquake. He explained that customs officers had been treating the culm as coal (the value of which was four times higher), charging duties of ten shillings a chaldron on cargoes carried in British ships and twenty-one shillings on cargoes in foreign ships, whereas culm exported to Ireland attracted duty of just one shilling.[15] Finally, he made the point that the high level of duties prevented William from selling his lime except at a loss, "therefore his kilns are become useless and his intention of aid in rebuilding the city of Lisbon abortive."[16]

When the Treasury considered the matter in February, it was decided that any reduction in export duties might lead to fraud, allowing "officers to pass coals as culm, the one not being distinguishable from the other, and thereby enable foreigners to supply their forges at a cheaper rate."[17] Dingley was furious. British and Portuguese diplomats supported William's request, he replied, and the export of culm was to Britain's advantage for the proposed duty of one shilling a chaldron would be "a considerable gain to the revenue." Neither William nor Dingley was "by any temptation whatever capable of fraud or collusion," while customs officers could easily tell the difference between coal and culm as the duty payable on trade to Ireland distinguished between them.[18]

There was no reply to this letter, so Dingley wrote again, explaining that continuing delays in the matter were likely to "put an end to the undertaking" and asking for permission to present his case to the House of Commons.[19] After a few anxious days, he "waited on the Duke of Newcastle, first lord of the Treasury, and his Grace was pleased to tell him that he had leave to apply to parliament for a Bill to empower him to export culm to Lisbon for a certain number of years, paying only a trivial duty."

Parliament considered the matter in April and, when the Bill passed to the House of Lords, several members accompanied it there, including William Pitt who "spoke very warm on the occasion, how glad the nation was to oblige the Portuguese, and declared that he would be willing to let culm be sent to Lisbon even without any duty."[20] The Culm Act was passed on 26 April 1758. For a period of fifteen years, exports to Lisbon would incur a token duty of one shilling a chaldron on condition that bonds were signed at the port of embarkation; these would be cancelled when the British consul confirmed that the cargoes had been landed.[21]

News of the Culm Act reached Lisbon in May. The first cargo incurring the token duty arrived a month later, after which ships began to arrive in increasing numbers.[22] William's spirits soared and, watching his workmen busy at the kilns and mule carts entering and leaving the site, he felt proud of his achievements. Indeed, he was heard to boast that his factory was a demonstration to the Portuguese of how the economy of the country could be improved.[23]

Sebastião de Carvalho, meanwhile, was consolidating his power. Viewing the earthquake as a natural phenomenon, he had been urging people to restore order and help clear the city, but his efforts were hampered by the clergy who considered the disaster to be punishment from God. As the first anniversary approached, the best-known Jesuit in the country, Gabriel Malagrida, published a pamphlet insisting that the earthquake was divine retribution for people's sins. "It is necessary to devote all our strength to the task of repentance," he wrote. "God is watching us, scourge in hand."[24]

Carvalho was irritated by the Jesuits, holding them responsible for the alarmist sermons that were terrifying the people of Lisbon. He denounced Malagrida's pamphlet as heretical, banished its author from the city, and accused the priests of using the disaster to "frighten feeble and superstitious minds." Meanwhile, several Jesuits began to plot against him, their intrigues mirrored in Dom José's court where the nobles also simmered with resentment, having been ousted by Carvalho from their positions of influence over the king.

One night in September 1758, as Dom José was returning to the palace after an assignation with the young Marquesa de Távora, several men emerged from the shadows and opened fire on his chaise. A bullet grazed the king's arm and, sensing an opportunity, Carvalho used his spies to collect evidence against members of the aristocracy and their Jesuit confessors. Servants were tortured to extract information about their employers, nobles tortured into betraying their friends. And maybe Carvalho remembered his youth in Lisbon when, as the son of a provincial cavalry captain, he had proposed marriage to a member of the Távora family and the Távoras, calling him a common adventurer, had ordered him out of their house.

Carvalho's main ambitions were to increase the commercial prosperity of Portugal and lift the country out of its medieval mind-set, but he also had a despotic side to his nature. He was certainly a man to hold grudges and, if the Távoras remembered the occasion when they belittled the tall young man, they would soon have cause to regret it. The Duque de Aveiro, too, had become an enemy. The most important nobleman in Portugal, he had never concealed his dislike of Carvalho; it was he who headed the opposition to the indolent manner in which Dom José ran his country – and to Carvalho as the king's first minister.

The suspects were arrested in December and found guilty on 12 January, nine of them to be executed the following day in Belém. Alcântara was no more than a mile from Belém and William lay awake that night, listening to carpenters building the scaffold. Next morning, the prisoners were brought from their dungeons. The executions lasted all day and William, at work in the lime kilns, heard the distant sounds of the proceedings. "The flower of the nobility was executed yesterday," wrote an English visitor. "The old Marquesa de Távora died first. She was beheaded. Her husband and two sons, together with the Duque de Aveiro, were broken upon the wheel, and an assassin burnt alive. All the dead bodies were consumed along with him and their ashes swept into the Tagus."[25]

Carvalho now turned his attention to the Jesuits. A number of priests had been arrested for complicity in the assassination plot (including Malagrida who had acted as confessor to the Távora family) and, in the autumn of 1759, the minister expelled all Jesuits from the country. Malagrida was handed over to the Inquisition, Carvalho himself drew up the indictment of heresy and, on a warm September night, the mad old priest was garrotted by torchlight in the central square of Lisbon.

Finally, Carvalho separated Dom José from his church, breaking off relations with the Vatican on the pretext that the papal nuncio had insulted the king (he had failed to illuminate his house for the marriage of the crown princess). The breach between Lisbon and the Vatican was to last nine years, during which the minister did his best to remove the church's stranglehold over national affairs. He created a secular state, placed the church under government control, and reduced the powers of the Inquisition. He knew that relations with Rome would be re-established but, as he told the British envoy, "when the nuncio returns, it will be with his claws clipped."[26]

Ten years after becoming a minister, with the co-operation of a weak and unintelligent king, Carvalho had collected supreme power into his hands. When Dom José succeeded to the throne, Portugal was ruled by the monarch, the church and the aristocracy. Now the aristocracy and church had both been suppressed and Carvalho had become the effective dictator of his country. The dungeons were filled with people suspected of further intrigues, people arrested and imprisoned without trial. Nobody dared discuss politics or criticise Carvalho's actions; it was illegal to even speak of the Távora conspiracy. As a visitor to Lisbon remarked, "so many have been thrown into jail on this account, that the poor souls are quite frighted at the mention of some names."[27]

The British disliked Carvalho's dictatorship almost as much as the Portuguese, for the minister continued his measures against the merchants, whittling away at their privileges. But there was one benefit: because of the reduced powers of the Inquisition, they could practise their religion with less fear than in the past (although they still had to worship at home or in the British envoy's house). Several years later, an elderly lady remembered the *autos-da-fé.* "They were a fine sight," she explained to a young man who had said how dreadful those events must have been. "It was like the processions, and the English whose houses over-looked the streets through which they passed kept open house and made entertainments."[28]

William was less disadvantaged by the new regime than most British businessmen in Lisbon. His factory was unaffected by the removal of trade privileges, but he was still dependent on the government for his lime concession and the government was (in all but name) Carvalho himself.

On 12 January 1758, while Charles Dingley was still appealing to the Treasury, William had a meeting with the minister to discuss the reconstruction which was expected to start a few weeks later.[29] He was apprehensive for he had promised to provide large quantities of lime for one of Carvalho's favourite projects, the rebuilding of Lisbon, a promise he might not be able to fulfil.

The minister was aware of his difficulties with British customs, and William was relieved when he merely unrolled plans for the main square by the waterfront and discussed the quantities of lime required by the builders. Hoping that Dingley would be successful, that his kilns would be working at full capacity by the time the reconstruction began, he asked for a loan to cover his operating costs. Carvalho agreed and, after the meeting, authorised an advance payment of eight *contos* of *reis* (financed by the four percent import tax imposed after the earthquake), to be repaid in consignments of lime for the Praça do Comércio, the arsenal and the custom-house.[30]

Most of this money was sent to London to pay for cargoes of culm which were despatched as soon as the Culm Act was passed in April. By September, eleven ships had arrived in the Tagus with culm from south Wales and, with his kilns in full production, William was ready to supply the state with large quantities of lime. But the euphoria he experienced during the summer of 1758 soon evaporated as it became clear that the reconstruction would not be going ahead as planned. By the autumn, the only work in progress was the clearing and levelling of streets in the city centre and, with no lime required by the builders, William had to sell to individuals (as he had done a year earlier when his furnaces were lit for the first time).[31]

He now had greater quantities to sell, so he produced an advertising leaflet with instructions for preparing lime for different purposes: mortar for walls, rough mortar for flat roofs, fine plaster for decoration. He made the point that although good quality mortar was used in previous centuries, lime-making in Portugal had deteriorated since then and was now believed to be the most inferior in Europe. However, the leaflet continued, "with lime from the new factory, a firm bonding will be achieved, similar to that obtained by the old methods."[32]

The lime produced in traditional kilns was brought into the city and sold at the fixed price of 1400 reis per moyo.[33] Because of reduced transport costs, William was able to charge a lower price (1200 reis per moyo) and this, together with his critical remarks about their product, enraged the Portuguese lime-makers and it is hardly surprising that they determined to put him out of business. They made derogatory comments about his lime; they said it was discoloured and contaminated by ashes. Lime from continuous coal-fired kilns was often a more brownish colour than that produced in traditional kilns and William's competitors were telling no more than the truth.[34] But when their comments reached the ears of his private buyers, most of them took their custom elsewhere and, since his lime was not required for rebuilding the city, he was forced to close some of his kilns.

Work in the city had been delayed for a number of reasons. The country was in economic depression and, with the mines of Brazil producing less gold than in previous years, state revenues were much reduced. The war in Europe was another factor. France was putting increasing pressure on neutral Portugal, and Carvalho, concerned that an alliance between France and Spain was imminent, feared an invasion by Spanish forces. He had to upgrade the defences of his country (which had declined into an appalling condition), with the result that men, money and materials were diverted from the task of reconstruction.

William was unaware of these problems of state and, as he continued to close his kilns, he became increasingly despondent. With determination and persistence, he had overcome all difficulties – but to little purpose since most of his furnaces were lying idle. By the autumn of 1760, work had started on rebuilding the arsenal, but the city remained in ruins and William wrote a petition to Dom José. The demand for lime, he explained, was much less than previously estimated. It had been assumed that sixteen kilns would be needed to supply lime for the reconstruction but, with only three kilns in operation, he was still producing greater quantities than he could sell. He was deeply in debt and begged the king to have pity on him and suspend repayments of his loan.[35]

On the verge of bankruptcy, he tried to diversify into a more profitable activity, joining forces with William Elsden (his agent in south Wales) who had discovered a deposit of anthracite in the Mondego region of central Portugal. In July 1761, William offered his factory to the state in repayment of his debts. Then he and Elsden suggested that the kilns could be fuelled more cheaply by culm from the Mondego, although they would need a government loan to exploit the mine.[36]

Carvalho was inclined to consider both these suggestions but, because of the preparations for war, there were no funds available. He agreed to make another advance payment for lime, but the reconstruction continued to be delayed and William knew that his factory would soon have to close.[37] The advance from the government had paid off some of his creditors but he remained deeply in debt, mainly to Charles Dingley to whom he owed over £40,000 in today's values.[38]

For the past five years, William had kept in touch with his siblings in England. The two older boys were living in Cornwall: Lewis with a cousin in Liskeard, John Lyne, rector of the nearby parish of St Ive; and Jedediah with John's sister in Saltash (who was married to a warrant-officer in the naval dockyard). Their sister, Philadelphia, lived with Thomas Cogan above his haberdashery in Cornhill, close to Christ's Hospital where John James was coming to the end of his schooldays.

In his letters to England, William had boasted about the lime he was making for rebuilding the city and his acquaintance with the first minister of the country. He never mentioned his difficulties or his accumulating debts, and his family believed him to be a successful and wealthy merchant. Now, just as William was contemplating the closure of his business, just as he and his uncle were without income of any kind, he received a letter from Thomas Cogan. John James would be fourteen years old in January, the age when boys in the Writing School were apprenticed to a trade or merchant house, and Christ's Hospital thought it appropriate that he should work for his brother at the lime kilns.

Too proud to admit the truth, William accepted John James as an apprentice and, since it was time to take responsibility for his family, suggested that Philadelphia, now ten years old, should travel from London with him.[39] He arranged apprenticeships for Lewis and Jedediah in merchant houses in Lisbon, and wrote to Liskeard, asking John Lyne to make arrangements for his brothers and sister to sail on the packet boat from Falmouth.

Interlude

England

While his future was decided in letters to and from Portugal, John James was applying himself to his final year of studies. He had retained his placid nature, obeying orders from the masters, and copying and doing sums on the long benches in the Writing School.

It was a tradition of Christ's Hospital that, after a coronation, the senior schoolboy should address the monarch in a ceremony in St Paul's Churchyard. George III was crowned in September 1761 and, a few weeks later, an enormous platform was erected in the Churchyard, large enough to accommodate all the children of the Hospital, together with the governors, masters, and school officials. On the morning of 9 November, John James took his seat alongside several hundred excited schoolboys and, after a long wait, the royal coach clattered into the Churchyard as the young king and his bride made their way to a banquet in the Guildhall.

As the horses came to a halt, George and Charlotte stepped down from the coach and were seated on gilded chairs under a canopy. "Most august and gracious sovereign," began the senior scholar, reading a speech composed by the master of the Upper Grammar School, "from the condescension and goodness which your Majesty displays towards even the meanest of your subjects, we hope you will accept the tribute of obedience and duty which we poor orphans are permitted to present you." He then read several sentences about royal patronage, before turning to the matter of the king's recent marriage: "Long may your Majesties experience the satisfaction of domestic life in every endearment of the most tender union, in every blessing of conjugal affection, and every comfort of parental felicity; and may a race of princes, your illustrious issue and descendants, continue to sway the British sceptre to the latest posterity."

Whatever the royal couple thought of this address, of the hopes for conjugal affection spoken by a schoolboy, they showed pleasure in the proceedings. And John James and the other boys sang "God Save the King" as the coach moved on.[1]

Five months later, on 17 March 1762, John James was discharged from Christ's Hospital, "the boy being sent to serve Mr William Stephens of Lisbon for seven years."[2] He removed the blue coat and yellow stockings, and was presented with £5 and several religious books, courtesy of past benefactors. Released into Thomas Cogan's care, he was taken to Cornhill and, the following day, he and his sister boarded the coach for Liskeard to be reunited with their brothers.

Together for the first time in seven years, the children were leaving the country of their birth and sailing to a new life in Portugal. A single fare on the Lisbon packet cost four guineas for embarkation and twenty-three *milreis* to the captain, a total of £750 in today's values.[3] Thomas Cogan paid for John James and Philadelphia, and the fares for Lewis and Jedediah were raised by cousins in Cornwall who were pleased that the problem of the orphaned Stephens boys had been resolved at last.

4

A Family Together

1762–1769

"I have been reduced to the most abject misery because of the great loss I sustained in the lime factory, which I built in good faith for the reconstruction of the city."
William Stephens, 1763

The boys and their sister embarked on the *King George* packet which sailed from Falmouth on 30 April.[1] They were placed in the care of Captain Bown and Lieutenant Oak who were, according to another passenger, "very kind and very civil; nor did I ever see people mind their business more closely than they do theirs. They are always upon deck, attentive to the sailors that each may stick to his respective duty."[2] Several sheep and a pig were kept on board, together with cages of poultry, sufficient to last the passengers and crew for a voyage of two months or more, and fish were caught to supplement the rations.

A year earlier, one of the Lisbon packets had been lost to a French privateer, so the voyage was an adventure for the teenage boys. The sailors talked of "delivering a broadside or two" should they encounter an enemy vessel, but the captains were forbidden to fight unless they had no choice. Their orders were to sail away from hostile shipping, to fight only if escape was impossible, and in case of surrender, to sink all mail and despatches overboard.[3]

The *King George* encountered no privateers and soon the brown hills of Portugal came into view. The young travellers sailed up the Tagus as their brother had done sixteen years before, but their first view of Lisbon was very different from his. No longer a city of magnificent buildings, the prospect from the waterfront was one of total devastation. "Nothing is to be seen," wrote an Englishman who landed here a few months earlier, "but vast heaps of rubbish, out of which arise the miserable remains of shattered walls and broken pillars."[4]

The children stepped ashore on a warm afternoon in mid-May. Met by the brother they had never seen (and still believing him to be a successful merchant), they gazed in amazement at the ruins and the few houses still standing, propped up by wooden beams. The workmen had made paths through the rubble and, in his mule-drawn chaise, William took his family through the ruined streets and western suburbs and through the camps of makeshift shelters outside the city.

He had closed his kilns in January and, as he brought the children to Alcântara, he had to explain why no furnaces were burning, why the site of his factory was deserted. John James failed to understand how he had been apprenticed to a business which had ceased to operate and William tried to reassure him. He was writing to the government, he told him, and hoped to be given a subsidy to reopen the kilns. In the meantime, John James could take over the clerical work and William would improve his education, teaching him to spell and write a well-turned sentence, giving him books to read and teaching him Portuguese. And a few days later, as John James and Philadelphia settled into the house in Alcântara, Lewis and Jedediah started work for their new employers.

William was more despondent than he had led John James to believe. Spanish troops had invaded the country on 5 May (a few days before his family arrived in Lisbon) and, as the city lived in fear of enemy occupation, he wondered whether he had been wise to bring his brothers and sister to Portugal. But the war in Europe was coming to an end; with the approach of winter, the invading forces retreated across the border and peace was signed on 3 November, eleven days after William reached the lowest point of his years in Alcântara.

Bailiffs had come to the house on 21 October to enforce an order instigated by Charles Dingley, and William watched from the yard as the men carried away his possessions. First through the door came the drop-leaf dining table and another table with panels of ebony embossed with gold; these were followed by twelve brazilwood chairs with leather seats, two sofas, and a side table. From the kitchen came the pine table, the dinner service, twelve pewter dishes and three copper casseroles. Finally, from the stables, came the chaise, the one-remaining mule, the donkey, and the tack.[5]

William was defeated. For six years, he had tried to make a success of the lime kilns, but now he sank into depression and it was not until early the following year that he raised the energy to write to Carvalho. He was, he informed the minister, "without means to support my person and my family, and without possessions of any value. I beg your Excellency to allow me to attend to the extreme misery in which I find myself." There was a quantity of lime at the kilns; if the government could send money for this, it would help sustain his family who, "since October of last year, have experienced the most terrible misfortunes."[6]

He received no reply to this letter, so he tried again a few weeks later, this time addressing his petition to Dom José: "I have been reduced to the most abject poverty because of the great loss I sustained in the lime factory which I built in good faith for the reconstruction of the city. Because of the war that ended the public works, the factory is useless and dead, and I have had the distress of selling the furniture of my house to feed my family of three brothers and a sister, orphans." This was stretching the truth (the furniture had been pawned to repay his debt to Dingley) but William was hoping to soften the king's heart by referring to his orphaned siblings. He had no other recourse, he continued, than to beg for clemency and, reverting to the request he had made almost two years before, he asked José to accept the factory in payment of his debts.[7]

But the invasion of the previous year had emptied government coffers and, for two years, William lived in poverty, helped by friends in the merchant community. It was not until the summer of 1764 that his fortunes began to change. With state finances improving, Carvalho turned his attention to the rebuilding of Lisbon. He gave thought to William's situation at Alcântara and, now the reconstruction was about to begin, he authorised an advance payment for lime.[8]

At last William could re-open his factory. He employed workmen, bought mules and carts, redeemed his furniture, and re-lit the furnaces. He ordered shipments of fuel from England and John James began his apprenticeship, writing bills of sale, paying rent and wages, and managing the accounts. And cargoes of culm began to arrive in the Tagus. Three thousand tons were discharged at the Alcântara quay in 1765, and a further 6000 tons arrived during the next three years as work on the reconstruction surged ahead and William's kilns worked at full capacity to provide lime for the builders.[9]

Meanwhile, Philadelphia busied herself in the house, looking after her brothers and her uncle who was becoming increasingly frail. When he died in June 1767, his body was taken on a mule cart to the Protestant cemetery in Buenos Aires. This peaceful square of ground was surrounded by cypresses (ordered by the Inquisition "to hide the burial ground of heretics from the sight of the faithful") and, in the dappled shade of Judas trees growing among the tombstones, the chaplain of the English Factory read the funeral rites as John Stephens was buried in the south-east corner of the cemetery.[10]

A few days later, William wrote to Carvalho. His exemption from duties on imported culm was due to expire in 1771 and he asked for an extension of this privilege. He had, he explained, been of considerable service to the state. He had built the kilns at his own expense and supplied lime for the reconstruction promptly and efficiently, but his costs had been excessive and his debts could not be repaid without a significant increase in time.[11] Carvalho looked kindly on this request and, on 27 July, the king signed an order extending the exemption for a further twenty years.

Guilt is not an emotion associated with Sebastião de Carvalho, dictator of Portugal, but perhaps he felt a little responsible for William's difficulties at Alcântara. It was he who had encouraged the Englishman to build his kilns on an industrial scale, to provide large quantities of lime for the rebuilding of Lisbon. In his enthusiasm, he had been convinced that the reconstruction would be underway the following year, but events conspired against him and work did not start until seven years later.

The minister was a good judge of the English in Portugal. He knew they were arrogant and self-serving and, although he was on good terms with British diplomats, he had little time for the merchant community. But he made an exception of William Stephens, a young man whom he liked and respected. William's first eight years at the lime kilns had been disastrous but, as soon as the reconstruction began, he proved to be an efficient supplier, providing large quantities of lime to order and on time. The factory at Alcântara could never be truly profitable while it relied on imported fuel and the end-product was sold at fixed prices, but maybe an opportunity would arise when he could put the Englishman's ideas and experience to better use.

Before the earthquake, William had become acquainted with John Beare, an Irishman who directed the royal glassworks at Marinha Grande, and he was on friendly terms with Beare's partner, Edward Campion, who was in charge of selling the glass in Lisbon. The factory was originally built near the southern shore of the Tagus but, in 1748, it was relocated north of Lisbon, close to the sawmill in the royal pine forest of Leiria.[12] Beare fell into debt at Marinha Grande; he began to drink heavily and the factory closed in 1767 when he declared himself broken. By this time, Carvalho had set up several new industries, granting loans to men of business who could compete with imported products, and after the bankruptcy of John Beare, he included the glassworks in this programme. The factory was to be reopened and enlarged to provide increased levels of production and, more important in the short term, to manufacture window glass for the rebuilding of Lisbon.

Several of the men chosen to run the new factories were foreigners; there was so little commercial activity in Portugal, and the country was so heavily in thrall to the church, that it was difficult to find competent Portuguese with business experience. Seeking an entrepreneur to reopen the glass-works, Carvalho's ministers discussed the matter with Edward Campion. And Campion, who had known William for many years, put forward the name of his friend, a man towards whom Carvalho felt some degree of responsibility.[13] The minister felt confident that William would be successful at Marinha Grande; the factory would burn firewood from the royal pine forest and, apart from window glass (categorised as a building material), its products would not be subject to fixed prices.

William, who was content now his kilns were in full production, was reluctant to leave his family and move to a small village seventy miles north of Lisbon. He was also reluctant to take on a factory that had bankrupted one entrepreneur and might ruin William himself for a third time. "During the years 1767 and 1768," he explained, "I was often asked by the secretary of state, Francisco Xavier de Mendonça, to rebuild the decaying glass factory near the pine forest of Leiria. I refused the invitation for fear of the ruination experienced by those who had previously attempted the project."[14]

In 1769, Mendonça approached William again, this time informing him that the request was made by order of the king. Dom José had seen the lime kilns from his carriage windows as he travelled between Belém and Lisbon, and knowing the factory was operating successfully, hoped that

William could achieve similar success with the glassworks.[15] He now had little alternative; it would have been difficult to disobey the king and Carvalho was not a man to cross. He was capable of imprisoning (or worse) anyone whose loyalty he suspected, Portuguese or foreigner, and it was courageous of William to have held out for so long.

When he accepted Mendonça's offer, "the minister ordered me to leave directly for the palace to inform the king of my compliance, for which I was granted a private audience. I kissed his Majesty's hand, thanked him for the honour of his request, and explained the difficulty of the enterprise. Dom José was greatly pleased by my acceptance and promised his immediate royal protection." The king told William to list his requirements and, if he needed help in the future, he should "make representations, either to the secretary of state or to his royal person, as the establishment and progress of the glassworks were very much in his royal interest."[16]

The following day, William drew up a list of his demands. He agreed them with Mendonça and submitted a formal petition to the king. And years later, when John James was an old man in Lisbon, he would tell the story of William's business ventures. "My brother's first speculation at the lime kilns," he explained to an English visitor, "was not of any pecuniary advantage to him. But his next speculation was of a far more profitable nature."[17]

PART TWO

William
The Years of Success

5

Marinha Grande

1769–1772

"William Stephens, man of genius and sound judgement who, although an Englishman, always showed the greatest interest in the advancement and prosperity of the Portuguese nation."
Jacome Ratton, 1813

"I never saw so excellent an establishment. Mr Stephens's will is law with the whole fabrick. No monarch ever had more absolute power. He reigns in the hearts of all the people; they only want to know what he likes in order to do it."
Antony Gibbs, December 1798

In 1769, William was more experienced than the young merchant who set up the lime kilns thirteen years earlier. He had learnt from his mistakes and his enthusiasm was tempered by caution and a strict attention to detail. He entered into partnership with John James (who would remain in Alcântara to manage the lime kilns as well as handling the sale of finished glass in Lisbon) and ordered books on glass production from his home country. Edward Campion had died the previous year and, since John Beare had returned to Ireland, there was no-one in Lisbon to teach him.[1]

On 7 July, Dom José signed a decree authorising the re-opening of the glassworks and ordering that William be given "all the help and favour that is necessary." It set out fifteen conditions under which the business would operate, including an interest-free loan of thirty-two *contos* of *reis* (£650,000 in today's values). To fuel the furnaces, he was given free use of decayed wood and branches from the royal pine forest and, for an initial period of fifteen years, he would be exempt from payment of all taxes on the sale of finished glass. The loan from the Junta do Comércio (financed by the four percent import tax) was to be paid in four instalments of eight *contos* of *reis*, the first to be handed over immediately and the balance paid in three six-monthly instalments. It was to be fully repaid after thirteen years, the first repayment falling due four years after the factory re-opened, followed by annual repayments over nine years.[2]

The first instalment of the loan was paid on 20 July and the following morning, as his baggage was loaded onto a string of mules, William's family gathered to say their farewells.[3] He had employed an armed guard to protect the money he was taking with him and, for three days, they rode along the rough tracks, taking refreshment at village inns. They travelled through the spa town of Caldas da Rainha, where the royal family took the waters, and towards the end of their journey, passed the great monasteries of Alcobaça and Batalha. William stopped to pay his respects to the monks and, as a protégé of the first minister of the country, was invited to stay at Alcobaça, a monastery renowned for its cuisine. This was an establishment of great wealth, referred to by the travelling aesthete, William Beckford, as "the most distinguished temple of gluttony in all Europe."[4]

The kitchen at Alcobaça was huge. "Through the centre of the immense hall," wrote Beckford, "ran a rivulet of the clearest water, flowing through wooden reservoirs containing every sort and size of river-fish. On one side, game and venison were heaped up; on the other, vegetables and fruit. Beyond a long line of stoves extended a row of ovens and, close to them, hillocks of flour, rocks of sugar, jars of the purest oil, and pastry in vast abundance which lay brothers were rolling out and puffing up into a hundred different shapes, singing all the while as blithely as larks in a cornfield."[5]

William ate well at Alcobaça and, after a comfortable night, he rode through the pine forest of Leiria and reached Marinha Grande during the afternoon of Sunday, 23 July.

The village was set in flat, sandy countryside and John Beare's workshops stood empty and derelict. The glass-workers, who had been unemployed for two years, had been awaiting his arrival and, as news of his coming spread through the village, many of them turned up at the inn to present themselves to the new proprietor of the factory.

The following morning, William introduced himself to the villagers and surveyed the buildings. On Tuesday, he set to work, recording details of his expenditure in a notebook.[6] He worked at a furious pace, spending long hours on paperwork and proving that, as Carvalho had suspected, he was an administrator of great ability. He had been given the power to acquire land at reasonable prices, but he preferred to work by negotiation.[7] He wrote numerous letters about legal and religious matters, for the transfer of land had its complications (one plot was owned by the Knights of Malta, another required regular masses to be read for a previous owner).[8]

Most of Beare's craftsmen had remained in Marinha Grande and William soon employed seven glass-masters, five assistants and three apprentices. He engaged twenty-five workers for other duties, while twenty-eight men agreed to supply firewood, cutting branches and dead wood in the pine forest and transporting it to the factory in bullock carts.[9] On 7 August, work began on the restoration of workshops and furnaces, an occasion celebrated with a feast for the craftsmen and labourers.[10] Potters began to make crucibles, Beare's tools and equipment were cleaned and restored, and William organised the collection of raw materials for the production of window glass: sand (available in the soil around Marinha Grande) and soda alkali (imported from abroad).

By early October, supplies of sand and soda had arrived at the factory, the workshop for window glass was ready to enter production, and a furnace had been lit to heat the crucibles. Two weeks later, after the glass-masters had gathered in the workshop and taken up the first melt on their blowing irons, William sent a letter to Mendonça in

Lisbon. "I started to make glass on the sixteenth of this month," he wrote, "and the first order is on its way for use in your Excellency's houses. I hope the establishment I have made here will be approved by your Excellency and by his Majesty, and that this approval will be even greater in the future when the glass-masters have perfected their work. To this end, I shall apply all my vigilance."[11]

At the same time, William was making arrangements for the production of tableware, for glass made with soda alkali was only suitable for window panes; it had a sea-green tint and hardened quickly on cooling. Crystalline glass required a slower cooling mixture (achieved mainly by substituting soda with potash) and production began in early 1770 in a second restored workshop, initially using John Beare's catalogue of designs for the moulds had remained at the factory.[12] And during the year, work proceeded on the construction of a stone-built workshop for crystalline glass, as well as separate buildings for the preparation of raw materials.

On 31 December 1770, William sent his first annual report to the government. Great advances had been made, for the glassworks now employed 150 men, with an additional seventy men collecting firewood in the pine forest. The factory had manufactured 12,000 sheets of window glass and sent over a hundred crates of crystalline glass to Lisbon. The new workshop had entered production a few weeks earlier and he enclosed plans for the factory complex. His next project was to demolish the workshop in which he was making window glass and replace it with another stone building.[13]

Meanwhile, a warehouse was required in Lisbon to stock the finished glass and provide storage for imported raw materials which arrived by ship in the Tagus. At first, William used space at the lime kilns but this was insufficient and, in the spring of 1771, he returned to the city. He was looking forward to a reunion with his family and he arrived in Alcântara in time for Philadelphia's twentieth birthday on 3 March, travelling south from Marinha Grande across rivers still swollen by winter rains.

Having decided to build a home for his family as well as a warehouse, he found a plot of steeply rising ground on Rua de São Paulo, close to the river a little to the west of Carvalho's major work of reconstruction.[14] He bought the land at auction and was summoned to meet Carvalho, now known as the Marquês de Pombal (a title granted after a papal nuncio returned to Lisbon, ending Portugal's long breach with the Vatican). After discussing the glassworks, William and Pombal drew up plans for a mansion house, warehouse and courtyard to be built on the site, a little square still known today as the Largo dos Stephens.[15]

Leaving John James in charge of the building work, William returned to Marinha Grande where the factory complex was taking shape with the construction of workshops and furnaces. He had impressed Pombal with his plans for the glassworks and, in January 1772, he was congratulated by the Junta do Comércio. "The great success of this factory," wrote the Junta, "despite the fact that the workshops are still incomplete, is very pleasing." Two months later, when the Junta authorised the final instalment of William's loan, he was informed that the government was "extremely satisfied" with the factory and had high hopes for its future progress.[16]

The compound at Marinha Grande covered an area of forty-four acres, enclosed by a wall. Inside the gates and beyond the porter's lodge lay a large courtyard which William had planted with trees to provide shade. By the summer of 1772, elegant stone buildings (in neo-classical style) had taken the place of John Beare's wooden structures. The main workshops occupied two sides of the courtyard, and behind them were several ancillary structures for carpentry, sawing and pot-making, as well as engraving, cutting and painting the glass. There was a large warehouse and several covered areas where firewood was stored.

On the third side of the courtyard, William had built a small but well-proportioned mansion house, "a pretty little palace," according to a Portuguese aristocrat, "with an exterior both grandiose and simple."[17] The rooms were partially tiled in blue and white *azulejo* tiles and the ceilings decorated with mouldings, including the Stephens family coat of arms over a minstrel's gallery on the staircase. The windows at the rear of the house overlooked a garden with a lake, beyond which lay orchards and vegetable plots.

The garden, planted with herbs, shrubs and low box hedges, was a small area of tranquillity in a busy factory complex. The front of William's house faced the courtyard where bullock carts arrived from the pine forest, their wooden axles creaking and grinding. Smoke rose from the factory chimneys and, while craftsmen laboured in the heat of the furnaces, other workers prepared the raw materials. The sand was washed, heated and sifted, before the materials were mixed together and passed through sieves of brass or copper wire. The mixture was then placed in crucibles and remained in the furnace for several days, after which the melt was cooled a little – to the consistency of treacle – before being taken up on the blowing irons.

It was hot in the workshops where the craftsmen transformed these blobs of molten glass into a great variety of shapes and sizes. They rolled the glass into round or cylindrical masses, blew them into bubbles shaped by swinging the blowing rods, then cut them with shears, tongs and pincers. Meanwhile, they were constantly reheating the glass through apertures in the furnace, the whole process requiring precision, dexterity and a fine sense of rhythm.

Crystalline glass was prepared plain or coloured by metallic oxides, then hand-blown and spun into shape or blown into clay moulds. After cooling, it was cut using wheels of iron and sandstone; engraved with diamond tools or copper wheels; polished, gilded, enamelled, and painted. Finally, it was checked, sorted and packed in straw. Crates of finished glass were sent to Lisbon containing a great variety of products (wine glasses and tumblers, decanters and vases, dishes and bowls, oil and vinegar dispensers, salt cellars and ink-wells, candlesticks and scent bottles), as well as sheets of pale sea-green glass for use as window panes.[18]

William was proud of his factory. His new buildings were elegant and functional, and output was growing as workshops and furnaces entered production.[19] But sales were affected by competition from imported Bohemian glass and, by the time the factory complex was completed, the warehouses were stocked with more than 300 boxes of unsold glass.

Fifteen years earlier, his enemies in Alcântara had told stories about the poor quality of his lime; now glass merchants in Lisbon were spreading rumours that his products were of lower quality than those imported from Bohemia. They had also reduced their prices, undercutting the price of glass from Marinha Grande. Shops in the cities were controlled by the merchants, stocking only imported glass, so people were choosing not to buy the more expensive domestic product.

As a young man, William had been defeated by the lime-makers of Lisbon; now, with royal protection from Dom José, he was in a stronger position. Determined to put the glass merchants out of business, he drafted a petition to the king and travelled to Lisbon in June 1772 to present it personally to the government.[20] It was a long petition and had taken several weeks to write, time well spent as William's description of his problems, and how they could be resolved, was so logical and detailed that the government was persuaded to accept almost all his recommendations.

He complained of the "malice and subterfuge" of the merchants and their attempts to destroy his factory, which had been reopened at the king's request "for the good of the public." He listed several reasons why glass production was cheaper in Bohemia (climate, cost of living, availability of skilled labour and raw materials), and made the point that the three-day journey from Marinha Grande to Lisbon, on roads consisting of rocks and stones, cost him twice as much as the merchants paid to ship Bohemian glass from Hamburg to the Tagus. And when his glass arrived in Lisbon, he was unable to show it to the public for the merchants controlling the shops had no intention of offering shelf-space to products from Marinha Grande. Sales were made from his new warehouse in Rua de São Paulo, where crystalline glass had to be sold in bulk, by the box rather than by piece.

Having explained his problems, William proposed a number of solutions. The glassworks were capable of meeting the total demand for glass in Portugal and its colonies, with an excess available for export abroad. Annual capacity would soon be over 2000 boxes of glass, valued by William at forty *contos* of *reis*, and to ensure that his achievements at Marinha Grande should not be in vain, he asked that measures be taken to reduce competition from Bohemian glass.

First, he requested an increase in import duties. Second, to compete more directly, he asked for permission to display his glass in shops (where his products could be sold to the public in small quantities). Third, to make his prices more competitive, he suggested that his factory be exempt from duties on imported raw materials. Finally, he asked for a prohibition on window glass arriving from Bohemia in pre-cut panes; only whole sheets should be allowed into the country, while the factory at Marinha Grande should be given permission to cut window glass into sections.

William had been exceeding his authority and selling pre-cut window panes for some time and, seven days after he submitted his petition, the glaziers of Lisbon made an official complaint against him.[21] It was, they explained, their exclusive privilege to cut window glass which, until recently, had always been sent from the factory in whole sheets. However, as William pointed out, "the public cannot be obliged, through a mere spirit of patriotism, to buy a whole sheet of glass from my warehouse to replace one window pane. This would be like a tailor prohibiting people from repairing their own clothes."

Production at Marinha Grande was reduced during the summer months (only the strongest workers continued their daily routine in the additional heat of the furnaces), so William remained with his family for several weeks. The mansion house on Rua de São Paulo was nearly completed and, since foreigners were not entitled to own lands or buildings in perpetuity, he applied to have the laws set aside in his case. In August, on Pombal's recommendation, the king signed two decrees permitting William to "own, retain and convey his properties to his heirs and successors, even if foreigners, notwithstanding any law and custom to the contrary which are all dispensed with on this occasion."[22]

William met with Pombal several times during his stay in Lisbon. They talked about imports of foreign glass and his petition to the government, they discussed the ownership of his estates and property, and William mentioned the Culm Act which was due to expire the following spring. The lime kilns could not operate profitably if export duties returned to previous levels, and John James was preparing a petition to the British government asking for an extension of the Act for twenty years.[23]

John James gave the papers to the British envoy, Sir Robert Walpole, who forwarded them to London in January 1773. "I cannot forbear recommending the cause of these gentlemen to your Lordship and the rest of his Majesty's ministers," he wrote. "The Marquês de Pombal has repeatedly assured Messrs Stephens that he desires me to recommend this matter as a measure agreeable to his Portuguese Majesty."[24] A few weeks later, Walpole wrote again, enclosing a letter from one of the secretaries of state. Dom José, explained the minister, wished to inform the British government that he supported the petition "in order to ensure the continuation of an establishment so necessary for the rebuilding of Lisbon."[25]

In March, Walpole told John James that the government was willing to grant the prolongation. A few weeks later, his petition was approved by the Treasury and the new Culm Act was passed in June.[26]

6

A Miniature Welfare State

1772–1775

"The genius of this worthy man has changed the face of the district and the character of its inhabitants. The workmen are clean and industrious, the habits of the people are civil, obliging and orderly, and labour and amusement are happily combined."
Dr William Withering, 1793

I see such marvels in the fields of Marinha...
If gratefulness can presume the future,
William, your name will live for all eternity.
Sonnet by Marquesa de Alorna (1750–1839)

William and Pombal became friends during the summer of 1772, despite an age difference of more than thirty years. The minister, now seventy-two years old, had a youthful approach to life. "Age," wrote an Englishman after meeting him at this time, "had not diminished the vigour, freshness or activity of his faculties. In his person, he was very tall and slender, his face long, pale, meagre, and full of intelligence."[1] The French ambassador also warmed to the minister. Pombal was, he wrote, "easy to get on with. His loquacity was such that it was difficult to get a word in edgeways. He was a good-humoured man, and one would not have guessed from his appearance that his character was strong and relentless. He gave me every reason to like him."[2]

The two men had much in common. They shared advanced ideas about education and social welfare, and soon William formed part of the group which advised the minister on his reforms, a group consisting of Pombal's family, a small number of aristocrats and liberal-minded clergy, and two foreign entrepreneurs (the other being Jacome Ratton, a Frenchman who had several manufacturing interests in Portugal).[3]

For the past ten years, Pombal had been trying to reform the system of education which, until their expulsion from the country, had been run by Jesuits. He founded a College of Nobles with an enlightened curriculum (foreign languages, mathematics and the sciences), opened a commercial college to teach book-keeping and commerce, and in 1772, instigated a major reform of the university of Coimbra. He commissioned new buildings, and created faculties of mathematics and natural science. He introduced Newtonian physics and ordered the construction of laboratories, botanical gardens, an observatory, university press, and museum of natural history. He updated the faculty of medicine, allowing the dissection of corpses (which had been banned on religious grounds) and the study of hygiene, "because it is easier to conserve health than to recuperate it once lost."[4]

Intending to instigate his reforms in person, Pombal made arrangements to travel to Coimbra in September (the only time he left the court during his years in power) and, during one of their meetings, told William that he would inspect the glassworks on his way north and spend the night in his mansion house. William returned to Marinha Grande in August, bringing his sister with him to act as hostess for the occasion. He ordered his workers to clean and tidy the factory complex and, under Philadelphia's supervision, the house was scrubbed and decorated, and staff employed to provide a banquet for the first minister of the country.

Pombal and his retinue left Lisbon on 15 September, travelling up the Tagus in a royal barge before continuing the journey overland. They reached Marinha Grande on 17 September, arriving in time for the banquet at midday.[5] This was served on the first floor of William's mansion; the windows were thrown open to the courtyard and musicians played in the gallery above the staircase. After the meal, the buildings swept and decorated, the workers wearing their best clothes, and the factory in its most orderly condition, William accompanied Pombal into the workshops. He explained the process of glass manufacture and introduced him to his craftsmen, who demonstrated methods of blowing the molten glass and cutting, engraving and gilding the finished pieces.

Later that afternoon, Pombal visited the forestry sawmill to inspect the machine used to cut timber from the pine forest, then returned to Marinha Grande.[6] Over refreshments served in the garden, he and William talked long into the night, discussing the minister's educational reforms and William's problems at Marinha Grande. The following morning, he continued his journey north, passing through the town of Pombal (where he inspected a hat factory) and the village of Soure (his birthplace), before reaching Coimbra.[7]

During their talk in the garden, the minister assured William that the petition he had submitted in June would be given favourable consideration; four months later, he heard that most of his recommendations had been accepted. In January 1773, the king signed two decrees. The first allowed William to pre-cut window panes in the factory and display his products in the shops of Lisbon. The second authorised a new customs tariff; import duties were doubled on crystalline glass and increased by varying amounts on window glass according to quality.[8] At the same time, Pombal approved a new price list for all types of glass from Marinha Grande.[9] Since the factory was the only glassworks of any significance in the country, William had been given a monopoly of glass supply in Portugal and its colonies, a monopoly which (together with his exemption from taxes) would make him one of the richest industrialists in Europe.

William's luck had changed immeasurably. In Alcântara, he had been confronted with almost insuperable problems; now, with the Marquês de Pombal to protect him, the Culm Act had been extended, the Lisbon glaziers had been over-ruled, and the government had removed all competition from his factory. He had won his battle with importers of Bohemian glass, but the merchants were angry in defeat and William was seen as a black-leg by traders affected by Pombal's new factories. When he offered hospitality to a Major Dalrymple travelling overland from Oporto to Lisbon, his visitor commented in his diary: "Marinha Grande is a village where one Stephens, an Englishman, has been given a grant from the crown and established a glass manufacture, to the prejudice of foreign commerce."[10] Another traveller had a different point of view. "A very flourishing glass manufactory has been established under the management of an Englishman named Stephens," he wrote. "It produces every kind of glass, but it is mortifying and disgraceful to the Portuguese that the abundant profits of this manufacture go only to enrich a foreigner."[11]

Philadelphia stayed in Marinha Grande after Pombal's visit, preferring the peace of the village to the noise and bustle of Lisbon. She took over the housekeeping in William's mansion, and befriended the glassworkers and their families. She visited them in their homes, brought food and blankets when they were sick, and wrote letters for those unable to write their own. A strong and courageous woman, she was an intelligent companion to her brother and they discussed the financial aspects of his operation, as well as matters of welfare in the village.

Pombal's visit had given William confidence. His monopoly would allow him to sell as much glass as his factory could produce and, aware that a happy and motivated workforce was the key to high productivity, he introduced a programme of social welfare to Marinha Grande, thirty years ahead of similar developments in Britain.[12] In 1769, he had found a poor village on the edge of the pine forest; this he turned into a prosperous community in which the population was able to grow beyond the national average.[13] He saw himself as patron and protector of his workmen, and acted more like a squire of an English village than a proprietor of an industrial concern. He paid good wages; opened an elementary school where his apprentices received an education (learning to read, write and draw, and studying geometry and music); provided a first aid post where sick or injured workers were treated free of charge; organised a relief fund for illness; and set up a generous pension scheme.[14]

His first three years in Marinha Grande were marred by drunkenness in the factory; new taverns were opened to serve the growing population and "intoxication and disorder" would stop production for many hours at a time. As well as reducing output, such behaviour was a fire risk and, in January 1773, William was given permission to close all taverns in the area, except for one inn adjacent to the factory which, under his control, restricted sales of alcohol to good quality wine and for cash payment only.[15]

Another problem was a shortage of meat. Local butchers were unable to meet the increased demand, so the glassworkers ("who, because of their hard physical labour, require substantial and vigorous foodstuffs") had to travel eight miles to the town of Leiria.[16] The journeys were made in their working hours, reducing productivity, while the meat in Leiria was expensive and of poor quality. William's solution was to provide a slaughterhouse and butcher shop in the factory complex, using animals sourced from farmers in the area, many of whom worked as part-time carters in the pine forest.[17]

At the same time, he provided a greater variety of fruit and vegetables, for his interest in horticulture (nurtured by his father's lessons in botany) had flourished since his arrival in Marinha Grande. Using the aqueduct which piped water to the factory compound, he created the lake behind his house and, from the lake, he built conduits leading to an orchard and vegetable garden. The orchard he planted with fruit trees (grown from seed imported from England), while the vegetable garden grew many different varieties, including salad vegetables new to the country: lettuce, radishes,

watercress, and chicory.[18] He was generous with his innovations and soon people in the area were enjoying salads for the
first time. As he wrote to Pombal, "When your Excellency
first sent me to this place, I found it difficult to find a lettuce
to eat. Now, in imitation of my vegetable garden and with
plants and seeds taken from it, Leiria, Batalha and
Alcobaça are well-provisioned with the most delicate
greens."[19]

And remembering his childhood on the farm in Pillaton, he
turned his mind to agriculture. "The land about Marinha
Grande," wrote one of his visitors, "is very unproductive, the
greater part being a waste of marsh or sand."[20] William's
estates totalled 15,000 acres, mostly areas of scrub and
heath, land which he used to extract sand for use in the
factory. Having seen the poor harvests obtained by local
farmers and the backward methods used to cultivate the soil,
he reclaimed some of his waste land and used it to teach more
up-to-date techniques of cultivation. Initially, he introduced
methods of agriculture that were in general use in England,
but the land was so sandy and sterile that the volume of crops
harvested remained low.

Then he heard of the achievements of Thomas Coke, an
agriculturist in England. Coke had inherited estates in
Holkham, close to the sea in Norfolk where soil conditions
were similar to Marinha Grande (barren sandy soil with little
vegetation). Within a few years, he had turned this
unpromising ground into land which grew wheat, barley
and corn, as well as pasturing the latest breeds of sheep and
cattle. He planted pine trees to anchor the shifting sands. He
adopted an improved rotation of crops which enriched the
soil. He dug deep pits to find seams of marl (a soft impure
limestone which, when mixed with topsoil, adds body and
lowers acidity), seams which lay buried beneath thick layers
of sandy soil. He introduced clover and forage grasses, so
that livestock could graze in the fields, and reclaimed large
areas of salt marsh and shingle from daily flooding by the
tides and prepared them for cultivation.

Coke organised annual gatherings of his farmers, events which soon expanded to include agriculturists and scientists from Europe and North America, as well as from all parts of England. News of these gatherings travelled to Portugal and William heard of Coke's success with growing excitement. He set up a farm three miles south of the glassworks, together with two smallholdings outside the factory complex. As Coke had done in Norfolk, he planted pine trees to stabilise the soil and he wrote to England to employ an adviser with knowledge of the methods used at Holkham. A few months later, an agriculturist sailed up the Tagus and made the journey to the glassworks, where William made him welcome in his mansion house.

The two men rode over the land at Marinha Grande, discussing its similarities to Holkham. They dug a number of exploratory holes until they discovered seams of marl which were mined for adding to the topsoil. The agriculturist advised William to raise windbreaks planted with bushes to shelter the growing crops, he told him about the new four-course rotation of crops (which eliminated the need for a fallow year), and suggested that he order mechanical seed drills and iron ploughs from England.[21]

William followed this advice and soon his large farm was growing wheat, corn, barley and oats, as well as root and leguminous crops for rotation, the smallholdings providing clover, grasses and alfalfa for pasturage and cattle feed. The marl-enriched land nurtured the growing crops, producing greater volumes at harvest time, and local farmers learnt to use the ploughs and seed drills. The alfalfa fields (the first in Portugal) produced several harvests a year, allowing more livestock to be kept on the land and increasing the supply of meat in the factory shop. And since alfalfa is pollinated by bees, he kept bee hives on his land, providing honey for the people of the village.[22]

As a result of William's efforts, his workers were healthier and better fed than in other areas of Portugal. His motto was "Ordem e Trabalho" (order and work), and he laid down a pattern for their daily lives: eight hours of work, eight hours of sleep and eight hours of leisure. Having closed the taverns, he provided cultural activities to occupy their free time. He employed teachers of music and dance, and built a small theatre to one side of his private garden. Plays were staged every Sunday as his craftsmen acted in plays of William's choice, often translations of Shakespeare or Voltaire. On one occasion, they performed Voltaire's *Olimpia*, translated by a Portuguese dramatist who directed the production and was "filled with admiration for workmen who had never seen theatre before, but who had the will and energy to commit themselves to this great and difficult tragedy." The production, he said, fell only a little short of those staged at court by professional actors.[23]

Every Saturday afternoon, there were concerts in William's music room, "never less than a harpsichord, a bass, two violoncellos, two horns, and four fiddles; no-one but a labourer in the factory is allowed in the band and there are some excellent performers."[24] And from time to time, William was serenaded by workers playing in the minstrel's gallery above the staircase, the ceiling decorated with musical motifs: a guitar, two trumpets and a violin.

William was proud of his achievements at Marinha Grande and he was much loved in the village. Every year on his birthday, after the workers had gathered in the factory courtyard, he emerged through the front door of his house, gave a speech to the assembled crowd, then walked amongst them, clasping their hands, putting an arm around their shoulders, and chatting to them with a general air of *bonhomie*.[25]

"The buildings of this manufactory are remarkably complete," wrote a visitor to the glassworks, "and the utmost regularity prevails in each department. The genius of this worthy man has changed the face of the country and the character of its inhabitants. The workmen are clean and industrious, men, women and children appear excited by a laudable emulation, and a general spirit of exertion pervades the whole district. The habits of the people employed in the factory are civil, obliging and orderly, and labour and amusement are happily combined."[26]

"I never saw so excellent an establishment," wrote another, "where such strict discipline is observed to the hours of attendance or more diligence appears through the work of the day. No drink but water is allowed in the factory during working hours and, generally speaking, the people here live to a great age. Mr Stephens might make a vast deal more money by the factory than he does. He is already one of the richest men in Portugal and there is not, I suppose, a better man in any country."[27]

Meanwhile, William's friendship with the Marquês de Pombal had brought him into court circles. Attending court was not a comfortable experience. Only the royal family could be seated in company; everyone else had to stand, an ordeal for the ageing Pombal who suffered from varicose veins and leg ulcers. Some of the courtiers knelt from time to time to rest their feet, others retired from the state rooms to lie down on the floors of antechambers.

Dom José remembered the young man he had persuaded to move to Marinha Grande a few years earlier, the young man convinced that reopening the glassworks would ruin him for a third time. But William had changed since then; his dress and demeanour had become more confident and he felt at ease in the king's presence. In 1774, he was asked to provide glass for the Great Room in the palace of Queluz, a newly-constructed room for official audiences with a large number of doors and windows opening onto the formal gardens.[28] Flattered by the request, he instructed his glassworkers to make sheets of the smoothest, thinnest window glass which he despatched direct to the palace, packed in large quantities of straw.

Appearances at court maintained his standing in government circles but William spent most of his time in Marinha Grande, directing every aspect of production and administration. The glassworks were a successful and well-run factory. The quality of finished glass had improved with the employment of a Bohemian master engraver, and three of William's apprentices had learnt their craft so quickly that he employed them as assistant glassworkers before their apprenticeship was completed. The workshops were operating at full capacity and sales were increasing as imports had declined to minimal levels since the imposition of higher duties.[29] William's operation had become extremely profitable but he still had a few problems to contend with, mainly concerning the supply of firewood and transport of finished glass to Lisbon.

Heavy rains during the winter months often made the roads impassable, covering them with mud and swelling the rivers and streams so that bullock carts were unable to ford them. "This obliges me," wrote William, "to send orders by the port of São Martinho, using open boats to transport the glass by sea." The boats had to negotiate Atlantic surf at the entrance to the harbour before sailing down the coast to Lisbon, a risky method of transport for such a fragile product (particularly since each cargo was worth almost £50,000 in today's values).[30]

He was also affected by the petty bureaucracy of officials in the pine forest. His contract allowed him to use wood which was of no value for building purposes, but the keeper of the forest refused to grant him a licence to cut branches. He had to make formal declarations that he had made maximum use of chippings from the sawmill and dead wood on the ground before his carters were allowed to cut from the tree. Even then, he had to declare that the branches were affected by fungal infestation and therefore useless for construction purposes. At the same time, officials were apprehending workers who (in their opinion) had infringed regulations; William's carters were often removed from the forest and it was sometimes difficult to obtain sufficient firewood to fuel the furnaces.

In the spring of 1774, William complained to Pombal about the activities of one official, a complaint which was promptly dealt with. Later in the year, he was troubled by a man named Azevedo; despite several protests to the keeper of the forest, no action had been taken and William included the matter in his annual report. "This man lives on stealing," he wrote, "and has made the most extravagant demands by pretending to be an official in his Majesty's service. He torments my workers, threatens the factory and, with the most scandalous words, has offended me personally in such gross ways that I feel obliged to inform your Excellency of them under separate cover."[31]

In his private letter to Pombal, William set out the abuse he had suffered from Azevedo, including an attack on his religious principals which, although Protestant in a Catholic country, were deeply held. "This kingdom has no need for glass," Azevedo was telling the people of the district, "and even less need for heretics. Even the parish priest of Marinha Grande is an infidel for he is friendly with the heretic William Stephens."[32]

During the previous three years, the minister had intervened in a number of William's local difficulties and now he came to his aid once again. Azevedo was arrested, an enquiry opened into the conduct of forest administrators, and officials instructed by royal order to assist the transport of firewood to the factory. A year later, the keeper of the forest was ordered to enlist a hundred carters to work solely for the glassworks, an area of the forest being set aside for their exclusive use.[33]

7

The Fall of Pombal

1775–1782

"Your Excellency has nothing more to do here."
Cardinal da Cunha to Marquês de Pombal, 25 February 1777

On 6 June 1775, a statue of Dom José was inaugurated in the Praça do Comércio, the great square by the Lisbon waterfront where merchants congregated to hear the latest news and discuss matters of business. The statue depicted the king in breast-plate and plumed helmet, his horse tramping on writhing serpents, the pedestal decorated with allegorical figures and a bas-relief of the Marquês de Pombal.

The Praça do Comércio was the centrepiece of Pombal's reconstruction of the city, although one side remained unfinished and this was hung with a replica painted onto canvas. The square was swept and sanded, the stands filled with dignitaries, diplomats, magistrates and military men. When the king and queen had taken their seats under a canopy, Pombal stepped forward and unveiled the statue to the sound of rockets and a salvo of guns fired from ships anchored in the Tagus.

A few days later, Pombal presented Dom José with a report on his achievements as first minister of the country. "Observant foreigners do not fail to remark," he wrote, "the many millions spent on public and private buildings after the earthquake. They see a most magnificent square, surpassing all others in Europe, with a costly equestrian statue in the centre. In the past, every manufactured article was imported from abroad, but now our native industries provide everything necessary for the dress of both sexes, for the furnishing of houses, for the rich and numerous carriages used on this most brilliant occasion; even the candlesticks and drinking glasses are made by his Majesty's subjects."[1]

Many of Pombal's new factories (particularly those run by foreign entrepreneurs) did operate successfully, but the articles they produced were of lower quality and more expensive than those produced elsewhere in Europe. "They only survive," explained a foreign diplomat, "because of the costly patronage of the government."[2] However, as the minister recognised, it was a step forward for the Portuguese to buy goods made in their own country instead of spending money on imports.

Meanwhile, William's operation was thriving. The glass-works were exempt from domestic taxes, competition had been removed by high import duties, and all obstacles to the smooth running of his factory were promptly dealt with. The only clouds on the horizon were the advanced age of the minister and the king's deteriorating health. Pombal was unpopular with the aristocracy, the clergy and the people, and it had long been surmised that he would fall from power on the death of Dom José.

A few months before the inauguration of his statue, José had suffered a series of strokes, leaving him partially paralysed. He attended the celebrations in the Praça do Comércio, but took little interest in the proceedings and showed no signs of pleasure when the great statue was unveiled. Eighteen months later, he was crippled by another, more devastating stroke and the atmosphere in the royal palace changed. Pombal attended his master every day, his tall frame bending over the sick-bed, but the ranks of courtiers closed around the king as soon as he left the room, and foreign diplomats wrote home to their governments that a change in politics was imminent.

Pombal was seventy-eight years old, and suffered from oedema and ulcers in the legs. He stooped slightly, but his great height was still impressive and old age had not impaired his vigour or his intellectual power. A few months earlier, the

French ambassador had written that the minister was "sound in body and mind, thinking himself immortal, talking of vast projects that not even his sons could hope to see realised."[3] But he had become increasingly ruthless. The people loathed him and, when his carriage rattled through the streets of Lisbon, they slammed their windows shut as he approached.

The king died in the early hours of 24 February 1777 and the following morning, when Pombal went as usual to the palace, he was greeted by Cardinal da Cunha (one of his former allies) with the words "Your Excellency has nothing more to do here." Barred from royal circles, the minister returned home to await developments, while priests hurried from house to house to pass on the news and people took to the streets, rejoicing.

Dom José was succeeded by his eldest daughter, Dona Maria, the first female monarch in Portuguese history. In accordance with a custom of the royal family, Maria was married to one of her uncles and, until the death of her father, she and her husband had been living quietly in the palace of Queluz, producing a family of several children. In a document signed shortly before his death, José had expressed the wish that Maria would "pardon the legal punishment of those state criminals she may judge worthy of forgiveness." Accordingly, the prisons were opened and more than 800 people emerged from incarceration in Lisbon, some after an imprisonment of twenty years. Crowds of sympathisers gathered at the gates as the priests, magistrates, and men and women of the aristocracy emerged from the dungeons. Pale and emaciated, their clothes in tatters, the prisoners were carried home to their families, and Pombal, hiding behind the shuttered windows of his house, became aware that his days of power were over.

On 1 March, he asked permission to travel to the small town of Pombal (twenty miles north-east of Marinha Grande), the town from which he had taken his title. This put Maria in a difficult position. Her priests and courtiers were pleading for his arrest and imprisonment, but she honoured her father's memory and Pombal had been José's favoured and trusted minister. For the present, she accepted his resignation and, on 4 March, she signed a decree allowing him to retire to the town near his birthplace and ordering him to remain there. The following day, he travelled to his estate in Oeiras a few miles west of the city; in the evening, the people of Lisbon burned him in effigy and marched singing through the streets.

From Oeiras, Pombal sent a letter to his eldest son who had been allowed to remain at court. He was, he wrote, "heavy-hearted and lonely, for I have not yet the consolation of your mother's company and the escort which is to accompany us on our journey has not arrived. You can imagine what my night has been like, when to the strain of the last weeks has been added a separation from my children whom I so deeply love."' Next morning, he was joined by his wife and, the following day, they started their journey north. They made slow progress. The roads were in an appalling state from the winter rains and, to avoid angry villagers, they made several detours which prolonged the journey. Pombal was too ill and depressed to leave the carriage but sometimes, to lighten the load on the mules, his wife was forced to walk. The party stumbled along, manoeuvring the carriage over the rocky tracks, and at night they kept moving by the light of torches.

They arrived in Pombal after a journey of eight days. The minister owned large estates in the area but had neglected to maintain his property in the town, so the only accommodation available was a small rented building, an old, dilapidated, single-storey house in the market square. The walls were damp from the rain, but Pombal and his wife settled in as best they could and unpacked the few possessions they had been able to bring with them.

William had long suspected that his friend would lose power on the death of Dom José but he was shocked by the speed at which he was banished from court. Drawn to the man to whom he owed his entire fortune in life, he grieved for the minister in his predicament. Nevertheless, he had his own position to consider. Many of Pombal's collaborators had been dismissed from their posts; others were deserting him to ingratiate themselves with the new regime. And because subsidies to the new industries were being reduced, it was essential that he act quickly to ensure that his factory retained its privileges.

In this difficult situation, William had the courage to act with honour as well as self-interest. He opened negotiations with Dona Maria and her courtiers, but remained loyal to his friend and began to correspond with him as soon as he had settled in his place of exile. To keep him up-to-date with foreign news, he sent gazettes from England (translating the more important items into Portuguese) and delivered baskets of asparagus, herbs and seeds, for the minister shared his interest in horticulture and was planting a vegetable garden on his land in Pombal.[5]

From time to time, William's carriage travelled the rough roads from Marinha Grande and Philadelphia accompanied her brother, forging a friendship with the Austrian-born marquesa who was finding it difficult to adjust to life in exile. "During the prosperity of the marquês," wrote a traveller who visited Pombal in July, "his wife had grandees at her feet, her house was a sort of court, and men would kneel to kiss her hand. Her vanity, flattered by so many marks of respect, cannot tolerate the solitude to which her husband's disgrace has condemned her. These sentiments she strove to conceal from me but they were too powerful to repress and, after ten minutes conversation, her eyes overflowed with tears." As Pombal watched his wife's face crumple with misery, he turned to his visitor. "That is natural in her sex," he told him. "To comfort her is one of my occupations."[6]

In September, William fell ill with malaria and, when Pombal heard the news, he sent a messenger to enquire about his condition. "Yesterday's fit of ague was small," William replied, "and I have started to take quinine." Four days later, when Pombal sent for further news, William was feeling stronger. "I have only suffered one fit of ague since I started the medication," he wrote, "and believe that the quinine has effected a complete eradication of my ills. As a precaution, I am drinking the extract of laxative plants, repeating the quinine at every change of moon and at each quarter. The illness, the blood-letting or the medicines have weakened my eyesight, but I am not too concerned about this because every day I am feeling better." William had intended to visit Pombal as soon as his health improved but his use of laxatives confined him to the house. "I have had no repetition of my ailment," he wrote at the end of the month, "but shall continue with the preventative medicines which means I find it embarrassing to go out." He hoped he would soon be able to call on his friend; meanwhile Philadelphia sent her respects to the marquesa.[7]

Three months later, Pombal received a pamphlet of letters published anonymously in London.[8] The pamphlet, which eulogised the minister and his achievements, arrived with a covering letter from John Blankett, his go-between in secret negotiations with the political opposition in England. Before the death of Dom José, Pombal had asked for English military assistance in his territorial squabbles in South America, a request the British government (busy fighting its own colonists in North America) had refused. Considering this to be in breach of the Anglo-Portuguese alliance, Pombal had informed the opposition that his country might be forced into alliance with Spain, with unfortunate consequences for England so far as trade and a safe harbour in Lisbon were concerned.

Despite his years as Portuguese envoy in London, Pombal was unable to read English (a language he felt was particularly difficult for a Portuguese).[9] Seeing his name quoted many times, he spent a frustrating few days before a note arrived from William who had ordered a copy for himself and knew that the pamphlet was complimentary to his friend. "In my dilemma," explained Pombal, "I received a

1   Sebastião de Carvalho e Melo (Marquês de Pombal) planning the
reconstruction of Lisbon, painting by Miguel Angelo Lupi

2   Packet ships at their moorings in Falmouth harbour, viewed from above the town, 1775

3   HM Packet *Walsingham*, 1823. Built in 1794, the *Walsingham* carried post and passengers to and from Lisbon for the next thirty years

4 Glass cut and engraved with a portrait of Dom José, attributed to Antonio Taibner, a Bohemian master craftsman employed at Marinha Grande, c.1772

5 The royal glass factory in Marinha Grande, engraving dated 1868

6 Inside the workshop for crystalline glass, engraving dated 1890

7 View of the glass factory, engraving dated 1890. The railway lines were built in 1862/3 to transport wood from the royal pine forest to the port of São Martinho

8 Bullock cart carrying firewood in the royal pine forest, c.1950. Little has changed since the time of William and John James (except the dress of the carter)

9   The mansion house in Marinha Grande (c.1772), photographed from the factory courtyard

10   The workshop for crystalline glass (rebuilt after the French invasion of 1810/11), photographed from the main gates

11 William Stephens, engraving by A Smith from drawing by Bouck, 1799

12   Liskeard from Beloytha Fields, engraving dated 1850

13   Charles Lyne dressed as a page to accompany William Stephens to Dona Maria's court, c.1778

14   Coat of arms of the Stephens family in the mansion house at Marinha Grande

letter from my friend, William Stephens, who informed me
that he was expecting a pamphlet of letters from London
which he would forward as soon as it arrived. The marquesa,
judging it to be the same as the one we already had, begged
me to send it to William Stephens with a request that he
would have it translated by someone who might be paid for
his trouble."[10]

Pombal took his wife's advice and wrote to Marinha
Grande, a letter to which William replied promptly. He was
pleased to have the pamphlet, for the ship carrying the copy
he had ordered from London had missed the Tagus and
sailed by mistake to Portimão, a fishing port on the south
coast. His office was short-staffed and no clerk was available
to do the translation but, "since the letters are in praise of
your Excellency, my sister has offered to translate them and
will do so with much pleasure, especially as the marquesa
also wishes to read them."[11] And so, as Pombal noted,
"Philadelphia Stephens, who has contracted a friendship
with the marquesa, took the translations upon herself and
forwarded them to us as soon as they were ready."[12]

Pombal spent long hours reading Philadelphia's translations, his suspicious mind looking for hidden meanings in
every paragraph. Unable to accept that the pamphlet was
written in his defence, he decided that it was drafted by the
opposition in England to criticise the government's handling
of the American War of Independence. "The more I analysed
the letters," he wrote, "the more I became convinced that
they were not written to instruct readers in the history of
Portugal. Nor was my personal praise, nor defence of the
calumnies written against me, the object of this work. My
name served only as a pretext to cover the thundering attacks
made on the British government."[13]

William was a little surprised at these conclusions,
although he admired the rigour of the old man's intellect.
And while he maintained his friendship with Pombal, he was
also in communication with the new regime. His annual
report for 1776 was incomplete when the minister fell from

power and he had taken the opportunity of sending it to the queen personally, an opportunity which allowed him to state his case for continued royal protection.[14] He received no reply and, in May the following year, he came under combined pressure from the Junta do Comércio and from foreign glass merchants who had lost their market when higher import duties were imposed six years earlier.

His first loan repayment had fallen due in the autumn of 1773, but he had succeeded in postponing payment until July 1775 when the Junta asked him to pay the money immediately as it was "long overdue."[15] William, who preferred not to lose the profits flowing into his account books, explained that he was unable to make repayments in cash because the money was tied up in the factory and in stocks of finished glass. However, since he was supplying lime and window glass for the reconstruction of Lisbon, he suggested that payments be made in kind. At the time, this was considered a reasonable proposition; it was, the Junta explained to Dom José, "the best means possible to obtain repayment of the loan without prejudice to the royal coffers, as well as encouraging the continuation of two factories which are so useful to the state."[16]

For almost three years, William repaid his loan in consignments of lime and window glass but, after the fall of Pombal, the reconstruction had come to a standstill. In May 1778, the Junta advised him that it could no longer guarantee the quantities required because, "by order of her Majesty, the greater part of the works are suspended. It is therefore necessary that you make repayments of the loan in money, to be paid over the contracted period." William appealed against this decision, reasoning that some rebuilding was likely to continue, but in July he heard again from the Junta: "The payment of the debt in the form of lime and glass is no longer viable because of the continuing suspension of public works in the city."[17] The buildings that remained under construction were of "little consideration," while the state coffers were empty, requiring prompt repayment of all outstanding debts.

Meanwhile, two importers of Bohemian glass had sent a petition to the queen complaining about high import duties and the inferior quality and high price of glass from Marinha Grande.[18] It was a critical time for William. He would lose his monopoly if the new regime sympathised with the merchants and reduced the duties on imported glass. Meanwhile, the reconstruction of the city (which had taken a significant proportion of his window glass) had been cancelled and he would have to repay the loan from profits made on his private sales.

William was confined to Marinha Grande during these months because of the illness of his administrator and the absence of a clerk. Never too proud to roll up his sleeves and work in the office when occasion demanded, he was doing the accounts, paying wages and invoices, ordering supplies of raw materials, and organising transport. "I am in this factory," he wrote to Pombal, "not only as owner but also as supernumerary, always prepared to work in positions which are vacant – so much so that I have been held captive in the office for the past twelve weeks." He had, he told his friend, been forced to dismiss his clerk for having taken up "the vice of hunting" so enthusiastically that he was frequently absent from work.[19]

By the autumn, most of William's worries had been resolved. On the advice of the Junta do Comércio, the queen rejected the petition from the glass merchants, maintaining import duties at high levels.[20] The administrator recovered from his illness and a new clerk was employed, freeing William from the office and allowing him to spend several weeks with his family in Lisbon. He made appearances at court, reminding Maria that her father had placed the glassworks under his "immediate and royal protection," he showed loyalty to Pombal by dining at Oeiras with his eldest son, and there were business matters to attend to, particularly at the lime kilns. The factory had lost its market with the cancellation of the building works and, as William explained to Pombal, "Unless new measures are taken (which I do not expect), it will be closed down."[21]

For many years, Maria had agonised over the fate of the Távora conspirators. She believed their execution to have been unmerited and unjust, although she knew that a posthumous pardon would damage the honour of her father, whose memory she held dear. These conflicting emotions caused the queen great anguish and she found it difficult to make a decision on the future of the exiled minister.

Maria and her consort had been excluded by Pombal from all contact with government; they had no knowledge of public affairs and their personal interests were limited to domesticity and the church. They were excessively religious, an English traveller commenting on the "gloomy and severe spirit of superstition" which formed the core of Maria's character. She was, he wrote, "tall and thin, of a pale and wan complexion that indicated melancholy."[22] Her consort, Dom Pedro, was an unintelligent man, "devout, reserved, and constantly engaged in prayers and processions."[23]

Maria was given little opportunity to forget the minister. Public rage had resulted in his plaque being torn off the statue in the Praça do Comércio ("I am happy to hear it," said Pombal, "it was a very poor likeness"),[24] and she was besieged by appeals for his arrest. In 1779, a nobleman laid a claim for damages against him. He accused Pombal of "having abused a despotic power to raise himself to the summit of honours and riches at the expense of the liberties of many innocent persons."[25] Pombal responded to this claim with enthusiasm, drafting a closely-argued defence of his actions. It was the king, he wrote, who had signed every order against the nobles and the Jesuits. He, the loyal servant, had merely been a passive instrument in his master's service.[26]

The queen was unhappy to see her father held responsible for such tyranny, and Pombal was delighted when he heard that Maria had asked to read the papers. "I am not displeased that my contradiction has been sent to the palace," he wrote to his son. "The documents will weight the consciences of those who read them, who will see that I ought not to be treated with such barbarity."[27] His hopes were misplaced, for Maria declared his defence to be a libel on her ministers and an insult to her father's name. She had spent long hours in prayer before consenting to the demands of her courtiers, but now she agreed that plans should be put in hand for his prosecution.

On 9 October, two judges arrived at Pombal's house to interrogate him on charges of abuse of power, corruption and fraud. A temporary courtroom was set up and the trial lasted for more than fifty days. Pombal's strength was fading; sometimes he fainted, sometimes he was carried into the courtroom on a stretcher, sometimes he was too ill to be questioned. But throughout the trial, he continued to assert that every cruel deed, every act of terror, had been instigated by the king who had signed all the relevant papers.

In January, a few days before the interrogations ended, William and a visitor to the glassworks, the poet William Julius Mickle, made the journey from Marinha Grande. "We waited first on two judges," Mickle wrote in his diary, "who were there on enquiries carried on with a degree of rigour against the great minister which indicates a desire for retaliation. This extraordinary man is now in his eighty-first year and retains all the spirit and memory of his youth, both of which are remarkably lively and strong."[28]

Pombal had been so weakened by the trial that he was unable to see anyone, not even his friend from the glass factory. "After an hour's conversation with the judges," the poet continued, "we went with the magistrate to the house of the marquês who has been much indisposed. His lady received our visit with the greatest affability and politeness, in which no person can be more accomplished than the marquesa. After three quarters of an hour, we retired with the magistrate with whom we supped and returned to Marinha Grande early next morning."

When the judges reported their findings, Maria was once more in a difficult position. While Pombal's enemies were clamouring for his punishment, he had proved that every one of his decrees had been signed by her father. Initially she hoped that Pombal would die but, although his physical sufferings were acute, the life force in the old man showed no signs of weakening. In March, she sent a doctor to report on his condition and was dismayed at the findings. "The marquês," wrote the doctor, "displays the vivacity of spirit, the lucidity and firmness of intellect, and the fresh and exact memory of a man not yet thirty years old."[29] This extraordinary statement may have been true of Pombal's mind, but his body was a different matter. His skin was ulcerated, his blood poisoned, and he suffered from fever and dysentery. The doctors prescribed asses' milk and viper-broth (local people brought snakes to his door in baskets) and he was dosed with quinine.

But still he lived and, in August the following year, the queen signed a decree. The Marquês de Pombal, she declared, was "an infamous criminal deserving of exemplary punishment. Nevertheless, out of regard for his advanced age and heavy infirmities, I have been softened by his prayers for pardon. Remitting all bodily punishments, I enjoin him to absent himself from the court at a distance of at least twenty leagues, my intention being only to pardon him the personal chastisement which justice and the laws require."[30]

Pombal died on 8 May 1782, a little more than five years after losing office. As his body lay in an open coffin, crowds of people filed through the house in the market square, crossing themselves at the sight of the recumbent figure with its long emaciated face. The clergy came too, to sing masses for his soul, and William and Philadelphia came from Marinha Grande to pay their last respects to the man who had befriended and enriched them.

On 12 May, the bells tolled as Pombal's body was taken to church in a hearse drawn by six horses, escorted by eight boys with lighted tapers. As the coffin was placed on a bier before the altar, William remembered his friend and mentor, the man who had given him so much help at Marinha Grande. The minister had had great charm. An advanced thinker, he was interested in the philosophy of the Enlightenment, the physics of Newton, the latest ideas about education and medicine, and he and William spent many hours discussing the social reform of his country.

William was also aware of the minister's dark side. As early as 1759, he had lain in his bed at Alcântara, listening to carpenters erecting the scaffold for the Távora conspirators, sawing and hammering through the night. Later, as their friendship matured, he had closed his ears to stories of courtiers imprisoned or deported without trial, of executions of those suspected of disloyalty, preferring to remember his friend for their wide-ranging conversations on philosophy, education and modern methods of agriculture. For the Marquês de Pombal was, as William told the poet William Julius Mickle, an extraordinary man.

8

The Largo dos Stephens

1777–1778

"The English in Lisbon are the most indefatigable dancers and the most inveterate casino players in all Europe."
Robert Southey, 1796

By the time of Pombal's death, William's family had been living in the mansion on Rua de São Paulo (the Largo dos Stephens) for almost ten years. John James left Alcântara as soon as the building was finished, Lewis and Jedediah moved in a little later, and the household was completed by Jane Campion, daughter of John Beare's partner in the glass factory. Jane's mother had been killed in the earthquake and, when her father died thirteen years later, she found herself alone in Lisbon, with no relatives, no money and no home. She was a shy young woman with little confidence, so William offered her shelter in his house at Alcântara, an offer which Jane accepted with relief.[1]

Jane was in charge of household management in the Largo dos Stephens and there was plenty of money to employ domestic servants. Apart from William's increasing wealth, his brothers were also doing well in business: Lewis had set up his own trading house; Jedediah was in partnership with a merchant from Exeter; and John James was proving to be a good administrator, handling the sale of glass in Lisbon as well as managing the lime kilns.

A few months after Pombal's fall from power, John James had found himself in difficulties with the British consul, Sir John Hort, over the custom-house certificates required to prove that cargoes of culm had been landed in Lisbon. As soon as these had been countersigned by the consul, they were sent to England to cancel the bond (for three times the value of the cargo) that John James's representative had signed at the port of embarkation. Hort was a pedantic official and, in the autumn of 1777, he decided that the wording of the culm certificate, which merely stated that the cargo had been unloaded, was inadequate. It was possible, he reasoned, for ships to have off-loaded some of their cargo in other countries and taken different goods on board. Also, "the means are not absolutely barred of fraudulently breaking bulk, whether at sea or in the same British port where they declare for Lisbon, by secretly conveying part of their culm on board some other ship."[2]

On 31 October, John James received a note from the consul: "You are to take notice for the future that, in all custom-house certificates under the Culm Act, it must be declared either that the ship brought nothing else except culm or, if it discharged anything besides culm, the particulars must be specified. It must also certify expressly that it was all unloaded for the manufactory of lime."[3]

John James replied a few days later: "As I am a great admirer of regularity in office, I must acquaint you that the Culm Act only requires a certificate testifying 'that such culm has been landed in Lisbon.' The other particulars are superfluous. As to the culm being 'all unloaded for the manufactory of lime,' it is a thing of course, culm being useless for any other purpose in this country."[4]

The matter came to a head on 9 November when the ship, *Four Brothers and Sisters* (owned by Lewis Stephens and named, a little inaccurately, after his family), arrived in Lisbon laden with culm. The cargo was off-loaded at the Alcântara quay and the customs officer completed the certificate, which John James sent to the consul.[5] It was returned unsigned, so John James sent it back. "Your secretary has returned the certificate of the *Four Brothers and Sisters* as insufficient," he wrote, "thereby depriving my friends of the means to cancel their bond as the Act directs. Is it not strange that, after twenty years, you should start these objections? Such scruples and trifling minutiae, Sir John, are the bane of trade and I lament meeting with them in a consul-general to the greatest commercial nation. Enclosed I return you the papers hoping that, on mature deliberation, you will send me the certificate as customary."[6]

After the certificate was returned unsigned for a second time, John James wrote again: "John James Stephens presents his compliments to Sir John Hort and requests that he will pass the enclosed certificate under his hand and seal of office, having been presented to him *such as it is*."[7] This time, his letter was returned unopened, the messenger informing John James that he should present himself at the consul's house for a conference.

William would have pandered to Sir John's sense of dignity to keep his business running smoothly, but the younger John James was more confrontational. "A conference cannot in any manner contribute to my indemnification should this matter be brought to a general issue," he wrote to Hort. "I therefore choose to avoid an interview until this affair is decided. I once more return you the papers, repeating my request of yesterday that you will send me a certificate of my having presented them to you, *such as they are*."[8]

No reply was received, so he sent a fourth letter to the consul: "I have represented and remonstrated, I have requested and entreated, without any effect, for a certificate from your office to cancel the bond given in England for the cargo of culm per the *Four Brothers and Sisters*, which I understand you are in duty bound to pass. Neither can I obtain from you any voucher to prove your refusal. I shall therefore, in consequence of your provoking silence, finish my epistolatory addresses and proceed to such judicial processes as may procure my indemnification."[9]

And this he did, sending his agent in London a letter addressed to the secretary of state, Lord Weymouth. After outlining the purpose of the culm certificates, he made the point that he and his brother were "uninterrupted importers of culm, with a character of probity unimpeachable, and most solemnly declare that we have never, nor ever will, abuse or deviate, even in thought, from the words there enacted." Hort had "arrogated to himself the power of prescribing a new mode for passing certificates," and his failure to sign the latest certificate was a breach of office. Finally, he made the point that he and William were "perplexed by these embarrassments as they cannot expect any person in England will give security for culm if proper returns are not readily made."[10]

A packet boat arrived in Lisbon towards the end of February, carrying a despatch from Lord Weymouth to Sir John Hort. "A form that has been used for near twenty years does not seem to have wanted amendment," it read, "and all innovations in these matters, unless essentially necessary, are inconvenient to trade. I therefore trust you will immediately re-establish the old form."[11]

John James heard from his agent by the same packet boat and immediately penned a letter to the consul. "Since you have been directed by the secretary of state to pass the culm certificates according to Act of Parliament without any innovation," he wrote, "this is to resume my former request for a certificate whereby they may cancel the bond given for the culm per the *Four Brothers and Sisters*."[12]

Hort, still smarting from Weymouth's rebuke, replied the same day: "Although it is not the custom of this office to engage in written correspondence with those of his Majesty's subjects who reside in this city and are able to attend their business in person, yet as you have found means to write me a few lines this morning unmixed with ill manners, I think it proper to acquaint you that I wrote by last post to your brother at Leiria to explain to him in what manner his business continues to be impeded."[13]

The letter reached Marinha Grande on 5 March and, as William read through the pages, he became increasingly angry. Hort complained of John James's attitude which he construed as arrogant and ill-mannered. He set out his reasons for refusing to sign the certificate, explaining how easily William and John James could abuse the Culm Act, and referred to John James's "improper letters, such as are not usually apt to forward any business within my knowledge."[14]

William put pen to paper the following day. "I am sorry to see," he wrote, "that the dispute between you and my worthy brother with respect to a culm certificate is not yet settled. I have maturely considered all the arguments you have offered, wherein you suppose there may be a possibility of evading the Act of Parliament by the culm ships going to some other country and unloading part of their cargoes, which suppositions, having no example, do not authorise you to stop our business. Besides which, they are so highly improbable that they require no refutation. These suspicions carried a little further would suppose more than you intend to say, but as yet I shall not take the argument up in that light. I am of the opinion that you have not the smallest foundation to refuse the certificate we have required. I am further of the opinion that you are under the highest obligation to my brother for proceeding so prudently in his complaint and through so proper a channel. The Culm Act, you know, was made in favour of this kingdom, so my brother might have made this dispute a court affair, but he very prudently avoided giving the court of Portugal any notice of your stopping the trade."[15]

This was not the reply Hort had expected, but the matter was soon of little relevance for Dona Maria put a halt to the reconstruction and, by the end of the year, the lime kilns had ceased production. It is significant that the consul only raised the issue when it became clear that the rebuilding of Lisbon would soon be cancelled. He reasoned that, unless William and John James had foreseen the situation and reduced the number of cargoes, they would be left with many tons of surplus culm, a type of coal with no other purpose than the burning of lime.

But the main reasons for the confrontation were Hort's bureaucratic nature and his sense of wounded dignity. As

William explained, "The real state of the argument is that you are displeased at my brother for not waiting personally on you for every certificate (notwithstanding you have always exacted the office fees contrary to Act of Parliament) and you are therefore determined to stop our business until he complies."[16]

Hort also remembered the time, four years earlier, when he had considered retiring from the post of consul and the envoy, Sir Robert Walpole, wrote to London suggesting that William might be a suitable replacement. Walpole had written twice on the matter. "I wrote to your Lordship some time ago," he explained in his second letter, "recommending Mr William Stephens to be successor to John Hort in case the latter should resign his post of consul-general. In a conversation I had lately with the Marquês de Pombal, I find that such a change would be highly agreeable here. I cannot forbear repeating this to your Lordship in case events should offer for such a measure which, I am sure, would be received here with the greatest satisfaction."[17]

Hort had not resigned, but he was aware of the envoy's recommendation. And Walpole's suggestion that William would make a better consul, and be more popular with the Portuguese government, was a lasting insult to his self-esteem.

The British community in Lisbon led an active social life. The merchants, explained an English visitor, "are as attentive to their counting-houses and business every day before dinner, as they are to their dressing, cards and other amusements in the evening. Any little moments they have to spare are towards the evening, and then the cards, the eternal cards, are constantly at hand to swallow it up."[18] Indeed, card playing and dancing were their main leisure occupations. The English Factory hosted a ball every fortnight, and dinners and entertainments were held in the homes of wealthier merchants. "All foreigners of distinction here," continued the visitor, "live on a very friendly footing with each other. They have public nights in their respective houses, when the master and mistress are glad to see all good company of their acquaintance without invitation. By this means, there is always one house, and often two, open every night of the week."[19]

Such entertainments were often held at the home of the consul, a man of stiff, formal manners as well as a pedantic turn of mind. Another Englishman described a musical evening at Sir John's house, an evening similar to many attended by the Stephens family (although John James was less welcome after the squabble over culm certificates). "We had some excellent music," wrote the traveller, "both vocal and instrumental. Sir John sang some charming duets with a Miss Cole, though when they first struck up I could hardly preserve my gravity, Sir John being a man of six foot two, very thin and upright as an arrow, Miss Cole a diminutive little creature of four foot and a half. The piece they commenced with was 'Drink to me only with thine eyes.' Nothing could have been executed in a more masterly style but the contrast in the figures, Sir John towering some feet above his companion upon whom he looked down most languishingly, was superlatively ridiculous."[20]

Meanwhile, much of the city remained in ruins, although the new grid of streets behind the Praça do Comércio was almost complete. Further west, reached by following the river or by climbing and descending one of Lisbon's many hills, was the corner of Rua de São Paulo and Rua das Flores. Here lay the Largo dos Stephens, a large four-storey house built on a steep incline from the river. Stuccoed and colour-washed, with wrought iron balconies, the mansion represented the growing wealth of the Stephens family.

In early 1778, when Lewis (the eldest of William's brothers) decided to expand his business, his thoughts turned to John Lyne, his cousin in Liskeard who had cared for him when he was orphaned. A sequence of two wives had provided John with twelve children and, to support his growing family, he was acting as master of Liskeard

Grammar School as well as rector of St Ive, a heavy workload for a man of fifty-four. His eldest son was a student at Oxford, destined for holy orders, but he had four more sons of school age and another still in the nursery.

More than twenty years earlier, John Lyne had taken pity on Lewis and given him a home and an education. Hoping to return the favour, Lewis wrote to Liskeard with a proposition: if John agreed, he would take two of his sons and bring them up in his merchant business. The boys would be employed as apprentices in Lewis Stephens & Company, they would have a comfortable home in Rua de São Paulo and, in time, they would become rich merchants in the city.

Interlude
Liskeard

1778

When Lewis's letter arrived in Liskeard, John Lyne had been rector of St Ive for twenty-four years and master of the Grammar School for fourteen. "I do not reside in my parish," he explained to his bishop, "but am the licensed master of the Grammar School at Liskeard which is distant but four short miles from my church at St Ive." Nicknamed "Short Mile Lyne" by his parishioners, his black-clad figure could be seen at weekends, riding along the road to St Ive, then back again to Liskeard.[1]

The school occupied a small building within the ramparts of the ruined castle, just two rooms overlooking the narrow streets of Liskeard. It had a high reputation and many boys from west country families were sent here for their education, several of them boarding with the master. John was a kind and learned teacher, "a good classical scholar," wrote one of his pupils, "with a taste for *belle-lettres*, particularly for poetry."[2] He took an interest in all his charges, encouraging the more intelligent to apply for scholarships at Oxford, and helping them find employment. "I improved greatly under his instruction," wrote one boy in later life. "He did me full justice as my preceptor and showed great kindness to me as long as he lived."[3]

Four of John's sons were attending the Grammar School, climbing Castle Hill every morning from the family house in Higher Lux Street. The eldest, Richard, was seventeen,

Charles almost fourteen, Joseph eleven, and Edward ten. They received a free education, while boarding and schooling for other pupils cost £14 a year, with additional fees for dancing and fencing lessons.[4]

Teaching in the schoolhouse, travelling the eight miles to and from St Ive, his house filled with his own children as well as several boarders, left John with little energy. He had hoped that all his sons would follow him into the church, but it was increasingly expensive to send young men to university (a degree from Oxford or Cambridge being a necessary qualification for holy orders). Meanwhile, England was suffering from inflation and those living on fixed incomes were the worst affected.[5] With his salary and stipend declining in value year by year, John was grateful for the opportunity to give two of his sons a good start in life.

After discussing the matter with his wife, he decided to leave the choice to the boys themselves, in order of seniority. Accordingly, he called Richard into his study and told him about the apprenticeship in Lisbon. "Which will you be," he asked his son, "a poor clergyman or a rich merchant?"[6] Richard, a pious boy with no ambition beyond holy orders, had no doubts. "A poor clergyman," he replied.

Now Charles came in. "Which will you be," John asked again, "a poor clergyman or a rich merchant?" Charles, who in later life always referred to himself as "a practical man," had not inherited the piety of his elder brother. "A rich merchant," he said.

Finally, the question was put to Joseph, who was too young to travel to Portugal but who looked up to Charles and copied him in everything he did. Eager to decide his future as Charles had done, he told his father that he would be a rich merchant too.

The following morning, John wrote to Lewis. Charles would leave for Portugal after his fourteenth birthday, Joseph would follow when he had finished his education. He disliked the idea of his sons travelling alone so, as soon as he received the letter, Lewis wrote to his sister in Marinha Grande, asking her to return to England to accompany Charles on the voyage.

Philadelphia had visited Liskeard sixteen years before, an eleven-year-old girl on her way to Portugal. She had grown into an intelligent and self-confident woman, and her poise and expensive clothing surprised her cousins when she returned to the small Cornish town. A few weeks earlier, in the spring sunshine at Marinha Grande, she had translated a pamphlet of letters for the exiled dictator of Portugal. Now, under gloomy skies, she was welcomed into John's house in Liskeard where she stayed for several weeks, passing on news of her brothers in Portugal, playing with the children in the nursery, and telling Charles about the south European city that would soon become his home.[7]

In May 1778, Charles said farewell to his parents (who were expecting a thirteenth child), and he and Philadelphia set out for Falmouth where they stayed at the inn for several days, waiting for an east wind. William Beckford suffered the same fate a few years later. "The glass is sinking," he wrote while waiting for the Lisbon packet, "the west wind breathing upon the water, sailors yawning at the door of every ale house. Navigation seems at a full stop, the captains lounging about with their hands in their pockets, and passengers idling at billiards."[8]

On 4 June, the winds moved to the east and Philadelphia led her young cousin on board the packet boat.[9] They stood on deck as the seamen made preparations for departure. The sails were raised, the ship began to move out of the harbour and, when Philadelphia went below to organise the cabins, Charles remained in the open air, watching the shores of his homeland recede into the distance until they dropped below the horizon and all he could see was water.

9

Dona Maria

1778–1788

"I have gone through this affair with great éclat. *It was an honour they have never done any of their own subjects."*
William Stephens, on the royal visit to Marinha Grande, October 1786

Charles sailed up the Tagus on 15 June, after a voyage of eleven days. Standing on deck as his Stephens cousins had done before him, he was entranced as the city of Lisbon came into view, sprawling over its seven hills, its white buildings reflecting the sunshine under a cloudless sky.

A chaise collected Charles and Philadelphia from the quay and, in the Largo dos Stephens, Charles was introduced to his cousins and Jane Campion and taken on a tour of the house to admire the spacious rooms with their wrought iron balconies and *azulejo* tiles, the elaborately carved and inlaid furniture, the view of the river from the upper floors of the building.

The following morning, he set out to explore the streets and squares of his new home. He discovered the hills of Lisbon, "such ups-and-downs," as an English visitor put it, "such shelving descents and sudden rises as occur at every step one takes."[1] He saw the ruins left by the earthquake, the heaps of fallen masonry that lay undisturbed in many parts of the city. He walked through Pombal's reconstruction near the river, with its wide streets and tall houses, and mingled with the merchants who gathered under the arcades in the Praça do Comércio to discuss the latest news and read foreign gazettes in the coffee houses.

As he wandered about the city, he became aware of women peering through latticed windows; he saw chaises drawn by mules trotting through the streets, men on horseback wearing cloaks and slouched hats, ladies on mules attended by servants. And there were men sitting in the street with baboons on their shoulders, freeing their heads from lice. "The baboons are very dextrous," explained a visitor to Lisbon, "and are the property of a man who gains his livelihood by thus employing them, exacting a *vintem* per head for cleansing it."[2]

Charles was given little time to explore, for Lewis soon put him to work in his counting-house. He wrote letters and orders destined for England and Brazil, and made copies of all correspondence, bills and insurance documents. "When I commenced my career in the counting-house of Mr Stephens," he told a relative many years later, "I sometimes worked on foreign post all night until I fainted from fatigue. Then, as soon as I recovered my senses, I took a bath and resumed my place at the desk."[3]

In August, when Charles was wilting from the heat, William arrived in Lisbon to decide the future of the lime kilns and be seen at Maria's court. Charles was a small, slight boy and William asked him to be his page. Given leave from the counting-house, dressed in silk and lace, a powdered wig and pale blue jacket with diamond buttons, Charles accompanied his cousin to the palace of Queluz and stood beside him in the gilded audience chamber. He was daunted by the formality and ceremonial, by the glitter of jewellery and richness of dress, for nothing in Liskeard had prepared him for such occasions.

On Sundays, the one day free from his duties, he attended morning service in the British envoy's house; in the afternoon, he wrote home to Liskeard in reply to letters which arrived on every packet boat. He learned that his new sister was born on 20 August (named Philadelphia after the visitor who had collected him from Cornwall), and his parents asked about their cousins in the Largo dos Stephens, whether they were likely to marry and have children of their own.

William was forty-seven years old, his brothers were in their thirties, and Philadelphia was twenty-seven. None of them had shown any inclination to marry but, in August 1779, Lewis (aged thirty-four) astounded them all, not least because his future bride was just fifteen years old. The daughter of a wealthy American merchant, Mary Bulkeley received a marriage settlement of twenty-four *contos* of *reis* and, on 27 November, after William and Philadelphia had made the journey from Marinha Grande, she and Lewis were married in the British envoy's house by the chaplain of the English Factory.[4]

A ball was held in the Largo dos Stephens to celebrate the wedding, to which William invited the poet, William Julius Mickle, who had recently arrived in Lisbon and been introduced to the Stephens brothers by the envoy, Sir Robert Walpole.[5] As members of the English Factory danced minuets in the ballroom, William sat at a window overlooking Rua de São Paulo, drinking wine with the poet from England. He told him about his glass factory in Marinha Grande and the miniature welfare state he had created there, he talked of his experiences in the earthquake and his friendship with the Marquês de Pombal. Mickle was curious about all things Portuguese and it was soon agreed that he would accompany William when he returned to the glassworks after Christmas.

They left Lisbon on 4 January, the poet anxious about the dangers of the journey. "This being the chief road to the northern provinces and no houses," he wrote in his diary after passing through an area north of Vila Franca, "naturally is a fit place for robbery and murder. The several crosses denote the spots where murders have been committed." William reassured him, having travelled the roads many times, and they arrived safely in Marinha Grande on 6 January. The two men enjoyed each other's company and Mickle stayed at the glassworks for the next three weeks, visiting the monasteries of Alcobaça and Batalha, and travelling to the town of Pombal to visit the exiled minister.[6]

William's careful handling of the situation at court, his wooing of the queen and her courtiers, bore fruit at the end of the year. As an Englishman, a protégé of Pombal and (worst of all) a Protestant, he had found it difficult to make a favourable impression. "Their present Majesties are so much given to piety," explained a visitor to Lisbon, "that there is no road to preferment but by the influence of the church. They and their ministers are constantly employed in masses and religious processions, and all other objects are over-looked or forgotten."[7] But William persevered; he attended court as often as time allowed, charming Maria with his intelligence and humour, and by the autumn of 1780, he had become her favourite industrialist.

In December that year, she proved her high opinion of William and his factory by endorsing the conditions agreed by her father in 1769.[8] Congratulating William and John James on the "zeal they have manifested for the great utility of my kingdom," her decree confirmed that the glassworks would continue to operate under royal protection, extended the exemption from sales taxes until 1794, and widened the definition to include export tax. The high duties on imported glass would remain in force and Maria conferred a new privilege (one which even Pombal failed to grant): the factory would be exempt from import duties on raw materials and utensils for a period of five years.[9] Finally, she stipulated that the glassworks should never be divided on the deaths of William and John James or their successors, nor were they allowed to admit other partners into the business. This, she explained, was to "conserve the integrity of this useful and beautiful factory for the benefit of this kingdom for ever."

After four years of uncertainty, William's factory – and his fortune – were secure. It was a time for celebration and his family made a special occasion of his fiftieth birthday on 16 May 1781, travelling to Marinha Grande to share in the festivities. A banquet was served in the mansion house, while musicians played in the gallery and the workers assembled in the courtyard. In the afternoon, they entered the house two-by-two. First came the administrator and book-keeper, then the glass-masters, assistants and apprentices, and finally the other workmen. William embraced them all and, as the last pair left the room, he followed them out of the house to find them re-assembled in the courtyard. The administrator removed a sheet of paper from his pocket and, as he recited a poem extolling William's achievements, his employer was overcome with emotion. "I shall remember this demonstration of affection," he told his workers, "to the very end of my days."[10]

William was well-known in Portugal and respected by most men in authority, with the notable exception of the clergy. Sixteen months after Maria confirmed his privileges, he became embroiled in litigation with the Bishop of Oporto who, angered at his tax exemptions, started legal proceedings on the grounds that glass sold in the city should be subject to an ancient tax (dating from 1120), the receipts of which were payable to the church. This was typical of the clergy's attitude towards the new domestic industries. ("It did more harm than good," said another bishop about a short-lived ribbon factory in Leiria. "It encouraged people to learn weaving and spinning, and many persons working together corrupt each other's morals. There is plenty of ground and let them till that. They will not starve and the less intercourse they have with strangers the better.")[11] The litigation with Oporto continued for almost a year and William drafted several petitions to the queen. His ability to write with logic and clarity served him well for, although the case involved one of her bishops – to whom she was generally subservient – Maria eventually found in his favour.[12]

Meanwhile, the Largo dos Stephens became home to another young Englishman as Joseph Lyne arrived from Liskeard in September 1782, allowing Charles (more than halfway through his apprenticeship) to take on more

responsible duties in Lewis Stephens & Company.[13] Eighteen
years old, Charles had become friends with John James and
was enjoying the social life of the English Factory which,
surprisingly, did not have its own Assembly Rooms until
John James negotiated a contract with the Marquês de
Marialva in 1783. Renting two storeys of a house Marialva
was building in Rua do Alecrim (close to the Largo dos
Stephens), the Factory asked John James to design the
interior; his plans included a ballroom the height of two
floors and a supper room stretching the length of the
building.[14]

Completed in 1785, the Assembly Rooms allowed
members of the Factory to meet every evening and amuse
themselves with cards, billiards, foreign gazettes and
conversation. Balls were held once a fortnight and, every
year, there were three gala entertainments when banquets
were served and dancing continued until morning. "Never,"
wrote the French ambassador after one such evening, "have I
attended such a beautiful and imposing assembly."[15]

William made the final repayment on his loan from the
government in 1786.[16] Profits from his monopoly were now
unencumbered by debt repayments but he was disappointed
that Maria had not imposed his tax exemptions for longer
periods. The exemption from sales taxes did not expire until
1794, but the exemption from import duties had expired the
previous December and he wrote to the queen asking her to
extend both these privileges. This was necessary, as he put it,
not only to protect the capital value of the factory, but also
"to preserve the good faith of our workers who, at present,
are not inclined to educate their sons in this art for fear that
the exemptions will soon expire, rendering their work useless
and obliging them, in their old age, to seek alternative
employment."[17]

In October, he attended Maria's court in the spa town of
Caldas da Rainha to deliver his petition personally and offer
condolences on the recent death of her consort. Maria had

been devoted to her husband; she was inconsolable at his loss but she gave an audience to her favourite Englishman. She agreed to extend his tax exemptions for ten years and, as she thanked William for his sympathy, he raised the courage to suggest a royal visit to Marinha Grande.[18] Touched by his solicitude, Maria agreed to visit the glassworks five days later when she would be staying at the monastery of Alcobaça.

William hurried back to his factory and, for several days, the workshops and open spaces were cleaned and tidied, creating an excitement amongst the glassworkers reminiscent of Pombal's visit in 1772. Philadelphia took charge of the organisation, cooks arrived from Caldas to set up kitchens, stables were prepared for the horses and mules, and arrangements made to feed the large number of servants that would accompany the queen and her retinue.

On the morning of 17 October, the royal carriages clattered through the gates, to be greeted by William on the steps of his mansion house. Maria was the first to alight, followed by her two sons and their wives. José, the crown prince, was (in royal fashion) married to one of his aunts; João's wife was the ten-year-old Spanish princess, Carlota Joaquina, a tiny mischievous child who scampered out of the carriage, intent on enjoying these hours away from palace protocol. Then came the aristocrats, the queen's confessor and other senior clerics, and the rest of Maria's household.

Refreshments were served (lemonade, iced tea and coffee, wine and liqueurs) before the royal party made a tour of the glassworks. The cooks from the palace had prepared a banquet and, after the queen visited the workshops, William accompanied her to the first floor of his mansion house. Maria travelled with her troupe of musicians, a choir of boy singers accompanied by an orchestra of violins, cellos, oboes and flutes; and as the royal party began to eat, the doors to the central staircase were thrown open and the musicians, crowded into the minstrel's gallery, played and sang for their queen.

Later that afternoon, the horses and mules were brought from the stables, carriages rumbled into the courtyard and servants hurried about, attending to the details of departure. "I have gone through this affair with great *éclat*," William told a visitor to the factory. "It was an honour they have never done any of their own subjects. I was therefore without a precedent to go by. I requested nothing from the palace but their cooks and the kitchen utensils."[19] And the day was, according to *Gazeta de Lisboa*, "all to the queen's satisfaction."[20]

Eighteen months later, when Maria and her court returned to Caldas, William made another visit to the spa town. His monopoly was under threat from foreign glass merchants who hoped to avoid import duties by building their own factories in the country. He asked the queen for confirmation that foreign factories would not be permitted on Portuguese soil and, as Maria gave him the assurance he needed, she hinted that she was willing to make another visit to Marinha Grande.

During his birthday celebrations on 16 May, William stood on the steps of his house to address the assembled workers. "This annual gesture of affection is very pleasing to me," he told them, "and I congratulate you on the industry and enthusiasm which have enabled this factory to reach the summit of its achievement. It is the admiration of your compatriots and fills the hearts of importers with envy and malice. But their efforts to build new factories will come to nothing. Our factory produces sufficient glass to supply the entire kingdom and its colonies, and her Majesty will not permit factories to operate with foreign craftsmen, for these would prejudice her subjects, the workers in this factory who have applied themselves so well to the art of glassmaking that they can compete with the most skilled glassworkers in Europe. When I went to Caldas, I was given the most clear demonstrations of kindness and encouragement from her Majesty. The care and contentment we show in our work have led to such high esteem at court that I hope she will deign to honour the factory for a second time with her royal presence."[21]

This hope was fulfilled in June, when Maria and her retinue stayed in Marinha Grande for three days and were entertained with a play performed by the workers in the factory courtyard. William spent over £10,000 in today's values on provisions and decorations, including four plumes of feathers to decorate the queen's chair, fifty yards of velvet, and a hundred yards of green and white baize to line the dinner tables. He bought fat oxen and calves and 400 gallons of wine.[22] "Her Majesty's attendants," wrote one of his friends, "together with the vast influx of persons from the surrounding countryside, formed an assembly of many thousands. Thirty-two cooks were employed and stabling provided for 853 horses and mules. To the credit of Portuguese honesty and sobriety, only two silver spoons were lost from sixty dozens in use and, although wine was placed in the apartments used by the servants, not a man was intoxicated."[23] When the visit was over, the queen gave a gift of money to the factory which William distributed among his workers according to rank and length of service.[24]

The summer of 1788 was the last period of normality for Maria. Still mourning her husband, she would soon be crushed by a second grief, an anguish from which she would never recover. In September, her eldest son, the relatively intelligent Prince José, died of smallpox and she retired to Queluz to mourn him in private. She had refused to allow vaccination for religious reasons, so she blamed herself for his death. José was known to have had anti-clerical sympathies and rumours were spread that the childless prince had been "allowed to die." The rumours arose from Maria's sense of guilt, rather than from any complicity in his death, but there is no doubt that João, her second son, was considered by the church and aristocracy as more suitable for the role of crown prince.

Three months later, the queen's confessor, Inácio de São Caetano, died at Queluz and Maria lost her main pillar of strength and support. Appointed to the role by Pombal, Caetano was an intelligent man with a store of great humanity. "I never saw a sturdier fellow," wrote William Beckford. "He seems to anoint himself with the oil of gladness, to laugh and grow fat."[25] When the queen confessed that she felt excluded from all hopes of salvation, Caetano would soothe her. "Be easy concerning your soul," he told her, "for I shall take that upon myself."[26]

Caetano was replaced by José Maria de Melo, Bishop of Algarve, who was described by Beckford as a young-looking man, "whose small, sleek, school-boyish head and sallow countenance were overshadowed by an enormous pair of green spectacles."[27] This new confessor, an ambitious and rather sinister priest, was addicted to preaching on the terrors of hell. He gave his queen no comfort, preferring to heighten her dread of hellfire which, he told her, was waiting for her just around the corner.

In the spring of 1789, the English Factory celebrated the recovery of George III from madness and soon Dr Willis, the man who treated the king of England, would be summoned to Lisbon to attend the queen of Portugal.[28] Already suffering from melancholy, the French Revolution added to her fears and, by 1791, plagued by constant nightmares, Maria was convinced she was damned and would burn forever in the infernal flames. William Beckford heard her screams one evening when he visited Queluz. "Ai Jesus! Ai Jesus!" she cried, the sounds echoing through the gilded rooms of the palace.[29]

10

A Time of Change

1789–1797

"From all that I have seen, Mr Stephens's glass bears the alternatives of heat and cold much better than any other I have had occasion to try."
James Watt to Sir Joseph Banks, November 1797

"I trust that, from the good example I have shown them and the great reputation of my merchant house, my cousins will continue the business with success... The method is to be honest, regular, punctual and frugal."
Lewis Stephens, July 1789

Most English travellers who visited the monasteries of Alcobaça and Batalha were entertained at Marinha Grande: poets (William Julius Mickle, Robert Southey), statesmen and diplomats (Lord Macartney, governor of Madras and leader of the first British embassy to the court of Peking),[1] and men of science and the arts (Dr Withering, the architect James Murphy, and William Elsden who designed several of Pombal's new buildings at the university of Coimbra). Marinha Grande was so convenient a stopping-place, and William so eager to offer hospitality, that the glassworks were included in English guide-books. "Batalha will be more conveniently visited from Marinha," explained *The Lisbon Guide*, "where the noble glass factory of Mr Stephens presents a picture of English liberality and industry, highly gratifying to the vanity of his countrymen."[2]

Visitors stayed in William's mansion house and those who made the journey in winter were glad of the fireplaces he had built in two of his reception rooms. These were almost unknown in Portugal and travellers arriving in the rain, cold and damp from long hours in the saddle or in a *liteira* (a

107

sedan chair slung between two mules), were welcomed by the warmth of a blazing fire, a sight they had not encountered since entering the country.

One of his more interesting visitors was William Withering, the doctor who discovered the benefits of digitalis in the treatment of heart disease. Withering stayed at Marinha Grande in 1793, bringing news of the latest industrial and intellectual developments in England. He was a member of the Lunar Society of Birmingham, a group of men from the Midlands who met monthly (near the time of the full moon) to discuss developments in science and technology; other members of the society included Erasmus Darwin, James Watt, and the pottery manufacturer Josiah Wedgwood. William, hungry for news of the most recent thinking in scientific matters, talked long into the night with Withering, their discussions including political developments in Europe, for his guest had been an advocate of the French Revolution and his house was targeted during the Birmingham riots of 1791.

Travellers were comfortable in Marinha Grande but the rigours of the journey were not always to their taste. "What would have been considered in England as only the journey of a day," wrote Dr Withering about the first fifty miles from Lisbon to Caldas, "was a formidable undertaking, from the miserable accommodation on the road and the difficulty in making progress."[3] James Murphy commented that "the inns were as indifferent as usual, yet the masters of these miserable hovels think them palaces in comparison to inns in other parts of the country."[4] Robert Southey was more graphic. At Cabeça de Montachique, where he stopped for a meal, a dead dog had been left decomposing outside the door and, in Alcobaça, the inn was "execrable, most verminous – and our next neighbour was a watermill insufferably loud... The fleas rendered it impossible to sleep."[5]

Southey's journey (accompanied by his wife Edith) was made at the end of winter. "One day, we rode twenty miles in the rain," he wrote to his mother, "and our army of attendants mutinied. They all ran into a wine-house and our own servant, sorely against his will, was the only one who followed us, growling all the way. Umbrellas and greatcoats kept us tolerably dry; poor I, completely wet in only one place – it was the seat of my pantaloons – was unable to sit down and walked the room in delicate distress." As for the mules which carried the party, "they have an ugly trick of lying down under their rider and rolling in dry sand. This happened three times to Edith, more to our merriment than terror at seeing them both sprawl together. She did not like it."[6]

William was also visited by the French entrepreneur, Jacome Ratton, a wealthy businessman who had set up several industries in Portugal, including a cotton factory at Tomar. The two men were of similar age and had a high opinion of each other, Ratton referring to William as "a man of genius and sound judgement who, although an Englishman, has always showed the greatest interest in the advancement and prosperity of the Portuguese nation."[7]

One of Ratton's projects was the preservation of the port of São Martinho, which William used to transport much of his glass to Lisbon and Oporto. The shallow circular harbour, protected from the Atlantic by two projecting arms of rock, was slowly silting up and Ratton believed that sand causing the damage was carried by two rivers that discharged into the basin. William was asked to investigate the problem and, after surveying the area, he recommended that the rivers be diverted along a canal cut through the hill to the south side of the harbour. He drew a map detailing the course of the new waterway and, not a man to be unnerved by a large undertaking, he hired a team of workmen and started digging through the rock.[8]

To his disappointment, the project was cancelled for lack of funds, although the port remained in use and glass from Marinha Grande continued to be transported in small ships from the harbour. In 1789, when he was building a second house on the north side of the Largo dos Stephens, William used the port to transport wooden beams from the pine forest. Sales of timber for building purposes were prohibited at this time (all tree trunks being reserved for use in the royal dockyard), so he acquired the fallen trunks which had started to rot but still had sufficient strength to be used as beams and props.[9]

Two years later, he was granted free use of the sturdier trunks to build an eight-mile road linking Marinha Grande with the new public highway from Lisbon to Coimbra.[10] The road, known as the *Estrada do Guilherme*, was completed by 1793, allowing him to send a greater proportion of his glass overland to Lisbon or to Vila Franca where it was loaded on to ships for transport down the Tagus. William had taken advice from engineers in England and his road was built to the highest standards of load-bearing and drainage.[11] Such techniques were new to Portugal and the road so impressed the authorities that it was used as a model for the later stages of the highway to Coimbra.[12]

At the same time, William was experimenting with the production of tempered glass (glass resistant to thermal change and used for scientific purposes). He showed Dr Withering some examples of his "tough glass" in 1793, and Withering sent details to Sir Joseph Banks, president of the Royal Society, and wrote to James Watt who tested the samples sent from Marinha Grande. "From all that I have seen," Watt reported, "Mr Stephens's glass bears the alternatives of heat and cold much better than any other I have had occasion to try."[13]

Banks requested a sample of William's tough glass but soon had to ask for more. "I fear it was my inexperience in manipulation which broke Mr Stephens's glass," he explained to Withering. "I shall heartily rejoice to have it in my power to do it more justice if you favour me with any part of the cargo you expect... I mean to put them into the hands of my chemical friends as soon as I get them. If they prove useful in the chemical, optical or any other line, I shall know how to thank Mr Stephens for having confided the receipt to me."[14]

To further fill his time, William made items of jewellery for his friends to send to England. Using Italian workmanship as a model, "he coined precious pearls for necklaces and earrings, knowing how vainglorious some of our English-women are and how fond of trinkets."[15]

As William continued his many pursuits at Marinha Grande, John James remained in Lisbon, handling the sale of glass and ordering raw materials from abroad. But when administrative or legal difficulties arose, it was William who took charge, for John James had a less incisive intelligence and was not as successful in business negotiations or in flattering the royal family.

In the spring of 1789, the brothers came under renewed attack from the glaziers of Lisbon, who complained that their exclusive right to cut sheets of window glass had been contravened by the decree of 1773 which gave permission for window glass to be cut at Marinha Grande. A petition from the glaziers was considered by the Junta do Comércio and, on the grounds that "cutting and preparing glass for use in window panes is an essential part of the glaziers' specialist trade," William and John James lost the right to sell pre-cut window panes in Lisbon, their largest market, but retained permission to do so elsewhere in the country.[16]

This represented a considerable loss of added-value. It also meant that William had to compete like-for-like with window glass from Bohemia, which was of better quality and (by defrauding the customs) still entering Portugal in significant quantities. Because of these illicit imports, William's sales of window glass had failed to keep pace with production for several years.[17] His stocks had been accumulating and, in 1792, he decided to fight the glass merchants, as he had done twenty years earlier when he persuaded Pombal to impose high import duties.

He prepared a set of accounts showing the annual value of glass produced between 1769 and 1792, together with the value of sales in Lisbon and Oporto. He then wrote a petition to the government. Capital was tied up, he explained, in more than 1000 boxes of unsold window glass, valued at over thirty-eight *contos* of *reis*. This was sufficient to meet two years' consumption in Portugal and its colonies, while the workshop continued to operate at normal capacity. To maintain employment, he asked that all imports of window glass be prohibited. This would, he wrote, "benefit the national industry and the numerous families who work in this factory."[18]

Although the petition was well-written and appeared plausible, the value given for unsold window glass was heavily inflated. Stocks had accumulated to less than nineteen *contos* of *reis* by 1791, but the value was boosted by estimated figures for 1792 which showed production of window glass increasing by more than fifty percent over the previous year, with sales remaining unchanged.[19] William, too intelligent to have increased production at a time when his stocks were accumulating, had exaggerated the figures to give greater force to his petition.

This was a time of turmoil and uncertainty at court. Rumours of the queen's illness had been circulating since the autumn of 1790 and, in March 1792, Prince João took over the reins of power. Taking advantage of this hiatus in government, William timed his petition well. No questions were asked about his estimated figures and, in January 1793, his monopoly was enhanced when a decree was issued prohibiting all foreign window glass from entering the country.[20]

This infuriated the merchants, prompting one of them (Manuel Joaquim Rebelo) to publish a criticism of William and his factory. William, he wrote, had acted selfishly. "If he had been less preoccupied with ambition, he would have been content with the privileges and exemptions already conferred on him and would not have prevented her Majesty from receiving taxes on imported glass while he pays no tax at all." Glass from Marinha Grande was of poor quality and "should not be protected with such diligence, as if it was the most important item in the kingdom, as if the happiness of the monarchy depended on it."[21]

William's glass had always been of lower quality than that produced elsewhere in Europe; with his monopoly position he had little incentive to improve standards.[22] A visitor to Marinha Grande commented on the high quality of the raw materials used and concluded that the factory failed to prepare them correctly. As a result, he explained, the final product "has neither the durability nor the brilliance of imported glass and it breaks easily."[23] William was certainly aware of the value of repeat sales, particularly at the lower end of the market. One evening, when he was staying in Rio Maior on a journey from Lisbon to Marinha Grande, he dropped his wine glass on the floor. Surprised that it remained intact, he borrowed a hammer from the landlady but the tumbler was so thick and strong that it required several blows to shatter it. Two days later, when he arrived at the factory, he ordered his manager to alter the composition of tavern glasses. "It is against our interests," he explained, "to make tableware that is difficult to break."[24]

With his tax exemptions having just three years to run and concerned that Rebelo's criticisms might damage his standing at court, William set out to charm another member of the royal family. Prince João was a placid man with a good heart. He shared his mother's high opinion of the glassworks, but he was slow-thinking and indecisive and it was over a year before William's fears were put to rest. In a decree signed in May 1794, João congratulated him on the road connecting Marinha Grande with the new highway. This was, he explained, "a gift to the country, an undertaking which has earned the benefit of my royal protection." The decree extended the exemption from sales taxes for a further ten years, but made no mention of import duties on raw materials.[25]

Meanwhile, William had employed a new manager at
Marinha Grande, José de Sousa e Oliveira, an efficient and
trustworthy administrator who was to give faithful service to
the Stephens brothers for more than thirty years. Sousa
moved into the mansion house, assumed responsibility for all
aspects of management, supervised the agricultural workers,
and with the help of "a clever fellow of a music master who
plays on several instruments and teaches the people,"
continued to stage weekly concerts and plays, as well as
monthly productions of Italian and Portuguese opera.[26] This
allowed William, now past his sixtieth birthday and in failing
health, to spend more of his time in Lisbon.

The people were sad to see him go. "Since my arrival
here," wrote one of his friends on a visit to Marinha Grande,
"several people have been lamenting with me that time
should have gone her usual course with him and brought on
old age so soon. His will is law with the whole fabrick. No
monarch ever had more absolute power; he reigns in the
hearts of all the people and they only want to know what he
likes in order to do it. I was always proud of his friendship,
but never so much as now. There is hardly a poor family in
the place."[27]

It took William a little time to adjust to the change in
lifestyle. He missed his garden bordering the lake, the activity
in the factory complex, the affection of his employees. He
missed his farms and vegetable gardens, but he enjoyed the
social life of Lisbon and the company of his family. William
and his brothers and sister were deeply attached to each
other, and it came as a great shock when Lewis, the eldest of
William's brothers, died suddenly and unexpectedly in
September 1795.

Lewis was fifty-one years old, and the last months of his
life were soured by the behaviour of his Lyne cousins whom
he had brought over from Liskeard and apprenticed to his
merchant house. The boys had worked well for their
employer and, in the summer of 1788, he took them both
into partnership. Charles, who had worked for Lewis for ten

years, resented this equal treatment. He had learned every aspect of the business and held a more responsible position than his brother who had arrived in Lisbon only six years earlier and should have served another year as an apprentice. He was also more capable than Joseph, but Lewis had made up his mind and the partnership agreement was signed in July.[28]

The following summer, Lewis travelled to England with his wife and sister, leaving the Lyne brothers in charge of his merchant house.[29] He was a prudent man and made a will before embarking on the packet boat to Falmouth, bequeathing a proportion of his wealth to his young partners. "I give these shares to my cousins," he wrote, "from the great love and regard I have for them and in consideration of the attention they have always shown to me and my business, in which business I have brought them up. I trust that, from the good example I have shown them and the great reputation and connections of my merchant house, they will continue the business with as much success for themselves as they have seen me meet with. The method is to be honest, regular, punctual and frugal, whereby they will continue the house in that rank to which it has risen, amongst the first class in the mercantile line."[30]

Lewis spent several months in England, staying with the Cogans in London and visiting John Lyne and his family in Liskeard. On his return to Lisbon, he found that his partners had taken care of the business, completing his mercantile transactions with skill and considerable profit. According to one of Joseph's sons (a most unreliable witness), one of the speculations was: "on a very large scale, I believe in tea, jointly with the Barings and the Hopes of Amsterdam. This speculation was brought to a successful close throughout the various markets of Europe, and the exchange operations were well managed during the absence of Lewis Stephens. It greatly increased his wealth and, I believe, gave to the Barings the power to rise higher and higher till they reached what Baring Brothers & Company are today."[31]

A few years later, Lewis moved his counting-house from Rua Nova d'el Rei to a more prestigious location in Rua Aurea, one of Pombal's new streets leading to the Praça do Comércio.[32] This was the street of the gold and silversmiths, and the Lyne brothers worked here until late 1794 when an altercation between Lewis and Charles's servant led to a break-up of the partnership. One evening, as Lewis climbed down from his chaise in the courtyard at the Largo dos Stephens, he saw the servant holding Charles's horse. Lewis rebuked him for not offering his help and was annoyed when the servant replied that he "worked only for Mr Lyne." "Remember," he said, "you and your master are both my servants."

Charles, already resentful at Joseph's equal position in the partnership, was enraged. He was a clever young man, whose efforts had done much to increase the profitability of Lewis Stephens & Company, but he had grown arrogant and would no longer be treated as a subordinate. After confronting Lewis, he left the partnership, set up in business on his own account and persuaded Joseph to join him.[33] They rented a counting-house in Rua da Madalena and, in May 1795, were both elected members of the English Factory.[34]

William and his family were distressed at the manner in which the Lynes had treated their benefactor, but they maintained friendly relations with their cousins who continued to live in the Largo dos Stephens. Shortly after Charles left the counting-house in Rua Aurea, Lewis's book-keeper had sought him out. "Mr Lewis Stephens will always have a kind feeling towards you," he said. Charles had disagreed: "I will sell to you for half-a-crown all that I get from the Stephenses."[35] He was right, for Lewis was angry and it was common knowledge that he planned to change his will, removing the Lyne brothers and substituting one of his friends, a merchant from Exeter named Antony Gibbs. As Gibbs was to write a few years later, "When my friend Lewis Stephens died, he left £30,000 to the Lynes, which many think he intended after his quarrel with them to have given me instead and would have done if he had not died so suddenly."[36]

As Lewis's body was laid out in the Largo dos Stephens, the family searched his apartment for the will which was normally opened immediately after death and read in front of witnesses by the British vice-consul. But the papers were missing, and Charles and Joseph spent a few anxious days before the will was discovered in the counting-house.[37] Luckily for the Lynes, it was dated July 1789; Lewis had prevaricated too long and made no changes since his cousins left the partnership.

On the morning after his death, Lewis's body was taken to the Protestant cemetery in Buenos Aires and buried in the south-east corner, close to the grave of his uncle John.[38] He had instructed his executors to "order a proper monument and inscription over my grave, as well for remembrance as to prevent the grave from being dug up too soon." Accordingly, an ornate oak-garlanded sarcophagus was ordered from the stonemasons and inscribed: "Lewis Stephens, having by an extensive commerce conducted with good sense and regularity acquired a most ample fortune in this city."

From the poverty of his childhood, Lewis had indeed acquired an ample fortune in Lisbon, and his will divided his residuary estate (£150,000) into fifteenths, three each to his brothers and sister and three to his young cousins: two to Charles and one to Joseph. He also left £30,000 to endow a charity school in Exeter, "for the purpose of teaching boys to read, write, cypher, and learn foreign languages, this being the best method to render poor people's children serviceable to their families and their country." The money was to be "laid out immediately in the purchase of estates in the counties of Devon or Cornwall, the income of which shall belong to my widow during her natural life."[39]

On 17 October, William and John James sent a letter to the mayor and aldermen of Exeter. "It having pleased the Almighty," John James wrote in his carefully-scripted handwriting, "to take to himself our very worthy and dear brother, Lewis Stephens, we now transmit to you a rough copy of the will for your present information. At the same time, we request your advice and assistance for investing the £30,000 as bequeathed. Your local knowledge of the counties of Devon and Cornwall will enable you to give us some light and instruction for the purchases, so the income for the widow may be the most improved. As soon as proper estates can be found, the money shall be paid and we think of placing the sum in public funds to be applied for the purpose as opportunities may offer."[40]

Twelve days later, they wrote again, enclosing an authenticated copy of the will and explaining that another copy was on its way to London to be proved in Doctors' Commons.[41] Jedediah was taking the will to London, sailing on the warship *Leander*, a safer vessel than a packet boat now that Britain and France were once again at war. During his time in England, he visited Cathedral Close in Exeter, then made the journey to Liskeard. John Lyne and his wife had both died since Lewis stayed here six years earlier, so he was offered hospitality by their son Richard, who was filling his father's shoes as master of the Grammar School.

Jedediah returned to Lisbon in the spring of 1796 and, over family dinners in the Largo dos Stephens, he talked of his cousins in Cornwall. Charles (who referred to himself as "a practical man") was unsentimental about his childhood but Joseph was nostalgic for Liskeard. He was in love with Charlotte Arbouin, daughter of a British merchant, and soon decided that he and Charlotte should sail for England, to be married in the parish church of his home town.

Charlotte, born and raised in Lisbon, was alarmed at the prospect of sailing across dangerous seas to marry in a small Cornish town. Five Lisbon packets had been captured by French privateers during the previous two years, and travellers were apprehensive of the voyage.[42] "Scarcely a day passed without some alarm," wrote an Englishman after arriving in Falmouth. "On more than one occasion, the enemy was deterred by finding the ship prepared for resistance, with every man at his post vociferating shouts of defiance and singing national airs."[43]

But Joseph was adamant and, in the autumn of 1796, he and Charlotte embarked for Cornwall where he was reunited with his family after an absence of fourteen years. The banns were read in Liskeard parish church and, on 1 October, Richard Lyne (the boy who had chosen to be a poor clergyman) officiated at the marriage of his younger brother who had made a different choice.[44]

Charles, meanwhile, was irritated by his partner's absence from the counting-house. There were angry scenes when Joseph returned to Lisbon and, a few months later, the brothers dissolved their partnership and set up separate trading operations in Rua da Madalena.[45]

As Charles watched Joseph settle into married life, his thoughts turned to Wilhelmina, daughter of William Tonkin, Lewis's partner in the wine trade. He had known the Tonkin family for many years but they had become closer during recent months as Charles (an executor of his cousin's estate) began to liquidate the business of Lewis Stephens & Company, disposing of goods in stock, selling shares in merchant vessels, and paying off agents in London and Brazil. He had spent several evenings in the company of William Tonkin, his wife and six daughters, but it was the twenty-year-old Wilhelmina to whom he was most attracted.

Wilhelmina returned his affections and, in the spring of 1797, the Tonkin family made plans for the wedding, a glittering occasion attended by the leading members of the British community. On 31 August, one of the hottest days of summer, Charles and his bride were married in the envoy's house by the chaplain of the English Factory. Charles signed the register with his arrogant signature, sweeping a large pointed loop under his name and blocking it in with ink. Wilhelmina then signed her name (a more modest signature), followed by John James and several other witnesses. Joseph took no part in the proceedings.[46]

After their marriage, Charles and Wilhelmina settled into the Largo dos Stephens, as Joseph and Charlotte had done before them. And soon, for the first time, sounds of new life rang through the little square. Joseph's first child was born in December 1797 and, four weeks later, the boy was baptised with the name of his principal godfather, John James Stephens.[47]

PART THREE

John James
The Years of War

11

The First Hostilities

1796–1801

"The state of Portugal is become uncertain and dangerous... The force of the country is absolutely nothing; no preparation whatever of magazines or even ammunition."
Robert Southey, February 1801

Britain and France had been at war for almost five years. Prince João had signed an agreement with England to provide "mutual aid" during the hostilities and, since the most important aid that Portugal could offer was a safe harbour in the Tagus, British naval ships were often seen at anchor near Lisbon.

In December 1796 (after Spain entered the war as an ally of France), a squadron arrived under the command of Admiral Sir John Jervis, with orders to report on the country's naval defences. Jervis was unimpressed. "The arsenal is unprovided," he wrote to the Admiralty, "owing to the neglect of the late minister of marine, the bad state of finances, and the supineness of the government which appears at a lower ebb than I ever remember it."[1] The following day, he wrote again: "The government of Portugal exhibits the most melancholy picture, and it becomes me to apprise you that no reliance whatever can be placed on the Portuguese marine for the defence of the country."[2]

The squadron stayed in the Tagus for a week, before leaving for an encounter with a Spanish squadron almost twice its size. The ships were intercepted off Cape St Vincent and the battle was a great victory for the admiral (and for one of his subordinates, Horatio Nelson, who succeeded in boarding two of the Spanish vessels). Lisbon was illuminated in celebration of the victory and, when the squadron returned to the city, naval officers were entertained in the homes of English merchants.

These early years of war passed without much danger in Lisbon. Merchant vessels sailed in armed convoys, but life for the English community carried on much as usual and William continued to worry about his tax exemptions. In 1794, Prince João had renewed the exemption from sales taxes for a further ten years, but the exemption from import duties had expired two years later and not been reinstated.

The prince had been signing documents in his mother's name since 1792, but it was not until July 1799 that the court gave up all hopes of the queen's recovery and João agreed to the formal appointment of regent. With the government on a more sensible footing, William tried again to have the exemption reinstated and, in October 1799, the regent signed a decree explaining that the Stephens brothers "deserve praise, not only for re-establishing the glass factory at Marinha Grande, but also for operating it with the utmost care and expense." Wishing to encourage them, "so the progress of the factory is carried to its ultimate and complete perfection," João reinstated the exemption for ten years. At the same time, he extended the exemption from sales taxes for a similar period.[3]

The glassworks were free from domestic taxes until 1809 and, with high duties on imported glass (and imports of window glass prohibited), William felt confident that the fortune he had made at Marinha Grande would continue to grow. In celebration, he planned a banquet in Lewis's counting-house on 1 June 1800, Corpus Christi, the day when a great procession wound through the streets of Lisbon. His family invited most of their friends and, when the poet Robert Southey arrived in the city to visit his uncle (who was chaplain to the English Factory), he was invited to join the party.[4]

The early morning of 1 June was filled with the sounds of bells, drums and trumpets as guests assembled on the first floor overlooking Rua Aurea. Servants had brought furniture from the Largo dos Stephens, cooks were preparing the banquet, and attendants were on hand to offer refreshments. The frontages of the houses, as high as the fourth and fifth storeys, were hung with crimson damask embroidered with gold, the roadway was sanded, and soldiers lined the route. Cheers were heard as the first marchers came into view and, for the next two hours, William's guests lent over the balconies to watch the procession pass along the street.

Southey was a priggish young man and found much to criticise. "The banners of the city led the way," he wrote. "I never saw banners so clumsily carried; sticks were stuck at right angles in the poles to carry them by. Nothing could be more awkward or more laborious for the bearers, some of whom were walking backward like lobsters and others crabsidling along."[5] The banners were followed by a statue of St George mounted on a horse, by knights of the different orders and a number of richly-caparisoned horses. Then came the monks and friars carrying the silver ornaments of their convents. "The brotherhood walked," wrote Southey, "an immense train of men in red or grey cloaks. I pitied the friars – it was hot, though temperate for the season, yet the sun was painful on their shaven heads."[6]

At the end of the procession, following the wafer in its silver container, walked Prince João, surrounded by aristocrats and dignitaries of the church. He was showered with rose petals from the windows and balconies, and as the procession passed down the street and out of sight, the crowds closed in behind it. The sounds faded into the distance and the party in Rua Aurea withdrew into the cool of the interior. The banquet was served and, after the guests had departed, ships in the harbour fired their guns, and rockets and fireworks crackled and banged through the night.

Charles Lyne and his wife had left Lisbon a few days before Corpus Christi, sailing to Falmouth with Antony Gibbs who had so nearly supplanted him in Lewis Stephens's will. The two men had become friends since then. "I go home with Mr and Mrs Lyne in May," Antony had written earlier in the year. "He has been a most excellent friend to me and is going to England to spend the handsome fortune he has made."[7] As well as the £20,000 inherited from Lewis, Charles was a highly successful merchant and was taking extended leave to enjoy his wealth in his home country.

There was a second reason for his departure: he was well-read in political matters, with an ability to forecast the trading climate. The closure of Portuguese ports to English shipping was a significant part of Napoleon's military strategy; it would not only disadvantage the British navy, it would also disrupt the lucrative Anglo-Portuguese trade which was helping to fund the war effort. In February 1801, nine months after Charles sailed for England, an ultimatum was delivered to the prince regent. If Portugal wished to remain in peace, it must abandon the English alliance and close its ports to British vessels. If it failed to obey these demands, it would be occupied by French and Spanish troops.

"The state of Portugal is become uncertain and dangerous," wrote Southey. "If France be resolved to shut these portals against England, there is nothing but famine to prevent her... The force of the country is absolutely nothing, no preparation whatever of magazines or even ammunition... The merchants are preparing to secure their property, those who can. To the many whose trade is selling to the natives it will be utter ruin."[8]

The Portuguese army, under the command of the eighty-year-old Duque de Lafões, was in an appalling state of neglect. Nothing had changed since Sir John Jervis described the situation four years earlier. "I have been at some pains to inquire into the state of the army," he had written to the Admiralty. "Though they have some 30,000 troops upon paper, I doubt whether they could bring more than 12,000 into the field and these would be without any necessary provision in opening a campaign; neither hospitals nor hospital staff, camp equipage or clothing except what they have on their backs."[9]

After a few weeks of indecision, Prince João refused the terms of the ultimatum and Spain declared war. In early March, a tax of three percent on domestic production was raised to pay for the defence of the country and, by the end of the month, hostilities on Portuguese soil looked increasingly likely. "We are threatened with speedy invasion," wrote Southey on 28 March, having just returned from a visit to Marinha Grande, "and the critical hour of Portugal has probably arrived. No alarm has been so general; they have sent for transports to secure us a speedy retreat. We shall soon and inevitably be expelled, unless a general peace redeem the merchants here from ruin."[10]

British merchants were sending a considerable proportion of their goods and money to England, and many families discussed the possibility of sailing for home. William had no intention of leaving the country; his duty lay with the people of Marinha Grande, ensuring that the glass factory remained in operation. He obtained exemption for his workers from military service and, when the high level of recruitment amongst peasant farmers resulted in a shortage of grain, he imported corn from England which was ground, baked into bread and distributed to the villagers free of charge. He also gave six *contos* of *reis* to the exchequer to help pay for military defences.[11]

The Stephens family had few relatives in England. John James and Philadelphia remained in touch with the Cogans in London, and Jedediah corresponded with Benjamin Tucker, son of the cousin in Saltash with whom he had lived as a child. Over the years, Jedediah sent money to allow the Tuckers to live in greater style than a warrant-officer's salary could provide. This enabled their son to buy a commission in the navy and, for the past three years, Benjamin had been serving as secretary to Sir John Jervis (now known as Lord St Vincent). Jedediah, recently retired from business, considered leaving for England but soon decided to remain with his family in Portugal. Joseph Lyne also chose to stay. Through the influence of Benjamin Tucker, he was acting as Lord St Vincent's prize agent in Lisbon, handling the cargoes of captured enemy vessels, a lucrative commission which he was loathe to lose.[12]

The invasion was brief. Spanish troops crossed the border on 20 May, Portugal capitulated three weeks later, and Prince João was forced to close his ports to British naval and merchant shipping. The government collected the new tax on production and William felt aggrieved that his thirty-two-year exemption from domestic taxes had been eroded. It was normal for a proportion of finished glass to be damaged during transport and, using these breakages as a bargaining lever, he asked for a reduction in the rate payable at Marinha Grande. João took the point and, in November 1801, he agreed to reduce the tax by one fifth on all domestically-produced glass, china and porcelain.[13]

Meanwhile, William and Philadelphia had returned to Marinha Grande, leaving Lisbon in early September to spend the winter at the glassworks.[14] A few weeks later, John James fell in love for the first (and only) time. He was fifty-three years old. "There is a marriage going on in the family of the Stephenses," wrote Antony Gibbs on 4 November, "but not a word must be said of it."[15] John James planned to tell William the news personally and, towards the end of the year, he made the journey to Marinha Grande to ask for his brother's consent.

He stayed at the glassworks for several weeks, then travelled home to Lisbon with William's approval. He went directly to his lover's house where, if report was true, he met an appalling sight. "During his absence," wrote one of his acquaintances, "the young lady died of a fever and, on the day of his return, the poor girl was to be buried. John James went to her house. The coffin had been brought in but was found to be too short, so they had cut the girl's head off and placed it on her chest. And Mr Stephens saw it. Can anyone be surprised that a man, by nature so kind, so true, so feeling, should have lived for the remainder of his days with such sorrow in his heart?"[16]

Interlude

England

1800–1802

As the ship carrying Charles and Wilhelmina moved north through the Bay of Biscay, Charles told his wife about Cornwall, the land of grey buildings, soft light and green fields that he had left twenty-three years before. He described the granite moors and ancient standing stones that lay a short distance from the market town of his birth. He talked of his father's school within the ramparts of the old castle, his days as a schoolboy learning Latin and Greek, and the family house in Liskeard which was always full of children. And every day, as they paced the deck watching sailors at work and scanning the horizon for enemy vessels, the weather felt a little cooler. A drizzle was falling when the English coast came into view and Wilhelmina saw her homeland for the first time, looking lush and green under an overcast sky.

Landing in Falmouth, they moved to an inn to await the stage-coach to Liskeard. Wilhelmina, tired after the voyage, was surprised at the constant activity. "The perpetual stir and bustle in this inn," wrote Robert Southey who arrived from Lisbon a few weeks later, "is as surprising as it is wearisome. Doors opening and shutting, bells ringing, voices calling to the waiter from every quarter. Everybody is in a hurry here. Either they are going off in packets and are hastening their preparations to embark, or they have just arrived and are impatient to be on the road homeward. Every now and then, a carriage rattles up to the door with a

130

rapidity which makes the house shake. The man who cleans the boots is running in one direction, the barber with his powder-bag in another. There goes the barber's boy with his hot water and razors, here comes the clean linen with the washer-woman, and the hall is full of porters, bringing in luggage or bearing it away."[1]

After a day or two at the inn and several uncomfortable hours in the stage-coach, they were met at Liskeard by Charles's brother in his clerical coat and hat. Four years earlier, Richard had welcomed Joseph and his bride to his home town and officiated at their marriage. Now he welcomed Charles and his wife; Wilhelmina was introduced to her brother-in-law and found him to be gentle, pious and unworldly.

Richard had been admitted to Exeter College, Oxford, a few months after Charles sailed for Lisbon. He graduated four years later and returned to Cornwall to act as curate at St Ive. In 1785, he became master of Liskeard Grammar School, succeeding his father who was too infirm to remain in the post. Here, according to his announcement in a west country newspaper, "the English, Latin and Greek tongues are taught, with geography and other branches of good and useful literature."[2]

Five years later, Richard moved to a house on Castle Hill which was, he informed the public, "a larger house than where he formerly resided, in an airy and pleasant part of the town, and well fitted up for the accommodation of young gentlemen. The Rev'd and Mrs Lyne make it their duty and pleasure to attend to the health and happiness of young gentlemen, as well as to their mental improvements. As the minds of young people are most ready to imbibe liberal sentiments when they meet with liberal treatment, such treatment will always be exhibited as part of the system of education adopted in Liskeard."[3]

In 1795, Richard resigned from the Grammar School to concentrate on private tuition. He was, he announced, "dedicating his attention to four private pupils at a charge of forty guineas a year for boarding and tuition in Latin, Greek and English Literature," and hoped that, "having been for many years the sole conductor of a large seminary, he is so much the better qualified for the office of private tutor to so small a number of pupils."[4]

Richard was an excellent teacher, as well as a kindly one. He was, in his own words, "a scholar, and a ripe and good one," but despite his high reputation, he disliked teaching. "It is so contrary to my tastes and feelings," he told one of his nieces, "that I never liked it, not even for an hour."[5] For Richard was, as his family described him, "a most simple-minded Christian, more fitted for the cloister than the open world."[6] According to one of his daughters, "Years of thought and meditation, of deep and silent study, had given a gravity to his demeanour. He was always accessible to the poor, to children (who greatly loved him), and particularly kind and gentle to the afflicted and meek of the earth. The expression of his eye and peculiarly sweet smile never failed to inspire confidence in those who beheld them, even in birds and beasts."[7]

Richard's first love died in 1785 and he soon fell in love with her cousin, Mary, whom he married three years later. For the rest of his life, he referred to these two women as equal in his thoughts and prayers. "There are two amongst the seraphs in heaven," he wrote towards the end of his life, "to their persons and society it has pleased God to so attract me, and my equal love for whom has, for more than half my life, been my constant study and delight. It is my greatest happiness to hope that I retain that rank in their esteem which I once had and which they will ever hold in mine. My bosom never glowed with a more ardent or youthful affection for either of them than it does now for them both, in what I trust I may call my constant heart."[8]

Mary became a quiet and self-sacrificing wife, and Richard often referred to her "deep humility, inoffensive and placid temper of mind, and surprising patience in bodily pain." When their second child was born, his wife's "travail in childbirth was always hard and long, yet my son was born within one hour after she asked for assistance, her pains having been violent all the night before but which she concealed for near twelve hours that I might be undisturbed, as I was in ill-health at the time and sleep was thought very necessary for me just then."[9]

Wilhelmina, still weary from the journey, soon found that the house on Castle Hill was no more tranquil than the inn at Falmouth. Richard and his wife had six children of their own, his private pupils boarded in the house, and Liskeard was not as quiet as Charles remembered it. A military camp was based in the town, where militia and volunteer forces were put through their paces, and there was much "drunkenness and licentiousness" in the streets.[10]

After a few weeks, the travellers left for Exeter, visiting Antony Gibbs and his wife Dorothea, and when autumn came, they settled in London. Charles took a house in Baker Street and investigated the possibility of working in the City, holding talks with Henry Roberts, partner in the merchant house of Hathorn & Roberts. Wilhelmina hated the cold weather and short days. "London does not by any means agree with Mrs Lyne," Charles wrote to Gibbs in January 1801. "She is not near so stout and well as she was at Exeter. I am therefore wishing for the month of March or April when we may go again into the country."[11]

Wilhelmina was expecting her first child when they left London in the spring. Returning to Cornwall, she and Charles were invited by one of Richard's acquaintances, John Lemon (member of parliament for Truro), to stay in Polvellan, his house near West Looe, eight miles south of Liskeard. This elegant house, built by Lemon on the banks of the Looe river, was described by the writer, William Makepiece Thackeray, as "the sweetest little snuggery as ever I saw."[12] The house overlooked a pond which filled with sea water at high tide, water which turned the local grist-mill as it made its way back to the sea. It was peaceful at Polvellan and Wilhelmina enjoyed sitting in the garden in the summer sunshine, watching the pond draining and filling as the tide ebbed and flowed in the river. And sometimes, in the evenings, the house was filled with the sound of music as Lemon (an accomplished musician) and his friends performed chants and psalm tunes of his own composition.[13]

On 4 October, Wilhelmina gave birth to a son and a message was sent to Richard in Liskeard, who arrived the following morning. "I name this child Stephens," he said as he dipped his finger in consecrated water and drew a cross on the baby's head.[14] Charles had decided that his son should carry a name that honoured all the Stephens brothers, although it was John James, his closest companion in the Largo dos Stephens, who was named as absent godfather.

This was a time of double celebration, for England had signed an armistice with France three days before Stephens was born and mail coaches decked with laurels were delivering the news to towns and villages throughout the country. By the end of the month, Charles was back in London, having further discussions with Henry Roberts and making arrangements for his return to Portugal in the spring. "Mr and Mrs Lyne and their little boy hope to sail for Lisbon on Saturday," wrote Dorothea Gibbs on 14 April. "He has bought furniture of every sort in London and of the very handsomest kind. He called here about three weeks ago and appeared in great spirits."[15]

The family sailed from Falmouth on the *Prince Adolphus* packet, a passage of just five days. "The water was smooth all the voyage," Charles wrote to Dorothea, "and Mrs Lyne, Stephens and myself are all the better for the little seasickness we experienced. I received your letter at Falmouth and we are rejoiced to find that your youngest child is so much improved. It is a great comfort to you that he cuts his teeth so easily. Our little fellow has not yet any signs of teeth but, in every other respect, is going on extremely well."[16]

12

Bereavement

1802–1807

"The factory thrived during the reign of Dona Maria and the regency of Dom João, God rest their souls. But most of the favours and protection that had been granted to the factory came to an end."
José de Sousa e Oliveira, April 1821

"No person called Mr John James Stephens a happy man."
Francis Lyne, 1878

The declaration of peace was greeted with much celebration in Lisbon. Traders brought back their goods and money, the harbour was reopened to merchant vessels, and imports of raw materials for Marinha Grande began arriving in the Tagus (after a hiatus of just four months). But Napoleon had not given up his territorial ambitions and, by the spring of 1803, it was common knowledge that a renewal of hostilities was imminent. This led to depression amongst the merchants, a depression exacerbated in the Largo dos Stephens by John James's blighted marriage plans and by William's deteriorating health. His body, grown fat with good living, was wasting away; the big square face had become thin and drawn.

On the morning of 11 May (five days before his seventy-second birthday), William's family gathered at the bedside to watch him take his final breath, to see his body twitch and stir for the last time. A few hours later, devastated by grief and loss, his brothers summoned the vice-consul who arrived in the early evening. John James knew the whereabouts of the will and, in accordance with custom, the vice-consul opened

135

the papers and "read the contents in an audible voice in the presence and hearing of witnesses."[1]

Written in March the previous year, the will appointed John James as sole heir and executor. "I recommend to my employees," William had written, "that they serve my brother and successor with the same zeal, fidelity and obedience with which they have served me during my administration of the factory." Under Maria's decree of 1780, John James was forbidden to find partners to help run the business and William (aware of his brother's limitations) reminded the state that the glassworks operated under royal protection. "Consequently," he continued, "I humbly request that the sovereign will not delay in making a decision on any representation my successor may make, for such delays would drain the enthusiasm and energy of any good-willed person."

Finally, he recommended that his brother should, at an appropriate time, "petition the sovereign to buy the factory of glass with all its belongings. Since the crown is the owner of the pine forest on which the factory depends, its perpetuity in private hands will need the continued protection of the monarch, or other protector at court, to avoid the malice and envy which I myself have experienced many times."[2]

After the will had been read, William's body was placed on a carriage shaft and pulled by mules to the Protestant cemetery in Buenos Aires. It lay overnight in the mortuary chapel and was buried the following day in a grave close to those of his uncle and brother.[3] The Judas trees were in bloom and, as the chaplain intoned the funeral rites, their purple blossoms glowed against the dark hue of the cypresses that ringed the burial ground. John James was distraught. His childhood had been a lonely one and, from the day he arrived in Lisbon, William had been a father to him, giving him affection, support and encouragement. For forty years, his brother had led and inspired him, and he knew that he could not direct the glassworks as William had done. He lacked the attributes which had made his brother so successful: his intelligence, assurance and charm, his fore-sight and sound judgement.

In the past, John James had acted with confidence, secure in the knowledge that his brother would stand by him. Now his courage evaporated. Never again could he refer to William for advice, or feel the strength of William's personality reinforcing his own. On his return from the funeral, he called the servants together. "My brother should not have died," he told them as he locked the door to William's study, explaining that the room must remain as his brother had left it. He included himself in this prohibition and the door would stay locked for twenty-three years while inside, gathering dust on the desk, were copies of royal orders affecting the glass factory and its privileges, as well as a pile of papers which required attention: correspondence, invoices, bills of exchange.[4]

At the same time, another decision formed itself in his mind. He had never enjoyed the journey to Marinha Grande, the jolting over rough roads, the nights in local inns, the bed-bugs that preyed on his body during the hours of sleep. William's study in Lisbon could be preserved intact and maybe, if he never saw the glassworks again, his brother's presence there could also be fixed in his memory. The administration was safe in the hands of José de Sousa e Oliveira, the manager who had run the factory for several years, and John James would ensure that William's welfare provisions remained in force.

Six days later, Britain declared war on France, deepening the sense of gloom in the Largo dos Stephens, a gloom that deepened further when news arrived in September that Jedediah had died "after a very short illness" in a friend's country house at Cabeça de Montachique. A bullock cart carried his body over the rough roads to the city and, for the second time in five months, John James and Philadelphia buried a brother in the cemetery in Buenos Aires.[5]

Their grief was mingled with renewed fear of invasion. Prince João (who had declared a state of formal neutrality) was coming under increasing pressure to break off the British alliance, Napoleon was encouraging Spain to re-enter the war against England, and the French ambassador was inciting anti-British sympathies amongst the Portuguese. On 2 October, at the "earnest entreaty" of the English Factory, the consul wrote to London requesting ships to carry the merchants and their families to safety.[6]

Remembering William's resolve in 1801, John James chose to remain in Portugal to ensure the continued operation of his glass factory. He was supported by his sister who agreed to stay with him. Joseph Lyne also chose to stay (mainly to protect his prize agency) but Charles made plans to return to England. He would join the firm of Hathorn & Roberts in London, a city where the dangers of war were less likely to impinge. French forces were assembling near Boulogne and England was also at risk of invasion, but Napoleon had no easy method of transporting his troops across the channel. Charles pinned his hopes on the British navy, confident that superiority at sea would prevent enemy soldiers landing in his home country.

Charles, Wilhelmina and their two children (a daughter was born in July) left Lisbon in late October.[7] "Some friends remained on board until the vessel was under weigh," wrote another passenger as his ship set sail for England, "others hoisted colours and waved handkerchiefs on the shore as she dropped down the river."[8] It was a painful departure, for Charles and Wilhelmina were leaving their friends as well as the city in which they had spent so much of their lives. They stood on deck as John James and Philadelphia waved from the river bank, John James lamenting the loss of a cousin who had been his companion for more than quarter of a century.

The invasion panic subsided a few weeks later and Philadelphia persuaded her brother to accompany her on a visit to England; since Jedediah had made no will, letters of administration were required to obtain the money he had invested in London. John James had returned home once before (in 1786 when he renewed his acquaintance with Thomas Cogan and his family) and Philadelphia hoped that another visit might improve his spirits.[9]

The voyage was laced with danger. "There are upwards of ten privateers cruising off the coast in wait for the packets," wrote a merchant recently arrived in Lisbon, his boat having been chased by a man-of-war as well as three smaller vessels.[10] "We were pursued by a large ship," wrote another traveller. "The captain put out great oars to paddle away but the darkness of the night was a better assistant. A few days after, we were in a heavy gale when an enemy schooner bore down upon us. The heavy sea exposed our hulk to their guns but the storm soon drove her away. Thus, after a boisterous and anxious voyage, we landed safely in Falmouth harbour."[11]

John James and Philadelphia arrived safely too, and stayed for a few days with Richard Lyne before taking the stage-coach to London. On 7 January 1804, they appeared before the probate authorities, estimating Jedediah's assets in England at £40,000 of which, as next of kin, they were each entitled to a half-share.[12] They visited Charles and Wilhelmina in their new house in Marylebone but spent most of their time with an old friend, James Palmer, treasurer of Christ's Hospital.

Palmer had been apprenticed to Thomas Cogan's haberdashery at the time when Philadelphia lived in Cornhill and John James was a pupil at the Hospital. He became Cogan's partner, took over the business on Cogan's retirement and, in 1798, retired himself to take the post of treasurer to the school.[13] He was, according to a colleague, "a man of few words, ungifted with eloquence. Enemies he had none. To his friends he was kind and constant. And his hospitality will long be remembered, for every visitor to Christ's Hospital found a welcome reception at the Treasurer's House."[14]

John James and Palmer had met only once during the previous forty years but their friendship was maintained by letter. They were similar in age and character, were comfortable in each other's company, and their reunion after William's death was a great comfort to John James. At the time of his visit, Palmer was updating the teaching in Christ's Hospital so that "young persons educated within its walls should find themselves qualified to compete with the middling and higher orders of society, in whatever business or profession they might be placed."[15]

This was not an entirely altruistic project. In the past, charity schools had taught the poorer classes to read, not to advance their learning but to train them "to know their station in life, how mean their circumstances, what duties they owe the rest of mankind, particularly their superiors."[16] These schools had improved over the years and, helped by the Sunday School movement, had raised the standard of education amongst the lower classes. As one of Palmer's colleagues put it, "If the humblest classes of society were instructed to read, write and calculate, some higher degree of knowledge would be required so that the middle classes might preserve their superiority in the scale of civilised life."[17]

John James enjoyed his stay with Palmer, his wife and three daughters, and despite the winter cold, took pleasure in walking with his friend in the walled garden behind the Treasurer's House. He renewed his acquaintance with his old school, watching the pupils in their cumbersome blue coats and yellow stockings. Every morning, a swarm of boys entered the Writing School, as John James had done more than forty years before when he sat on the long benches, copying documents day after day. Now, thanks to James Palmer amongst others, they enjoyed a wider curriculum than the copying and accounts that had consumed so many of his childhood days.

On his return to Lisbon in the spring of 1804, he requested confirmation of his ownership of the glassworks and asked that his tax exemptions be prolonged for a further twenty years. The factory was in good financial shape at the time of

William's death and John James should have acted sooner to protect its profitability, but he had been too miserable to think about procedure or to flatter Prince João as his brother had done.[18] Meanwhile, the delay was affecting his privileges, for some of João's advisers had joined the French faction in Lisbon and were absorbing their anti-British attitudes.[19]

The Junta do Comércio considered his petition in July and, in a critical report to the prince regent, made two recommendations: that John James be approved as successor to his brother, his privileges for the next five years (as already granted) being confirmed but not extended, and that the prohibition on imported window glass be revoked with immediate effect. This would, the report explained, "benefit the royal exchequer and the convenience of the people, both of which have been sacrificed to the interests of the Stephens brothers. No other factory in the kingdom makes window glass, so they have had no competition and have made incalculable profits. It must not be forgotten that this factory seems more English than Portuguese, for the owner has taken to England immense sums of money that have been made over the years, at the expense of our nation."[20]

William had never taken money to England but John James had done so during his recent visit to London, entrusting the funds to Samuel Aislabie, a stockbroker in Green Lettuce Lane.[21] He had thought it prudent to protect his fortune from the threat of occupying forces, but it played into the hands of those who congregated around the French ambassador and were hostile to British interests in Portugal.

In 1805, a new ambassador arrived from Paris (to replace Marshal Lannes). General Junot had not wanted the posting. "I am not calculated for diplomacy," he told his wife, "and Lannes tells me that the court of Lisbon is a perfect beargarden."[22] Spain re-entered the war soon after his arrival and, for the next few months, Junot continued to stir up anti-British feelings. He was recalled in October, shortly after Nelson's victory off Cape Trafalgar broke enemy sea power and ended the danger of a French army crossing the channel to England. When news of the victory reached Lisbon, British ships celebrated by firing their guns all night, "just as if," complained Madame Junot, "they had been at home in Portsmouth harbour."[23]

Trafalgar had lifted the threat of invasion from English shores but it increased the danger for Portugal, for the closure of its ports to British shipping was of renewed importance in French military strategy. Pulled by Britain and France in different directions, the weak and frightened prince did his best to please both sides. For a short time he fell ill from stress, suffering from faintness and bad memory, and the court feared that he might (like his mother) be going insane. This fear was fostered by his wife, the Spanish princess, Carlota Joaquina. The tiny mischievous child who had made two visits to Marinha Grande twenty years before had grown into a malicious, vindictive woman who hated her husband for his lethargy and indecision. On his part, Prince João avoided his wife's company and the couple lived apart, he in the palace of Mafra, she at Queluz or in her country house in Cintra, fifteen miles west of Lisbon.

In the summer of 1806, a British squadron arrived in the Tagus under the command of Lord St Vincent. Its mission was to ascertain whether Portugal had any intention or capability of defending itself and, if not, to persuade Prince João to sail to Brazil where he could continue to govern from overseas. The passive and home-loving prince, who disliked change and was wary of any kind of decisive action, hoped to appease the French. He was terrified by the idea of a sea voyage and separation from the only land he had ever known. "The reluctance to remove," wrote the secretary to the mission, "was universal and deep-rooted. No result of invasion would be more hateful than banishment across the Atlantic to those whose excursions had hitherto been confined to the journey between their town and country palaces."[24] As for defences, St Vincent did not mince his words. "The army is very much diminished since I was last in Portugal," he wrote to the Admiralty, "13,000 ill-armed infantry is the most that can be counted upon and the cavalry beggars description, both as to horses and men."[25]

Meanwhile, great parties were held on the flagship, HMS *Hibernia*. "We were in perpetual masquerade the whole time," wrote St Vincent, "not less than a thousand Portuguese on board the *Hibernia* every day. All the ministers, domestic and foreign, dined on board, except the Spanish and French. The principal nobility also dined on board and we had very pretty dances, Captain Ricketts having the best taste for turning a quarter-deck into a ballroom that I ever saw."[26]

The squadron left Lisbon in October, having concluded that Portugal was unable to defend itself and that no British force of any practicable size could prevent an invasion. As the Admiralty wrote to St Vincent, "It is vain to hope to defend a country totally incapable of exertion in its own defence. All that can be done in such a case is to render the conquest as little prejudicial to ourselves as possible."[27]

During the mission, John James and Philadelphia had dined several times aboard the *Hibernia*. St Vincent remembered them well; they were cousins of his secretary, Benjamin Tucker, and he had been entertained at the Largo dos Stephens after the defeat of the Spanish squadron in 1797. When John James explained that he wished to safeguard more of his money in London, he was offered a passage on one of the warships sailing for England.

Arriving in London in November, he spent the next two months with James Palmer in the Treasurer's House at Christ's Hospital. For the past three years, Palmer had acted as his agent, collecting interest and dividends on the money invested by Samuel Aislabie in East India stock and Bank of England annuities, and now John James handed over more money for Aislabie to invest.[28]

He returned to Lisbon in early 1807, refreshed from his sojourn in London. But it was unwise to have been out of the country at this time, for one of the ministers of state, the

Conde de Vila Verde, had taken a particular dislike to John James, and his operation at Marinha Grande was facing a number of difficulties, none of which had been resolved.[29] Vila Verde was influenced by the French faction in Lisbon; he had been on friendly terms with the ambassadors, Lannes and Junot, and as president of the Junta do Comércio, was responsible for the scathing report submitted to the prince regent in July 1804.

Vila Verde had removed John James's privilege of free use of firewood from the royal pine forest, ordering the factory to pay the sum of eighty *reis* per cartload.[30] And Prince João had acted on the recommendation of the Junta and revoked the prohibition on imported window glass in November 1804.[31] Sales of window glass from Marinha Grande had declined since then, a situation exacerbated by a misunderstanding with the customs which was impounding consignments of all types of glass for non-payment of taxes.[32]

Out of his depth without his brother to support and advise him, John James had lost his ability to think clearly. The day-to-day operation of the glassworks was in the capable hands of his manager, but it was John James who was responsible for ensuring that the factory retained its privileges and that glass from Marinha Grande passed freely through the custom-houses of Lisbon and Oporto. This he was failing to do. The customs were under the impression that his exemption from taxes (other than the three percent tax imposed in 1801) had expired in 1804 and that he should, since that time, have been paying all other domestic taxes. The administrator had demanded many times that John James show proof of his exemption and, since this had not been provided, he was refusing to release the consignments of glass until he had seen papers which confirmed that taxes had been paid on them.

The customs were acting on a false assumption for, in October 1799, Prince João had extended the factory's exemption from all taxes then in force for a period of ten years. It was this decree that John James should have presented as proof that the exemption still applied but the document was on William's desk, locked up in the study, and he refused to enter the room to look through the papers. Instead, he presented the decree of November 1801 (which reduced the newly-imposed tax on production by one fifth to allow for breakages) as evidence that all relevant taxes had been paid, claiming that this tax included within it all other taxes. This was not an effective strategy to use with officials familiar with domestic taxes; it certainly failed to convince the administrator who accused John James of subterfuge.

The argument continued through the spring and summer of 1807 until it was taken to the Junta do Comércio for arbitration. With the submissions of both parties based on incorrect assumptions, the decree of 1799 was also over-looked by the arbitrators. This was a time of great uncertainty in Portugal and the officials can perhaps be excused for the oversight. But John James should have been better informed about the privileges granted to his factory, particularly since, in July 1804, Prince João had approved the Junta's recommendation that he should "continue to enjoy for a further five years the privileges already conceded to him."[33]

After considering the matter, the Junta reported that John James's reasoning was faulty and that his exemption from taxes had indeed expired in 1804. However, since "the glass factory deserves the protection of his Highness because of the great benefit it provides to the country," it recommended that this should be reinstated. It also recommended that the customs should release the boxes of impounded glass.[34]

These conclusions were presented to the prince regent on 17 November 1807, by which time Prince João had more important matters on his mind.

13

Invasion

1807–1808

"You cannot conceive the dejection that reigns here, nor how melancholy it is to see such numbers of families obliged to liquidate their affairs, selling their furniture and effects, and obliged to quit the country."
Henry Gallwey, 10 October 1807

1807 was a year of increasing danger for Portugal. France was demanding that Prince João close his ports to English shipping and expel British subjects from the country, while England insisted that the royal family should sail to safety in Brazil. The regent felt himself pulled this way and that. To appease France, he sometimes pretended that he had a mind to expel the British, then he promised England that he would honour the old alliance and agree to leave the country.

In the summer, Napoleon issued an ultimatum: João must obey his demands, including the arrest of British residents and the confiscation of their property, or French forces would cross the Spanish border. As the prince continued to prevaricate, an invasion force gathered in Bayonne under the command of General Junot (whose brief embassy to Portugal had ended two years earlier). The British envoy did his best to persuade Prince João to sail for Brazil. "During an interview of nearly an hour and a half," he wrote in early September, "I employed every argument in my power and, although I have not succeeded, I trust I have weakened his reluctance."[1]

The British community was once more in a state of panic. On 25 September, the English Factory held a meeting at which members were advised to take immediate measures for the security of their property.[2] "We are in a most alarming situation," wrote one of the merchants. "Most British subjects are preparing to be off before a French army comes forward, which we have no doubt will take place very precipitately."[3]

On 1 October, when the French and Spanish ministers left the country, Prince João informed the people of his "well-grounded hopes that their absence will be temporary and that no hostile act will follow." English merchants were more realistic and, since the envoy advised them to "lose no time in removing their persons and property," the consul arranged for a convoy of sixty ships to take them home to England. "I am in hopes," he wrote on 4 October, "that the greatest part of our merchants will soon have embarked with their families. As to their property, there is much capable of being removed, but there are many British subjects who will be severe sufferers and some totally ruined. There are those who have debts in this country which it is feared will now become irrecoverable, and others who must relinquish their mercantile establishments, the success of which is their sole dependence."[4]

On 6 October, the English Factory held its last meeting, disposing of funds and paying off its agents. "You cannot conceive the dejection that reigns here," wrote a merchant four days later, "nor how melancholy it is to see such numbers of families forced to liquidate their affairs, selling their furniture and effects, and obliged to quit the country."[5] John James had raised the courage to stay in Portugal, partly in honour of William's memory and partly to protect his interests at Marinha Grande, but he would be alone in the Largo dos Stephens. Philadelphia, Mary Stephens, Jane Campion, and Joseph Lyne and his family were all packing up and making plans for departure.

The convoy sailed on 17 October and John James stood on the river bank, watching the ships sail down the Tagus and disappear around the bend of the river at Belém. He was not the only Englishman to stay in Lisbon; a few of the merchants also chose to stay, perhaps hoping that the invasion would be as short-lived as that of 1801. "There are very few British remaining here," wrote a merchant after the convoy had sailed. "In a day or two, we expect to have a declaration of this port being shut against the English flag, the consequence of which will be dreadful to this country."[6]

João closed the ports on 20 October and, two weeks later, a notice was delivered to the Largo dos Stephens. The consul had received a letter from the envoy ("in which his Lordship recommends British subjects to adopt without delay the most efficacious measures for the security of their persons and property") and he urged all Englishmen remaining in the city to "remove from Portugal without loss of time."[7] John James stared at the notice, then put it away. He had made his decision and no advice from envoys or consuls would change his mind.

Meanwhile, the envoy was trying to force Prince João into immediate emigration but the regent refused to leave, explaining that "every feeling of religion and duty forbids him to abandon his people until the last moment."[8] He remained sanguine about Napoleon's intentions and it was only when he was shown an announcement in *Le Moniteur Universel* ("the House of Bragança has ceased to reign, a new proof of the inevitable ruin of all who attach themselves to England") that he realised the full gravity of the situation.[9] Hoping it was not too late to appease the French, he implemented all the terms of the ultimatum.

A decree ordering the arrest of British residents and the sequestration of British property was signed on 8 November, after which the authorities began the confiscations and John James was "visited by an officer from the intendant of police, who acquainted him that he is no longer at liberty to quit this country without permission from the prince regent."[10] But João had prevaricated too long. Junot had received his final instructions three weeks earlier with orders to march on Lisbon, take possession of the Portuguese fleet, and imprison the royal family. His forces had crossed the border into Spain and were on their way to Portugal.

On 17 November, an English fleet arrived at the mouth of the Tagus to escort Prince João to safety in Brazil. The British envoy took refuge on the flagship and, a few days later, the consul escaped to a frigate. The Portuguese fleet was anchored in the river but João continued to wait, still refusing to leave until the last possible moment. On 22 November, news arrived that the invading army had crossed the border; two days later, it had reached Abrantes, less than sixty miles from the city. Only then did he make the difficult and painful decision. It was time to leave.

The next two days were ones of intense activity. The royal family, the aristocracy, government ministers and officials, together with their families, friends and servants, all were going, leaving behind a council of regents nominated by Prince João to rule the country in his absence. Offers to join the convoy were made to a small number of people outside these circles and John James, as owner of a factory under royal protection, was favoured with an invitation, the prince "causing it to be signified to Mr Stephens that, if he thought proper to secure his property and personal safety by accompanying him to Brazil, arrangements should immediately be made for his doing so."[11]

Six weeks earlier, after his family and friends sailed for England, John James had returned to empty apartments on Rua de São Paulo. His servants were kind and attentive, but he had never felt so lonely since he entered the gates of Christ's Hospital more than fifty years before. Now, faced with an uncertain future under enemy occupation, he was tempted to accept the prince's offer, although he soon remembered his brother's strength of mind in 1801. Having regained his courage, he instructed his servants to purchase food and provisions, and strengthen the doors and windows of his property. He had collected the equivalent of £20,000 in cash and, wrapping the money in an old cloth, he buried it beneath the floorboards of his mansion house.[12]

On the morning of 27 November, Prince João arrived at the quay in Belém where a galley was waiting to row him to his flagship. He was followed by his family (including his mother, the mad queen, who had a violent attack on the quayside and, screaming about infernal fires, had to be carried aboard by force). After the royal family had embarked, the servants brought the luggage. More than 700 vehicles transported the trunks and treasure chests to the waterside, for most of the contents of the royal palaces were on their way to Brazil: furniture, jewels, books, silver and paintings, as well as all the state papers.

Next came the aristocrats, government ministers, and large numbers of officials, priests and friars. There was great confusion on the quays as the courtiers and their families arrived in carriages, bringing with them their most valuable pieces of furniture as well as chests packed with their belongings, while crowds of people gathered on the river banks hoping to find a place on the thirty merchant vessels and fifteen men-of-war anchored in the Tagus.

By the evening, the embarkation was complete. Over 10,000 people were on board the Portuguese fleet but a strong wind was blowing from the west, trapping the ships in the harbour. They lay at anchor all the following day, unable to sail for the mouth of the river, while Junot and his forces were marching closer by the hour. It was not until the morning of 29 November that the wind shifted to the east and the ships began to move down the Tagus to join the English fleet waiting outside the bar. The refugees were safe, but only by the smallest of margins.

After the government had boarded ship in the Tagus, Lisbon became, for almost three days, a lawless place. Bands of armed men roamed the streets and John James forbade his servants to leave the house. He closed the shutters, locked the doors, and waited for the invasion force to arrive. Outside, he could hear shouting and the occasional pistol shot, but mostly he heard the feral dogs barking and fighting.

The first contingent of Junot's forces straggled into Lisbon on 30 November. They had marched over 600 miles in forty-three days, traversing mountain paths and fording swollen rivers with their gun-carriages and tumbrils. Under-nourished and drenched by winter rains, large numbers had died on the journey and many of the survivors walked barefoot into the city. "The state we were in when we entered Lisbon is hardly credible," wrote a general who was offered hospitality by William's old friend, Jacome Ratton. "Our clothing had lost all shape and colour; I had not changed my linen since Abrantes; my feet were coming through my boots; and in this guise I took possession of one of the handsomest suites of rooms in the capital."[13]

As the general explained, "Junot took possession of Lisbon without having a single trooper, a single gun or cartridge that would burn; with nothing but 1500 grenadiers remaining from the battalions of his advance-guard. Fagged out, unwashed, these grenadiers no longer had strength to march, yet the commander-in-chief must walk them all over town, in pouring rain, for six hours. The rest of the army dropped in at intervals of one or two days in still worse condition, some even falling down dead at the gates."[14]

British assets had been returned to their owners on 26 November when Prince João rescinded the sequestrations before boarding ship in the Tagus. Seven days later, they were confiscated again as Junot ordered the council of regents to "seize all possessions of any kind, personal property, jewellery and silver, as well as real estate, belonging to British subjects in Portuguese territory."[15] Collaborators passed on information and, on 7 December, the factory at Marinha Grande was sequestrated by order of the occupying forces.

Possession was taken by the chief magistrate of Leiria, accompanied by his secretary. They introduced themselves to the manager, José de Sousa e Oliveira, and the secretary made an inventory of the buildings and their contents. Orders were given to extinguish the furnaces, the workers dismissed and sent home. The factory had ceased to operate, explained the magistrate; it no longer belonged to John James Stephens.[16]

As soon as John James received the news, he wrote a petition to Junot. The closure of the factory, he explained, would not only result in a huge loss to the operation, it also meant that his workers were unable to feed themselves or support their families. Junot took the point. "Being informed," he wrote on 17 December, "that the glass factory at Marinha Grande provides employment for 500 people, and wishing to protect and encourage all useful establishments in Portugal, I order that the activity and control established by its founders be observed in the continuation of work at the factory. All people employed prior to its sequestration are directed to return to work."[17]

Junot delegated the matter to a magistrate of the Supreme Court in Lisbon, José Diogo Mascarenhas, a collaborator with the occupying forces who was in charge of all dealings with British subjects, including property under sequestration. Mascarenhas sent specific orders to the authorities in Leiria. They were to travel to Marinha Grande and check the inventory, for which Sousa was to sign a formal receipt. They were to inspect the factory every week, examine its records of production, and send copies of their reports to Mascarenhas in Lisbon. They should also ensure that lands belonging to the factory were farmed efficiently, informing Mascarenhas of the volumes of crops harvested.[18] And since Sousa required money to run the factory (sales being at a standstill), Junot ordered him to obtain a loan from the tobacco monopoly in Leiria.[19]

Two weeks later, the Largo dos Stephens was sequestrated. The chief magistrate of the district arrived in Rua de São Paulo on 7 January and John James led the way through the buildings as the secretary listed their contents.[20] Most British residents had been imprisoned by this time but, on condition that he behaved well and complied with regulations, Junot was willing to allow the occupier of a "useful establishment" to remain under house arrest.

Meanwhile, no decision had been taken about his tax exemptions and the crates of glass impounded by the customs. Prince João would certainly have agreed to the recommendations made by the Junta do Comércio but, when the council of regents considered the matter, they refused to take action in favour of an Englishman. On 9 January, they signed their names to the Junta's report. "*Escusado*," they wrote in the margin, "petition rejected." A separate document referred to John James's request for free passage through customs. "*Indeferido*," they wrote, "not granted."[21]

John James was disappointed by this decision (although it made little difference under enemy occupation). Angry at the weakness of the regents and concerned that he might be accused of collaboration, he broke the terms of his house arrest. On 13 January, he was collected from the Largo dos Stephens and taken to the British hospital in Buenos Aires, which had been requisitioned to house English prisoners.[22] The windows had been fitted with bars to prevent escape, and John James was to spend four months and eleven days incarcerated in this building which stood within the precincts of the Protestant cemetery. As he lay awake at night, listening to the snores of his fellow Englishmen, he thought of his three brothers lying in the south-east corner of the burial ground, their bones just yards from his makeshift bed.

The prisoners made such a nuisance of themselves over the next few months that most of them were allowed to return to their homes.[23] The release papers were signed by Mascarenhas (the magistrate who had organised the re-opening of the glassworks) and John James was given his freedom on 24 May, on condition that he signed a document guaranteeing good behaviour and presented himself to Mascarenhas on the first and fifteenth of every month. He was also ordered to pay bail which, since his assets had been taken from him, a Portuguese merchant paid on his behalf.[24]

Returning to the Largo dos Stephens, he found French officers billeted there, eating his food, drinking his wine and giving orders to his servants. Moving back into his home of thirty-five years, he had to endure this situation as best he could, for the house was now in French ownership and the terms of his parole meant he could cause no trouble. But the news from abroad had improved and, over the next ten weeks, his spirits lifted whenever he received information from his servants or from officers in the house.

The king of Spain had been forced to abdicate in the spring and, when Napoleon placed his own brother on the throne, the country rose in rebellion against its ally. French troops were attacked and a deputation arrived in London requesting money and arms for war. By early July, peace had been signed between England and Spain, and arrangements made for English troops to be sent to the peninsula. Meanwhile, the rebellion had spread to Portugal and Junot sent troops north from Lisbon to suppress the uprisings. For several weeks, 4000 soldiers were stationed near Leiria, looting the town of Pombal, burning the coastal village of Nazaré and, according to an English intelligence officer, "committing great excesses in Leiria."[25]

John James became anxious when he heard the news; Marinha Grande was only a few miles from Leiria and soldiers were known to have ravaged the countryside in search of food and booty. But relief was on its way. English forces had embarked for Portugal and news of their progress filtered through to Lisbon. Under the command of Sir Arthur Wellesley, the troops landed at Mondego bay (twenty-five miles north of Marinha Grande) in early August. They reached Leiria a few days later, then moved south, marching through Alcobaça to Caldas da Rainha.

Junot sent reinforcements to impede their advance and on 15 August, when he left Lisbon to head his army, John James broke the terms of his bail. He was due to report to Mascarenhas at one o'clock that afternoon, but he knew the city would soon be liberated and he no longer had to comply with humiliating and petty regulations.[26] Although he fretted for news of his factory, it was not a good time for Sousa to send a messenger to Lisbon; the countryside north of the city was full of soldiers and there would soon be major battles in the area.

Wellesley defeated the French twice during the third week of August, victories which gave him an opportunity to rout the occupying forces and advance on Lisbon. He was over-ruled by two senior commanders who had followed him to Portugal and, when a French general was sent to negotiate an armistice, Wellesley had no choice but to sign the terms agreed by his superiors. These were highly advantageous for the enemy: Junot's army, together with its guns, horses and property, would be repatriated on British transports and there would be no reparations. Wellesley disapproved of the details, as he made clear in a letter to London on 23 August. He agreed that the French should be evacuated from Portugal with their property, but "I should have wished to adopt some method of making the French generals disgorge the church plate they have stolen."[27]

As French soldiers retired to Lisbon to await the transports, Junot put them to work, minting into coin the gold and silver looted from churches and monasteries (the terms of the armistice allowed them to take as much specie as they wished out of the country). They stretched the definition of the word "property" to include all their booty, everything they had looted from churches, shops and houses, a large proportion of which was stored in the British Assembly Rooms in Rua do Alecrim. "Plate, books, indigo, cotton, everything that was moveable," wrote an English officer, "was crammed up in this building."[28]

As soon as the British army was informed of the looting, General Beresford was sent to the city to head a committee of enquiry. He saved a little of the church plate and a few religious paintings, and rescued the contents of the Royal Library and Natural History Museum, all of which had been crated ready for sailing. But his activities made little difference. As he wrote on 18 September, "The conduct of the French has been marked by the most shameful disregard to honour and probity. They have only refunded what they were compelled to disgorge and were absolutely prohibited from carrying off."[29]

The armistice (the Convention of Cintra) was ratified on 31 August and greeted with outrage by the small English community which had lived through the occupation. John James was particularly incensed. He had watched French troops pile up their booty in the Assembly Rooms, the rooms he had designed more than twenty years before and in which he had spent many an enjoyable evening, dancing, drinking and playing cards. Soon he would see soldiers carry their stolen treasure out of the building and into transports waiting in the Tagus. It was Wellesley who had signed the terms of the armistice and it was he who bore the brunt of public opinion, returning to England in September to defend himself against his critics. John James would forgive the British commander (referring to him in later years as "the Great Lord"), but he never forgot the humiliation visited on the Portuguese as their silver and gold was carried away by enemy forces defeated in battle.

A few days after the armistice, a messenger arrived from Marinha Grande reassuring John James that his factory was safe. Relieved at the news, he applied himself to the restitution of his assets: his property at Marinha Grande, the Largo dos Stephens in Lisbon, and as many of his possessions as he could extract from the hands of the French.

It was not an easy time to move about the city. In the heat of summer, 25,000 French soldiers were camping in the streets, many of them in the nearby Largo de São Paulo, where "the infection proceeding from their uncleanliness was so great as to cause occupants of neighbouring houses to dislodge."[30] To make matters worse, local people were killing the soldiers whenever they had the chance and the dead men lay as they fell, in open spaces as well as in dark corners of the city. Much as John James would have preferred to remain indoors until the French had departed, the restitution of his assets was more important than the noise, smells and dangers of the streets. Closing the leather curtains of his chaise, he was driven to the headquarters of the British army where a two-man committee had been set up to organise the restitution of sequestered property.

The English member of this committee was Colonel Trant, who had worked as an intelligence officer with the Portuguese militia before the arrival of Wellesley's forces. He did the job of restitution well, his senior officer commenting that his "zeal and ability in this duty were most meritorious,"[31] while Trant's young daughter remembered that "so great was the gratitude felt by the Portuguese nobility that it was facetiously expected, in the next calendar of saints, that he would be *canonised*."[32]

On 14 September, Trant signed a paper ordering that "no obstacle is to prevent John James Stephens, from this date onwards, entering into full possession of the lands, buildings, factories, animals, cattle and stock, furniture and utensils, and all goods of whatever kind which belong to him and which were seized by the French authorities."[33] The city was liberated the following day, and John James and his servants cheered from the balconies as British soldiers marched down Rua de São Paulo. They were greeted by ecstatic crowds, ringing bells, firing pistols, and throwing flowers from every window and balcony along their route. "Long live the English!" they shouted, "Death to the French!"

The celebrations continued for several days, with rockets and firecrackers exploding throughout the city. "All ranks appear in high glee," wrote a medical officer when he visited Lisbon on 19 September, "and very civilly salute British officers as they pass along."[34] Meanwhile, in the western suburbs, the invading army was preparing to leave. "The great quay at Belém was crowded with French troops," continued the medical officer. "They were embarking in boats to get aboard the transports, while the Portuguese were grinning at their departure. Our sailors were acting the part of masters of ceremonies, which they performed most ludicrously."[35]

Now the occupation was over, John James hoped his family would return to Lisbon. He disliked living alone. He had no inclination for running a household, overseeing servants, or organising hospitality. He missed all three of the women with whom he had lived for so many years but, most of all, he missed his intelligent and capable sister. A few days after the liberation, he wrote to Philadelphia in London, begging her to return to the Largo dos Stephens. He was lonely, he told her, and much in need of her friendship and her company.

Interlude

London

1807–1808

Philadelphia was living with Mary Stephens and Jane Campion in a house in Marylebone.[1] She had not enjoyed the English winter, but most of her friends lived nearby and she had an active social life. "There is a whole host of Lisbon families in London," wrote Antony Gibbs in January. "I have been invited to dine tomorrow with two parties of Lisbonites, one to meet at Mr Lyne's, the other at Mrs Stephens's."[2]

After his flight from Portugal, Joseph Lyne re-established his merchant business in Finsbury Square. His departure from Lisbon involved significant losses and, despite the bad feeling between them, Charles helped his brother during his first few months in London.[3] But they had little social contact and Joseph rarely came to the house in Devonshire Place where Wilhelmina had given birth to two baby girls and would soon become pregnant with her last child, a fourth daughter.[4] "Mrs Lyne seems quite stout again," wrote a young merchant who visited the house in the summer of 1806, "and you can have no idea how ridiculously they spoil their children. The boy Stephens does just what he pleases."[5]

Charles had joined Henry Roberts and George Hathorn in their counting-house in Finsbury Square in early 1804; with his mercantile skills and experience of trade in Portugal, he was the senior partner of the renamed firm of Lyne, Hathorn & Roberts. An office was opened in Liverpool and the partnership turned over an average of £140,000 a year

159

during its first three years of operation.[6] In late 1806, trade had been affected by Napoleon's Berlin Decree, which closed the ports of continental Europe to British vessels (only Portugal refused to comply), and trade with Lisbon came to a standstill during the French occupation. With turnover declining from £186,000 in 1806 to a mere £36,000 in 1808, Charles and his partners were in the process of diversifying into the Brazilian market.[7]

The ports of Brazil had been opened to direct trade with England as soon as Prince João landed there in January 1808, a significant advance for English merchants who were to take a monopoly of Brazilian trade for the rest of the war. By the summer, Charles was exporting a variety of products to this new market and bringing back cotton and tobacco, a vigorous commerce that would enrich the partnership and allow it to move to more imposing premises at 33 Old Broad Street.[8]

Charles worked long hours in his counting-house, but he stayed home in February 1808 when Wilhelmina fell ill with chicken-pox. Having nursed her children as they lay hot and itching, she became infected herself, a dangerous disease for an adult. The doctors feared for her life and, when she recovered, they suggested a move to the country. Accordingly, in April, Charles rented "the best and prettiest house in Richmond," where he planned to live for a year, driving to Old Broad Street every day except Sunday.[9]

Philadelphia was a frequent visitor to their house by the river and, when John James's letter arrived in October, she and Wilhelmina discussed the possibility of her return to Lisbon. Mary Stephens and Jane Campion had chosen to stay in London but Philadelphia felt drawn to Portugal and, with Wilhelmina's listening ear, she made her decision. She owed John James her loyalty and her help and, to avoid another winter of short days and grey skies, she packed her belongings and made arrangements for the journey.

14

Devastation

1808–1811

"The inhabitants of the country fled and hid. Most of them were roving in the woods, eating grass and wild fruit. Good God! What shelter did these unfortunates find? How many must have died during the six months we remained in this country?"
Jean-Jacques Pelet, aide-de-camp to Marshal Masséna, c.1817

"It is beyond everything horrid, the way the French have treated the unfortunate Portuguese. Almost every man they get hold of they murder. The women they use too brutally for me to describe. They even cut the throats of infants."
George Simmons of the Rifle Brigade, 26 March 1811

Philadelphia returned to the Largo dos Stephens in time to spend Christmas with her brother, happy to be back in the country which had been her home since she was eleven years old. From the balconies on Rua de São Paulo, she looked out over the river and watched the activities in the streets below: the monks and friars in their different habits, the strings of loaded mules, the chaises and bullock carts, the lemonade sellers, the Galician water carriers with their wooden barrels, their shouts of *"agua"* alerting householders to their arrival.

There was a coffee shop in Largo de São Paulo, frequented by English and American merchants and British army officers. "While sipping my coffee in the light cheerful room which looked out on the quay," wrote an officer taking breakfast here, "I commanded a view of the harbour crowded with vessels. Pilot and fishing barks with their large handsome sails were coming up or going down the river and, nearer the shore, small boats with white or painted awnings were transporting passengers from one quay to another or to the more distant suburbs of Alcântara and Belém."[1]

Another officer described the view from the German hotel in Largo de São Paulo, looking across the fish market to the Tagus. "All sorts of people strolled round this market," he wrote, "soldiers, priests, idlers, chefs and cooks, Greek seamen in red caps and short wide trousers, Algerians and Tunisians in their turbans, velvet waistcoats and yellow slippers. Beyond was the Tagus, filled with warships, transports and merchant vessels, their bright flags and pennants fluttering in the breeze."[2]

With his sister to accompany him, John James joined in the social life of the English community which had resumed after Junot's forces left the city. The British hosted a ball in the Opera House to celebrate the liberation, the Assembly Rooms in the Rua do Alecrim were reopened, several merchants returned from London, and the English Factory was holding regular meetings.[3]

During their evenings at home, they sat in the long room overlooking Rua de São Paulo, Philadelphia passing on news of their friends in London, John James telling his sister about the occupation and voicing his many concerns about the glassworks. The system of using local carters to transport firewood had been disrupted by the invasion and, with insufficient fuel, the factory was operating well below capacity. At the same time, his difficulties with the customs remained unresolved and crates of glass were still impounded for supposed non-payment of taxes.

The council of regents had been re-established after the armistice, but its members were proving to be inefficient, corrupt and timid. They were, explained a British officer, "as lame a government as well could be, mostly old generals who have never seen an enemy or lawyers who are entirely ignorant of politics and finance."[4] And since the regents were referring all matters relating to royal favour for João's personal consideration, long sea voyages were involved in any correspondence about the glass factory and its privileges.

The progress of the war was equally discouraging. The British army (under the command of Sir John Moore) had moved into Spain in November, but Spanish resistance collapsed by the end of the year and Moore fell back to Coruña on the northern coast, where his army embarked on transports for England. French forces had followed the British and it was assumed they would turn south for a second invasion of Portugal. English merchants were warned to be "ready to depart at a moment's warning," and Philadelphia wondered whether she had been wise to return so soon. "Great alarm amongst the merchants," wrote a visitor to Lisbon on 5 January, "many of whom are dispatching their property on board ships. Many French spies are suspected to be about under the disguise of priests and friars."[5]

In early March, Wellesley (now exonerated for his part in the armistice) persuaded the English government to concentrate its efforts on Portugal. The second invasion came less than three weeks later, when a French army marched south from the northern border and occupied Oporto. During the first two weeks of April, several thousand British soldiers landed in Lisbon and, when Wellesley arrived to take command, he was given a tremendous reception. "No words can convey the delight exhibited by all persons," wrote one of his officers. "All day long, the streets were crowded with men and women congratulating one another on the happy event and, at night, the city was illuminated, even in the meanest of its lanes and alleys."[6]

Marching north, Wellesley's troops reoccupied Oporto on 12 May and the French retreated across the border. Two months later, as the British army moved into Spain, reinforcements arrived in Lisbon and embarked on boats for transport up the Tagus. "I shall never forget marching through the streets of Lisbon," wrote an officer who left the city on 28 July. "They were filled with people, the windows crowded with faces; loud, long and continued *vivas* were poured forth; shawls, handkerchiefs and hands were waving from every balcony; and women threw flowers and garlands on our heads. From the quay of the Praça do Comércio, the men sprung into boats and our little fleet was soon sailing up the river under a favourable breeze. It must have been a beautiful sight for those on the quays: the polished arms, the glittering cap-plates, and the crimson dress of the soldiers crowded into the open barks.'"[7]

Another invasion overwhelmed, another march into Spain; the people of Lisbon breathed a sigh of relief and English merchants returned to their work and their entertainments. But a few weeks later, most of Wellesley's troops were back in Portugal, forced to retreat from lack of supplies and the size of the French army ranged against them. Now (and for the rest of the Peninsular War) British officers were constantly seen in Lisbon. They visited the opera and theatre, attended dinners and balls, and frequented the coffee house in Largo de São Paulo. Some were invited to dine in the Largo dos Stephens but, however indiscreet they might have become with wine and good company, John James and Philadelphia would have heard little about Wellesley's plans for the defence of Lisbon, plans so secret that few of his officers had any idea of their ultimate purpose.

During the autumn of 1809, Wellesley (now known as the Duke of Wellington) spent several weeks riding over the countryside north of the city, devising lines of defence near the small town of Torres Vedras. Built between the Tagus and the sea, the lines would provide a defensive area north of Lisbon behind which British troops could be withdrawn in relative safety. Detailed orders were given on 20 October and, during the following year, three lines of batteries and redoubts (running for thirty miles through a range of hills) would be built by a team of military engineers and a workforce of thousands of local labourers.

His plans completed, Wellington returned to Lisbon where the English Factory appointed John James, the consul and three other merchants to prepare an address. On 25 October, they attended Wellington's headquarters and offered their:

"congratulations on the brilliant successes which have marked the splendid carèer of your military glory. Their happy effect in restoring the liberty and legitimate government of this country, and the renewal of its commercial relations, call forth the gratitude of the Portuguese nation. This sentiment we, as British subjects established in this city, particularly feel and beg leave with the warmest admiration to express."[8]

John James attended this occasion with patriotic pride but his spirits remained low. None of his difficulties at Marinha Grande had been resolved. He was unable to obtain sufficient firewood and, although it was two years since the Junta do Comércio had reported on the matter, no decision had been taken on his tax exemptions and the glass impounded by the customs. Aware of the mistake he had made in 1807 (remembering that his exemptions did not expire until October 1809), he had sent a petition to Prince João asking him to lift the sequestration on glass impounded before that date. It was not until May 1810 that his request was granted, by which time the exemptions had genuinely expired and the customs were continuing to demand that taxes and import duties be paid on all consignments of glass and raw materials.[9]

John James wrote another petition. He had hoped, he explained, that his tax exemptions would have been prolonged at the same time as the sequestration had been lifted. He now had to face a further delay and, in the meantime, his business was stagnating to the detriment of the people of Portugal who were in need of glass. To save time, he begged the prince to communicate directly with the customs which should be ordered, as soon as the exemptions had been reinstated, to pass his glass and raw materials freely through the custom-houses.[10]

This was delivered to the Junta do Comércio on 28 May, by which time the country was once again under threat of invasion. A French army, under the command of Marshal Masséna, was gathering in Spain (close to the border with central Portugal) and the people of Lisbon were becoming increasingly anxious. French sympathisers planned to take control of the city and, on 15 August, an English officer was told by his servant that "British sick and wounded are to be put to death this night, and the people are to take the forts and declare in favour of the French."[11] But news of the plot had leaked; armed soldiers roamed the streets and warships in the Tagus shifted their positions, ready to fire broadsides into the city.

The plot was foiled, but Masséna had led his army of 70,000 men across the border the previous day. Wellington moved his troops forward to meet them, then began to retreat, leading Masséna towards the trap he had prepared at Torres Vedras. While British forces were supplied from the rear (by trains of bullock carts and river boats), French armies lived off the land, requisitioning food from local inhabitants. Wellington's strategy was to remove all provisions from areas through which enemy soldiers would pass on their march towards Lisbon, depriving them of food once they were trapped behind the lines at Torres Vedras.

"To give effect to this plan of defence," wrote a British officer, "it was necessary, not only that the army should retire to Torres Vedras, but that the whole country between the lines and the frontier should be abandoned by all classes of inhabitants. Everything which might contribute to the subsistence of the enemy should be carefully removed. My pen altogether fails me. No powers of description can convey the afflicting scenes, the cheerless desolation, that we daily witnessed on our march to the lines. Wherever we moved, the mandate which enjoined the wretched inhabitants to forsake their homes and remove or destroy their little property had gone before us. The villages were deserted, the churches were empty, the cottages stood open and untenanted, the mills were motionless and silent."[12]

Wellington's army marched through towns and villages, "sweeping before us all the resources of the country."[13] They were followed by the French who found a barren countryside, stripped of all food and stores. "We crossed vast districts without seeing a single inhabitant," wrote one of their officers. "Such an exodus had not been seen within human memory."[14] On 2 October, having passed through Coimbra and Pombal, the British army reached Leiria where Wellington set up temporary headquarters. "This beautiful town looked terribly devastated," wrote a commissary. "The order that all inhabitants should take flight had been carried out with the greatest speed. Except for some sick people, and a few who had gone mad through shock and grief, the town was deserted."[15]

The army bivouacked near Leiria until the morning of 5 October, when orders were given to resume the retreat. That evening, Wellington reached the monastery of Alcobaça and it was after this short journey, when the right flank of the army passed close to Marinha Grande, that one of his officers described the plight of the inhabitants. "It was most distressing," he wrote. "A crowd of men, women and children, the sick, aged and infirm as well as the robust and the young, covered the roads and fields in every direction, the wayside strewn with bedding, blankets and household furniture which the weary fugitives were unable to carry further. Those who forsook their dwellings did so under the persuasion that they would never see them again, and the agony which this excited exceeds my attempt at description."[16]

The army continued to fall back from Alcobaça to Torres Vedras and, during the last days of the retreat, the rains began. "Yesterday was the most uncomfortable day of my life," wrote an army surgeon on 9 October. "It blew and rained with the most dreadful violence, and in a very short time rendered the roads nearly impassable."[17] Soldiers and Portuguese struggled through the dampness and the mud, the peasants driving their stock of animals before them: bullocks, sheep and pigs. Now the lines of Torres Vedras came into view, every hilltop crowned with a fort, every valley cleared, every ditch and hollow filled. Slopes had been scarped into precipices, rivers and streams dammed to flood the plains, and there was no cover in any low-lying area against cross-fire from above.

On the morning of 8 October, Wellington began to shepherd his army into the area protected by the lines. Each contingent took up its appointed position and, three days later, all were in place. On 14 October, the advance guard of the French army arrived within riding distance and, as soon as Masséna was informed of the defences, he rode out to see for himself. During the British withdrawal, he had been convinced that Wellington was in retreat, that he was taking his men to a fleet of transports waiting in the Tagus. Now he returned to camp dispirited; the lines of defence were impenetrable with the number of men at his disposal.

Meanwhile, the people of Lisbon believed themselves to be in serious danger. They had no knowledge of the lines at Torres Vedras and, with French forces marching towards the city, enemy occupation seemed inevitable. "You can have no conception," wrote Admiral Berkeley from his flagship in the Tagus, "of the consternation which prevails in this great city."[18]

English merchants formed themselves into defence corps, and marched and drilled in handsome uniforms. They also made preparations for flight but there was no space for them on the British fleet. "Although it is my most anxious wish to embark the merchants," wrote the admiral on 5 October, "it is not in my power to accommodate them with any part of the transport tonnage in the river. They must therefore look to providing themselves with the means."[19] And provide for themselves they did; the packet boats (which had cabins for thirty passengers) took bookings from over a hundred people for each sailing.[20]

At a meeting of the English Factory on 17 October, it was resolved to form a committee, all members attending daily in rotation, to organise the chartering of vessels for "distressed British subjects" (those unable to pay their passage home) and to buy food for their journey.[21] John James attended three of these meetings but found it hard to concentrate. Not only was he concerned about the glassworks, situated in the path of the opposing armies, but he was alone again in the Largo dos Stephens, his sister having sailed for England in one of the overcrowded packet boats, fleeing from French invading forces for a second time.

The panic began to subside when it became known that the French had come to a standstill, although it was not until Wellington held a ball in the palace of Mafra (mid-way between Lisbon and Torres Vedras) that the city felt safe from enemy occupation. The ball, held on 7 November, was a great success. "It inspired confidence," wrote one of Wellington's officers, "and produced a most happy effect. The inhabitants of Lisbon naturally felt that, if the commander of the forces could give a fête when the enemy's advanced posts were almost within hearing of his revels, the danger could not be very pressing."[22]

Several merchants who had booked passages to England cancelled their reservations and the city became: "intoxicated by a strong feeling of security. Lisbon was crowded with objects of misery, yet at no time had its theatres been better filled, its societies more gay and brilliant, than when 70,000 enemies lay within miles of the city, panting for the plunder of it."[23] While the people of Lisbon felt secure in their homes, the city and its suburbs were indeed crowded with objects of misery, with thousands of refugees who had obeyed Wellington's order to abandon their homes and retreat behind British lines.

When this order arrived in Marinha Grande, the craftsmen and their families had prepared to leave the village, not knowing if they would ever return. Sousa had extinguished the furnaces, closed the factory, and made his way to the city where John James offered him hospitality in the Largo dos Stephens. Most of the glassworkers also arrived in Lisbon, having made the journey from Marinha Grande on foot or by bullock cart, and John James instructed Sousa to find them and ensure that each man received his regular wages.[24] A few of his workers had disobeyed the order and remained in their homes but, since all communication north of Torres Vedras had been severed, there was nothing John James could do to help them.

The French army stayed behind the lines for four weeks until Masséna ordered a retreat to Santarém, twenty-five miles to the north-east. His troops would remain here for nearly four months, drenched by the rains and with few provisions, their suffering shared by the Portuguese who had stayed in their villages. "The inhabitants of the country fled and hid," wrote Jean-Jacques Pelet, Masséna's aide-de-camp. "Most of them were roving in the woods, eating grass and wild fruit. Good God! What shelter did these unfortunates find? How many must have died during the six months we remained in this country, maintained by food that extreme necessity forced us to wrest from them."[25]

Soldiers roamed the countryside, torturing and killing people to reveal their hoards of food. For the first few weeks, Marinha Grande was left in peace (being over thirty miles from the French army) but, towards the end of the year, a garrison was set up in Leiria and a detachment of 800 men arrived in search of supplies. As well as persecuting the inhabitants, the soldiers burnt their abandoned houses. "They would set them on fire," wrote Pelet, "and the flames soon spread, resulting in frequent conflagrations. No-one was there to put out the fires when they started and no-one came for assistance or help. These careless soldiers would allow the fire to feed itself...Thus the magnificent convent of Alcobaça and an immense factory still full of woven cotton were burned, and the horrors of war increased in this unfortunate country."[26]

In February, Masséna made plans to cross the Mondego river and, on 5 March, his troops decamped and marched north. They reached Leiria two days later, setting fire to the city before continuing their march towards Pombal and Coimbra. On their heels came Wellington's army and, although British troops could be brutal too, plundering, looting and raping, they were genuinely shocked at what they saw.

"The French set on fire almost every town and village in the line of march," wrote one officer, "while peasants hanging upon trees, whole families murdered in their houses, and others lying dead by the roadside exhibited dreadful witness of these relentless invaders."[27] "It is impossible," wrote another, "to describe the scenes of horror. The city of Leiria had been eleven days on fire, and burning still. The images in the churches were in pieces, the graves opened for the sake of plunder, and we found none but a few Portuguese perishing with hunger and ill-treatment."[28]

On 13 March, harassed by British soldiers, with rains swelling the Mondego river and Portuguese militia defending the bridge at Coimbra, Masséna gave up all hopes of crossing the river into a region well supplied with crops and livestock. Instead, he turned east and set out for the Spanish border. Five days after his army crossed into Spain, Wellington issued a proclamation: "The Portuguese are informed that the cruel enemy has retired across the Agueda river. The inhabitants of the country are at liberty to return to their homes."[29]

15

Reconstruction

1811–1813

"We scarcely saw a house or a village but showed evident proofs of their barbarous wanton destruction. We saw many people and children absolutely starving, and living on nettles and herbs they gathered in the fields."
William Warre, January 1812

"The history of these atrocities is almost unparalleled and shocks every feeling of humanity. During their retreat, the French set on fire, not only the beautiful city of Leiria, but almost every town and village in the line of march."
Samuel D Broughton, May 1813

Cannons were fired in Lisbon to celebrate the French withdrawal from Santarém and soon details of the devastation north of Torres Vedras began to arrive in the city. As John James and Sousa heard about the destruction of life and property, they became increasingly fearful for the glassworks, not only for the factory complex but also for the villagers who had remained in their homes.

As soon as it was safe to travel, Sousa set out for Marinha Grande and, after passing through the lines, he rode through a depopulated countryside, every village devastated, every house in ruins. Colonel Trant and his young daughter, Clarissa, travelled the same route on a journey to Oporto. "We passed many ruined villages which appeared totally deserted," recalled Clarissa in her journal, "and seeing much evidence of the cruelties committed by the French army. Not a living being was to be seen, except here and there a little child attracted by the noise of carriage wheels, with nothing but a ragged shirt to protect it from the sun."[1]

On their way north, they visited the church where the Marquês de Pombal had been interred. "We were shown a vacant space where the tomb had stood," wrote Clarissa, "and on the wall the words *'respectez ce tombeau'* traced in chalk, but such an order was not likely to have been regarded by soldiers who respected neither the dead nor the living. They had broken open the coffin in hopes of finding treasure and scattered the contents in an adjoining courtyard." Clarissa helped her father collect the relics ("some fragments of bones, a pair of faded morocco slippers and a bag-wig") and gave them to two elderly friars for safekeeping. It seemed strange to her that "the duty of seeing these relics properly disposed of should have devolved upon a British officer and a little insignificant English girl."[2]

Sousa did not travel as far as Pombal. He turned left before Leiria onto the *Estrada do Guilherme* and, when he reached the factory, he found it, in his own words, "in a state which would have saddened and discouraged the bravest of men."[3] The workshop for crystalline glass (the great building which contained three furnaces for melting the mixtures, three ovens for heating crucibles, and several rooms for mixing ingredients and packing glass) had been burnt to a shell, its blackened roof beams lying in a heap of rubble. The covered yard and the factory's stock of fuel had been reduced to ashes, the crates of glass broken open, their contents smashed.[4] The mansion house had been looted and William's little theatre burnt to the ground. In the village, many houses had been destroyed; others were roofless and uninhabitable, their doors and windows, tables and chairs, taken by the French for firewood.[5]

Sousa sent a messenger to inform John James about the factory. He also wrote about the ruined houses and rows of makeshift graves, for the people who stayed in Marinha Grande had suffered the same atrocities as the inhabitants of every town and village behind the lines. Seventy-four had been killed by the French; many more had died from starvation or from epidemic typhus, a disease which feeds on war and famine.[6]

Typhus still gripped the area, infecting many of the villagers who had obeyed Wellington's order and were now returning to their homes. They would lie sick and dying in roofless houses, while nothing could be done to alleviate their suffering. The land was deserted. Crops and grain stores had been burnt or plundered, all livestock stolen or killed. Before the invasion, the glassworks had supported over 2000 people; only half this number would survive the months of war, famine and disease.[7]

Sousa wrote frequently to his employer in Lisbon, letters to which John James replied several times a week. There was no doubt in his mind that the factory should be rebuilt as soon as possible, to revive William's achievements and provide employment for the people of Marinha Grande. Villagers were still dying from disease, but boys appeared to remove the mess from the factory complex, a carpenter was hired to replace window frames, and broken glass in the warehouse was collected and stored for later use as cullet.[8]

John James continued to support families in the village, particularly those which had lost their wage-earner. He sent money to help local farmers restore their land and bought a hundred teams of oxen from the Oporto region (on condition the farmers repaid him by transporting cartloads of firewood at two-thirds their normal payment).[9] In this way, they could clear the land of debris and charred remains, and prepare it for crops and livestock. Seed and farm animals were provided by a programme of British aid and Philadelphia sent £50 from London, with instructions that her brother should buy textiles (baize, linen and bombazine) so the women of the village could make clothes.[10]

In early June, Sousa returned to Lisbon and, for the next three months, he and John James prepared plans and estimates for the reconstruction of the great workshop, an exact replica of William's building of the 1770s. A petition

15 James Palmer, treasurer of Christ's Hospital and friend of John James
Stephens, portrait by Sir Thomas Lawrence

16 The rectory at Little Petherick, photographed before alterations were made in the 1880s

17 Polvellan in West Looe, built by John Lemon (MP for Truro). Stephens Lyne Stephens was born here in 1801

18   Richard Lyne of Little Petherick, portrait c.1825

19 Chicksands Priory, lithograph by J D Parry, 1827

20 *The Melton Breakfast*, engraving from original painting by Sir Francis Grant, 1834. Stephens Lyne Stephens is sitting towards the back of the sofa, sixth from the left

21 Yolande (Pauline) Duvernay in *cachucha* costume, lithograph from original painting by J F Lewis, December 1836

22 Yolande Duvernay, pastel by Antonin Moine, mid-1830s

23 Yolande Lyne Stephens,
    1858/9

24 Count d'Orsay, drawing by
    Daniel Maclise, 1834

25 Stephens Lyne Stephens,
    mid-1850s

26 Stephens Lyne Stephens,
    late 1850s

27   Yolande Lyne Stephens, portrait by Edouard Dubufe, 1853

was sent to the council of regents, emphasising that the factory had been placed under royal protection and asking for as much assistance as the government could offer. On 12 July, John James was granted free use of mature tree trunks from the royal pine forest[11] but, although public money was used to rebuild the towns, no subsidy was made to the glassworks. The restoration was funded by John James from his personal fortune.[12]

Sousa set out for Marinha Grande on the first day of September and work soon began on the reconstruction.[13] Six months later, the roof of the new workshop was finished, work had begun on the interior, and Sousa was trying to reassemble the workforce, most of whom had fled to Lisbon before the invasion and received financial support from John James until the following spring. Despite this generosity, not all the glassworkers were proving loyal to their employer and Sousa was finding it difficult to retain the services of a sufficient number of craftsmen.

A few of John James's workers had been killed by the French or become too weakened by famine and disease to return to their duties, but most of those who left the factory believed that better opportunities lay elsewhere. Some had sailed for Brazil; others were employed in a new glass factory in Lisbon. They were earning higher wages in the city and intended to remain there, a situation which saddened John James as he expected more gratitude from his employees.[14] Sousa appealed to the government, listing the benefits the workers received at Marinha Grande and the help John James had given them when they were refugees in Lisbon. He asked that they be sent back to Marinha Grande by royal order, a request which was granted in June.[15]

The glassworks re-entered production in October 1812[16] although, because of the shortage of craftsmen and lack of transport from the pine forest, it would be almost two years before they could operate at full capacity. Before the invasions, a hundred carters were employed to transport firewood to the factory; by 1812, this number had been reduced to seventy-three, many of whom were at risk from military recruitment.[17] But at least John James's privileges had been reinstated. In November 1810, Prince João had re-established his right to obtain firewood free of charge, and restored and extended his tax exemptions for a period of twenty years.[18]

Meanwhile, the area north of Torres Vedras was receiving financial aid from England, distributed by a committee chaired by the British consul. (The English Factory had ceased to exist in 1810, when a commercial treaty abolished English Factories in Portuguese territories, and merchants in Lisbon renamed themselves the Society of British Merchants & Factors.)

Charles Lyne was appointed to help raise the money in England and, in May 1811, the committee in Lisbon met for the first time, with John James and four other merchants forming the British contingent. An initial sum of £5000 was sent to cover immediate needs and used to buy cattle, seed, clothes and blankets.[19] During the next two years, as larger amounts arrived for distribution, John James followed the progress of Wellington's army in the peninsula, sending details of battles and troop movements to Sousa in Marinha Grande.

In January 1813, Wellington made a three-day visit to Lisbon, his first since the retreat of Masséna's army almost two years before. On a fine, sunny afternoon, he arrived at the south bank of the Tagus and was rowed across to the Praça do Comércio in a royal barge. Ships in the harbour were decorated and the river was filled with boats, their sails illuminated by winter sunshine. "A salute from the flagship announced Wellington's approach," wrote an English officer, "the signal for a scene of tumultuous joy: shouts of *viva* from the Portuguese; varieties of bands playing as many different tunes as there were instruments; squibs, crackers, and all kinds of fireworks; and horses, mules and donkeys braying and prancing in all directions."[20]

John James wrote to Sousa about the festivities in the city. He described the scene in the Praça do Comércio as Wellington mounted the steps from the royal barge. He described the celebration in the Opera House that evening, although he chose not to attend the performance, nor the ball in the envoy's house the following night.[21] Alone in the Largo dos Stephens and missing his sister's company, he was not in the mood for parties, although he did sign a letter of welcome from the Society of British Merchants & Factors. The members offered Wellington their: "warmest congratulations on your arrival in this capital. We rejoice that, under your counsels and conduct, the Corsican despotism has received a vital blow by victories which rival the glory of Agincourt and Crécy."[22]

Four months later, Wellington left his Portuguese base for the last time, marching into Spain in an advance which would, within a year, defeat the French and send Napoleon into exile on the island of Elba.

Part Four

John James
The Years of Solitude

Interlude
London

1810–1813

When Philadelphia returned to England in the autumn of 1810, she moved into her sister-in-law's house in Marylebone. A year later, one of John James's friends visited London and suggested that she accompany him on the voyage home, but she was feeling unwell at the time and told him she would sail for Lisbon in the spring. And when spring came, she chose to stay in London and rent a house of her own.[1]

She remained on good terms with Charles and Wilhelmina, and also visited Joseph in Finsbury Square. After his first wife died in 1810, Joseph married his Portuguese children's nurse and started a second family.[2] Meanwhile, his older boys were in the care of their uncle, Richard Lyne, in his private school on Castle Hill.[3] They remained there until 1812 when Richard was offered a living as rector of Little Petherick, a village near Padstow in north Cornwall.

At last Richard could afford to give up teaching, a profession he had never found congenial, but his wife had little time to enjoy their new home. A few months after they arrived in Little Petherick, Mary took to her bed for the last time. "Her illness," wrote Richard, "was a chariot of fire, exceeding painful. In the last fortnight of her life, she was, from extreme debility and agony of pain, several times delirious, but there remained the same gentleness in her manner and that placidity of temper of which nothing could deprive her."[4]

Twenty-two years earlier, Mary had silently endured the pains of childbirth to avoid waking her husband; now, just hours from death, she still deferred to his well-being. "Shortly before she expired," explained Richard, "in the height of summer when the air was hot and sultry and she was in great difficulty of respiration, she desired that the door and windows be opened. This was no sooner done than she required them to be closed again, recollecting that I was in poor health and fearing I might suffer from the draught of air."[5]

England was now at war with the United States and, soon after his brother moved to Little Petherick, Charles started a campaign to halt the trade in North American cotton. In recent years, he had sourced most of his cotton from North America but, when war broke out in June 1812, he transferred his source to Brazil. Meanwhile, cotton from North America (which the millers preferred to all others) continued to be imported in neutral vessels, and the government was granting licences for these imports under the terms of an unrepealed Act of Parliament.

Charles wrote to the foreign secretary in February 1813, explaining that the unrepealed Act had caused "great clamour and discontent" among merchants importing cotton from Brazil.[6] A week later, having done his calculations in detail, he wrote a further letter which he published as a pamphlet. There was no need to import cotton from an enemy country, he explained, for there was "sufficient cotton-wool in England, and in the Brazils, West Indies, Surat and Bengal, to last until 17 July 1815 at normal cotton spinning capacity." And he added a disclaimer: "Although I am personally interested in the stopping of the North American export trade, I can assure your Lordship that I have taken up the question more on public grounds than on any of a private nature."[7]

Since his return from Portugal, Charles had gained a reputation as a shrewd and able merchant, and in the spring of 1810, he was called to give evidence before the select committee investigating the high price of bullion. Because of declining stocks of bullion, payments in gold had been suspended in 1797 and the Bank of England converted to a paper currency. For the first time, it was able to increase the issue of banknotes and, when the opening of South American markets to British commerce led to over-speculation, it began to manufacture large amounts of paper money. Meanwhile, stocks of bullion continued to decline as gold was sent abroad to fund Wellington's campaigns in the peninsula and to pay for imported foodstuffs.

The Bullion Committee interrogated a number of expert witnesses (Charles gave evidence on currencies and exchange rates in Portugal and Brazil) and presented its report to the government in June.[8] It concluded that the over-issue of banknotes had led to depreciation of paper money against the price of gold, and recommended a return to the gold standard no less than two years in the future. These conclusions were not considered by parliament for almost a year, allowing plenty of time for each faction (bullionists and anti-bullionists) to issue a spate of pamphlets.

Charles had no time for theorists and, when the politician, William Huskisson, wrote a pamphlet restating the principle that over-issue of banknotes led to depreciation of paper money, he published a pamphlet of his own. Exasperated by what he perceived as ignorance, he explained that Huskisson's opinions were: "erroneous and dangerous in the extreme. Never was a doctrine more pregnant with evil nor, thank God, one founded upon more fallacious principles. If Mr Huskisson would condescend to make a few enquiries of practical men, he would draw very different conclusions."[9] He then gave a complicated description of exchange rates between countries, and shipments of bullion from one country to another, to explain the high price of gold against paper money. "Mr Lyne lays considerable stress upon the state of exchanges between the different countries of Europe," wrote another merchant after reading the pamphlet, "which I am persuaded hardly any man in this country can comprehend."[10]

Parliament rejected the committee's recommendations in May 1811. The price of gold continued to rise and, in need of bullion to cover the increasing costs of the Peninsular War, the government asked the Bank of England to buy gold to the value of £2 million.[11] Impressed by Charles's trading experience with South America, the Bank employed Lyne, Hathorn & Roberts to import half this amount from Brazil. Charles was given a commission of six percent, of which one-third was passed to his agent in Rio de Janeiro, and since the Bank covered all transport and insurance costs, his profit was £40,000 (over £1.3 million in today's values).

In August, Charles wrote to his agent in Brazil. After detailed instructions about types of gold to be purchased, weighing and measuring techniques, insurance and shipping matters, he urged him to strict secrecy: "We can conceive that an operation of this nature may be viewed with no small degree of jealousy. It is therefore our most particular desire that you exert your utmost skill to do the transaction in that circumspect, careful, quiet manner, so that no person but yourself shall ever know the extent to which you are to carry out your operations. Nothing further should be known, even to your confidential clerks and assistants, than what may be absolutely necessary. The management and execution of the operation must be confined to as few of your clerks as possible and the greatest secrecy be enjoined, not only to them, but also to the captains and officers of the ships which take off the gold."

"This is the first trial of our being employed as commissioners," he continued, "and the skilful and honourable discharge of our duty throughout the whole execution will determine whether we shall be preferred for such operations on future occasions." And he hoped the commission would "form the basis of a series of transactions that will most probably take place from time to time."[12]

Shortly after writing this letter, Charles became ill and spent several months at home in Devonshire Place. He had retained his youthful arrogance and would regale his visitors with a constant flow of advice. When William Gibbs (son of Antony Gibbs) visited him in April 1812, he received a long tirade of instruction. "It would have amused you to have heard him talk," William wrote to his brother, "just the same as ever, only more in his peculiar way than before. It struck me that, having been ill and having no-one to pour his advice upon for some time, he thought it a good opportunity of giving it all to me. First, I was to remove to his part of town and ride into the City with merchants of the first eminence who lived in the same neighbourhood. Then I was never to attend a gambling club – no, no, it must never be said that I was even seen at such a place. And it was a bad custom too – which many young men had – of lounging away their evenings at playhouses."

Charles gave him more advice, mainly about business matters, and invited him to dinner a few days later. "I dine there on Friday," concluded William, "when I suppose I shall have an improved edition of my conversation with him this morning. He is certainly a very sharp and clever man, and although he carries his line of dictating to others to a disagreeable length, yet I believe he means well." There was another lecture on Friday evening, a lengthy one which caused Wilhelmina to fall asleep on the sofa. "It is astonishing what a deal of information one gets out of the little man," wrote William the following morning, "although the half of it may not apply to one's own case."[13]

16

An Uneasy Peace

1814–1820

"It may be difficult to conceive the degree of soreness and jealousy which is felt here at anything that looks like subservience to Great Britain."
George Canning, April 1815

Meanwhile, John James continued to hope that Philadelphia would return to Lisbon. He was lonely without her and, although she wrote several times a month, he longed for her physical presence, for his sister to sit opposite him at the dinner table, to be his companion during the long evening hours when he felt most alone. But Philadelphia was enjoying herself in London and seemed reluctant to sail for Portugal.

The early months of 1814 were severe in England. Roads were impassable, the Thames was iced over, and she wrote to John James sitting close to the fire and apologising for the quality of her handwriting. She could barely hold the pen for cold, but had learnt to enjoy the English winter and would not yet embark for Lisbon. In February, she wrote that she would return after the war but, when peace was declared in May, she found another reason for staying. After attending the launch of a battleship in July (her acquaintance with Lord St Vincent providing a seat in one of the best naval tents), she wrote that the rough water at Portsmouth had made her fearful of a sea voyage.[1]

John James was discouraged by these delaying tactics and began to suspect that Philadelphia had little intention of returning to Lisbon, a sense of disappointment shared by the people of Portugal who were also hoping for the return of an émigré. After the defeat of France, it was believed that the

prince regent would sail home to re-invigorate a country
exhausted and disorganised after eight years of war. The
council of regents wrote to Brazil asking for details of João's
return, and ordered window panes from Marinha Grande to
repair the palaces of Queluz and Ajuda.[2] And the British
government appointed George Canning as special ambassador to Lisbon. Only a chargé d'affaires was based in the city
and Canning (a senior politician out of government office)
was a suitably eminent person to receive the prince regent on
behalf of the British nation.

Canning disembarked in December 1814, landing at the
steps of the Praça do Comércio to be met by English
diplomatic and military staff, and by members of the Society
of British Merchants & Factors. It was a wet day, with a
leaden sky unleashing torrents of rain on the city, and John
James stood cold and damp by the waterside. Canning
suffered from gout and, watching the politician wince from
pain as he climbed the steps from the river, John James hoped
that his arrival would improve Anglo-Portuguese relations
which had deteriorated rapidly over recent months. The
Portuguese felt resentful at the gratitude expected for their
liberation, while English merchants believed that Britain's
efforts to save the country had been forgotten.

Canning absorbed these attitudes during his first weeks in
Lisbon and in January, when he was entertained to a dinner
by the Society of British Merchants & Factors, he tried to
build a few bridges. At the end of the meal, John James (the
most senior member of the Society) stood at the high table
and, on behalf of the British nation, congratulated Canning
on his arrival in Lisbon and offered a toast to his health.[3] He
then sat down, while the ambassador rose to his feet.

Canning spoke of victory over France and the part played
by Portugal in the defeat of Napoleon. "From this nook of
Europe," he told the assembled merchants, "proceeded that
impulse by which its mightiest kingdoms have been set free.
In this sterile and unpromising soil was deposited the seed of
that security whose branches now overshadow mankind. I

cannot behold the traces of desolation in this country, and of suffering among the people, without rendering homage to the character of the nation which, by all that it has done and all that it has endured, has raised itself to a pitch of moral eminence far beyond the proportion of its territory, population, or power."

"I am anxious," he continued, "to state the principle of our connection, and of our claims upon each other, in terms not of comparison but of equality. Portugal would not have been saved without England, it is true; but Portugal was to England an instrument for the mightier task which England had to perform. We brought hither councils, arms, discipline and valour. We found here willing hearts and active hands, a people brave and enduring. The arm of England was the lever that wrenched the power of Bonaparte from its basis; Portugal was the fulcrum on which that lever moved. England fanned and fed the fire, but Portugal had reared the altar on which that fire was kindled and from which it mounted, brightening and widening, until the world was illumined with the blaze."

At these words, John James, seated next to Canning, thought of the flames which had devoured his factory at Marinha Grande, brightening and widening until the great workshop had been reduced to a blackened shell. He watched Canning's face as the ambassador continued to speak, referring to the enmity between the two peoples. "It is naturally to be expected," he explained, "that having accomplished the overthrow of its enemies, the nation should carry itself with a bolder and freer port, even towards its friends. We have no right to feel this sorely; it would be neither just nor becoming in us to do so. To Portugal, on the other hand, I would say that there is no humiliation in national gratitude, that a grateful mind is at once indebted and discharged and recovers its level by an acknowledgement that there is no room for commercial or political jealousy. The world is large enough for both Portuguese and British commerce; and Britain, while she has never been wanting to her ally in time of need, seeks no other reward for her exertions and sacrifices than mutual confidence and common prosperity."[4]

Canning finished his speech and sat down to enthusiastic applause from the merchants. Over the next few months, he did his best to fulfil his role as special ambassador; he involved himself in diplomatic and consular matters and, after Napoleon's escape from Elba, spent several weeks trying (without success) to obtain the services of the Portuguese army in Britain's renewed campaign against France. As he explained to the foreign secretary in London, "it may be difficult for your Lordship to conceive the degree of soreness and jealousy which is felt here at anything that looks like subservience to Great Britain."[5]

Meanwhile, Prince João was reluctant to return home. He enjoyed life in Rio de Janeiro and, dreading the thought of another sea voyage, he soon decided to remain in Brazil. Canning's appointment was revoked in June and, before he left office, he set down his thoughts on Anglo-Portuguese relations. "It would be vain," he wrote to London, "to expect that a strong sense of national gratitude would long survive...Perhaps the burden of obligation, and the consequent sense of inferiority, have quickened the desire to emancipate themselves from a connection which is felt by them, however unfairly, as one of humiliating and painful dependency."[6]

The main reason for this sense of dependency was one man, William Beresford, the general who headed the enquiry into French plunder in 1808. Later that year, the council of regents asked that an English general should take command of the Portuguese army. Wellington recommended Beresford; he was given the rank of marshal and, with a small band of officers, disciplined the soldiers and recruits into a fighting force which gained the respect of British commanders. "The appearance of the Portuguese troops has really astonished me," wrote one general in 1811, "it is in every respect equal to our own and in some instances finer."[7]

After the war, Beresford settled in Lisbon and retained command of the army. This had grown to 100,000 men (having quadrupled in size since 1810) and the cost of its maintenance consumed three-quarters of state revenue. The army dominated domestic politics and Beresford, as commander-in-chief, controlled much of civilian life. The higher classes were jealous of his authority, the council of regents saw him as a power-hungry rival, and the people, sensing themselves under British occupation, resented his vice-regal powers. "*El rei Beresford*," they called him, "*este Britânico odioso*."[8] Beresford, meanwhile, lived in style in his palace on the banks of the Tagus (where it was said that senior appointments were made through the favour of his Portuguese mistress).

In March 1816, Dona Maria died in Rio de Janeiro and, when celebrations were held in Lisbon to acclaim the succession of Dom João VI, only the nobility made any effort to attend. John James rose to the occasion, watching the processions wind through the streets and attending a ball in honour of the new sovereign,[9] but there was little enthusiasm for the event and few people bothered to illuminate their houses. "All hope of the king's return has now ceased," wrote the British chargé d'affaires, "and the people consider themselves dwindled into a province of a South American kingdom."[10]

The first seeds of revolution were sown in 1817 when General Gomes Freire instigated a plot to take control of the country. Beresford was informed of the conspiracy, the plotters were arrested and, as their trial dragged on through the summer and autumn, the people of Lisbon began to perceive them as heroes. Found guilty of treason, the conspirators were executed in October, Freire garrotted outside the fort in which he had been held prisoner, his followers hanged in the Campo de Santa Ana.

One of Freire's complaints about Beresford was his constant use of military recruitment. "This ridiculous adventurer," he had written a few months before his arrest, "is making yet another recruitment, to do his country the service of annihilating our commerce, arts, and all native industry."[11] The methods used to obtain recruits were similar to the press-gangs which manned British warships. "The men are pressed like seamen in England," explained an English officer, "and, bound together, are conveyed immediately under escort to the army."[12]

John James had experienced problems with recruitment since the glassworks reopened in 1812 but this latest round-up was particularly serious, with officers combing the pine forest to swell the ranks of the military. At risk of losing the carters who transported firewood to the factory, he wrote a petition to Beresford, a man with whom he was on friendly terms. The marshal had been entertained to dinner at the Largo dos Stephens in October 1816 and the two men had met twice the following year, first at the ball to celebrate Dom João's accession in April, and again in June when John James was invited to Beresford's palace to celebrate the birthday of George III.[13]

John James prepared his petition in October, hoping that Beresford would look kindly on the request of a fellow Englishman. Remembering the mistakes he had made in 1807, he enclosed (in the words of the Junta do Comércio) "excessive proof," full transcriptions of every decree and provision affecting the use of firewood since 1775, a total of eleven documents. He explained that the glassworks operated under royal protection and, to prevent "the factory becoming, for a second time, a building in a deserted site, with ruin and misery to its people," he asked that exemption certificates be issued to a hundred carters so they could work safely in the pine forest.[14]

Beresford showed little interest. He passed the petition to the minister of foreign affairs, explaining that he had no legal powers to deal with the matter (although he found it "extraordinary" that a hundred teams of oxen were required to transport firewood to the factory).[15] The minister forwarded the petition to the Junta do Comércio and, in April 1818, as a temporary measure, the chief magistrate of Leiria signed papers exempting a hundred carters from military recruitment.[16]

For a more permanent decision, the Junta referred the matter to Dom João and the documents were sent to Brazil in July. No reply was received and, in the spring of 1820, John James asked the Junta to resubmit his original petition. "Almost two years have passed since this request went to the royal presence," he wrote, "and still it has not been resolved." Workers in the pine forest were again under threat from recruitment and the matter required the king's urgent attention, so that the factory remained in operation "to the benefit of the state and the many families that subsist on it."[17]

The Junta wrote again to Dom João, but political developments were underway which would solve the problem without the king's intervention. A few years earlier, an underground organisation had been set up in Oporto to discuss the principle of constitutional government and, as these ideas spread through the country, Beresford sent an emissary to the king asking for the return of at least one member of the royal family. His request was refused and, by the spring of 1820, he had become increasingly uneasy. To prevent further unrest, he needed an extension of his powers, a seat on the council of regents, and money for the army. Deciding to appeal to the king in person, he sailed for Brazil in April and warned Dom João that there would be revolution unless he was granted additional authority. The king gave him the powers and money that he asked for, and Beresford set sail again for Lisbon.

Revolution was indeed imminent, more imminent than even Beresford suspected. He was on his return voyage when the military council in Oporto demanded a parliament based on a constitution. As the Oporto regiments marched south, the garrison in Coimbra declared in their favour and, on 15 September, the revolution spread to Lisbon. The council of regents was deposed and one of the first rulings of the new (provisional) government was the expulsion of all British officers from the Portuguese army, a measure that included its commander-in-chief, Marshal Beresford.

When his ship arrived in the Tagus on 10 October, Beresford was refused permission to disembark. The following day, the constitutionalists from Oporto and Coimbra made a triumphal entry into the city. The old regime was dead; the centuries of absolute rule were over; the shouts of *"Viva a constituição"* had given birth to a new age. Seven days later, still aboard his vessel in the Tagus, Beresford admitted defeat. He transferred to a packet boat and sailed for England, where he settled down to right-wing politics in the House of Lords.

Despite Beresford's inroads into his labour force, John James continued to admire the marshal, referring to his "eminent services to this country, his valour and great ability in the cabinet as well as in the field, which merit praise and my admiration."[18] It is surprising that he thought so highly of him, for it was Beresford's arrogance, his assumption of vice-regal powers in an independent country, that led to such strong anti-British sentiments in Portugal. These contributed to the constitutional revolution and also affected the profitability of the glassworks.

George Canning wrote a report on the government in 1815. There were four members of the council of regents: two were in ill-health, one was of "unexceptional character," and the fourth was "a decided enemy to British influence and most active in devising means to get rid of it." Two government ministers also voted on matters that impinged on their responsibilities. The minister for home affairs had "long entertained a feeling of acrimonious dislike towards Britain," while the minister for foreign affairs had "a desire to create for himself the reputation of a good Portuguese by disparaging the usefulness of the British alliance."[19]

These were the men who ruled on all matters connected with commerce and, according to Canning, they had begun to make decisions based on anti-British principles as early as May 1814. Their rulings were founded on reports from tribunals and administrators, and in 1815, the custom-house in Lisbon was authorised to impose a tax on glass arriving in the Tagus by sea.[20] Since the public highway to Lisbon had deteriorated since the war, most of John James's glass was shipped from São Martinho and the tax was a drain on his profitability. At the same time, his sales were declining because of an increased level of imports.

Although duties on imported glass had been reduced some years earlier, the war in Europe disrupted trade and reduced the amount of foreign glass entering the country. But after the peace of 1815, imported glass began to arrive in increasing quantities and at decreasing prices. The industrial revolution had brought prices down in the manufacturing countries of Europe, while costs of raw materials and transport had fallen with the ending of hostilities. By 1820, imports of mass-produced glass had been competing with products from Marinha Grande for five years; they had also taken much of the market in Brazil which had been opened to direct trade with all nations in 1808.

John James's prices were higher than those for imported glass; they had been set by William and approved by Pombal as long ago as 1773 when Marinha Grande had a monopoly of glass supply. In order to compete with glass from abroad, John James should have reduced his prices, but this he declined to do, threatening to sack his employees if they sold glass at a discount.[21] He also declined to cut back on production. As a result, his stocks began to accumulate; by December 1816, the warehouse in the Largo dos Stephens was so full that he wrote to Sousa asking him to send no more glass to the city.[22]

John James refused to acknowledge that his problems were caused by high prices. Instead, he attributed them to lower import duties and the tax on glass transported by sea (he was charged at a rate of three percent, while imports from England paid only half this amount). In 1818, when two Portuguese aristocrats were planning a visit to Marinha Grande, he hoped they would "take note of the boxes of glass rotting in warehouses because of the tax imposed by the customs."[23]

In failing to accept that he should lower his prices to compete with imported glass, John James showed little understanding of market conditions. He even refused to depreciate the value of his older stocks as glass was broken because of poor storage and transport from one warehouse to another. He merely instructed his clerks to add the value of the stocks to the capital value of the factory. As the financial situation deteriorated, as profits began to slide into loss, he made up the shortfall from his brother's fortune. By the time of the constitutional revolution, he was subsidising the entire running costs of the factory, his stocks of glass accumulating at a rate of £40,000 a month in today's values.

His motives were to maintain the factory exactly as it was during William's lifetime. He had failed to change the designs to keep pace with fashion, and forbidden the introduction of more efficient machinery as the technology of glass-making evolved. There was a water-mill which broke down the pebbles and rougher grades of sand, but the kneading of clay to make crucibles was still done by the stomping feet of a dozen men and sand was still washed by hand in the factory courtyard. "No-one was concerned about the situation," explained a report written in 1827, "because the glass was simply packed and stored in warehouses, filling the accounts with imaginary value."[24]

The glassworks were overstaffed too. John James did his best to prevent workers leaving the factory (considering such men to be "ungrateful to the organisation which trained them and supported them during calamitous times,")[25] while his fortune provided full employment for the people of Marinha Grande. Sons of craftsmen had a right to work in the factory, their wives and daughters employed to wash the sand and select and pack the glass. "As a result," the report continued, "the establishment became overladen with workers, three times more than was necessary."[26]

The factory was in operation solely for the benefit of its employees, for no advantage accrued to John James when all finished glass was stockpiled in warehouses and he was subsidising the entire cost of production. Meanwhile, William's welfare state was thriving. Retired workers received generous pensions, a weekly collection was organised for widows and orphans of workers who had died in service, a surgeon was on call to treat the sick of the village, and a pharmacist employed to dispense medicines.[27]

Every January for some years past, Sousa had sent his annual report to the Junta do Comércio with a request that imported glass should be prevented from entering the country. No notice had been taken of these requests and in April 1821, in the vain hope that the constitutional government would take a more lenient view, he prepared a detailed petition. "All the benefits to the state and to so many individuals from preserving this factory," he wrote, "are in imminent danger of coming to an end unless prompt and efficient measures are taken." Estimating the stocks of glass at the equivalent of £2 million in today's values, he explained that a prohibition on imports was the only solution. "The factory maintains the same standards today as in the time of the greatest consumption of its products," he concluded. "Production has not been reduced and payments are made regularly and efficiently. But however great the wealth of the owner, he may not be able to withstand such losses. So far, he has borne them with perseverance and courage, but who knows whether he will continue to bear them in the future?"[28]

Interlude

England

1816–1820

After the declaration of peace in 1815, John James had sent constant requests for Philadelphia to return to Portugal. She had given many excuses for refusing: her weak health, the weather, the companionship of her friends in England. His hopes revived in November 1816 when she wrote that she might embark for Lisbon in the spring, but she was tired of her brother's entreaties and asked him to stop pleading for her return.[1]

This was the last letter in her own handwriting. A few weeks later, she suffered a major stroke and Charles broke the news to John James. Two doctors and a nurse were in attendance, he wrote, and his sister was making a good recovery.[2] During the winter, she was well enough to be taken for short carriage rides, but her mind was affected and she quarrelled with her paid companion, accusing her of theft. She also insisted on moving house, this time to Montagu Square where she was looked after by a widowed friend.[3] Her health improved during the spring but there was a setback in the summer. Taken ill on a visit to Windsor Castle, she began to suffer from "delirium and fever." The doctors feared the worst, the last rites were administered, and John James expected to learn of his sister's death with the arrival of every packet boat.[4]

Philadelphia's physical health recovered from this second stroke, but not her faculties. Fit enough to manage a two-hour walk every day, she had, as John James put it, "lost her memory and forgets everything."[5] By October, she was in need of constant care and James Palmer brought her to the Treasurer's House at Christ's Hospital, where she could be looked after by his three unmarried daughters. To make the news easier to bear, he wrote to one of John James's friends in Lisbon, asking him to go personally to the Largo dos Stephens to comfort John James when he told him that his sister had lost her senses.[6]

Charles and his wife were attentive to Philadelphia, but they were unable to help when she was moved to Christ's Hospital for their eldest daughter (just fourteen years old) was lying dangerously ill in Devonshire Place. She died on 5 November, the same day that Princess Charlotte died in childbirth. Only child of the future George IV, Charlotte was immensely popular and, as Charles and Wilhelmina interred their daughter under the parish church of St Marylebone, their distress was mingled with the pomp of a state funeral and the grief of an entire nation.[7]

A few months later, still in mourning for his daughter, Charles retired from business.[8] He was fifty-four years old. He bought a property in the fashionable resort of Weymouth and, after clearing his desk in Old Broad Street, he and his family travelled to Dorset for the first of many summers in their new house overlooking Weymouth Bay.[9] As his wife and four surviving children swam in the sea and played on the beach near the house, Charles read the newspapers and drafted letters to members of government, many of which he issued as pamphlets.

In January 1819, he published a letter to the prime minister, Lord Liverpool, restating his case against a return to the gold standard, a policy the government was finally planning to implement. "The idea of gold against paper money is so very prepossessing to uninformed minds that we ought not to be astonished at many being misled," wrote Charles. "But surely those who so earnestly advocate this measure cannot be serious or cannot have sufficiently considered the subject."[10] Lord Liverpool took exception to the tone of this letter; according to one of Charles's nephews, "it made the prime minister very angry, saying it was a pity that gentlemen of the City should waste their time writing on subjects they do not understand."[11] A year later, Charles published another pamphlet, this time addressed to the foreign secretary. Referring to the "tremendous evils concomitant on the speedy return to a gold currency," he hoped that the measure would soon be repealed. "Happy would it have been for the prosperity of the country," he wrote, "had the evils predicted by practical men been more regarded, more candidly met, and more openly discussed."[12]

Charles wrote this pamphlet in January 1820, during a cold winter when the streets of London lay under snow, a winter when his wife took to her sickbed. Her health deteriorated through the spring and the family remained in London during the summer as she was too weak to make the journey to Weymouth. She died on 23 August (her twenty-third wedding anniversary) and, eight days later, her body was interred close to her daughter in a vault under St Marylebone church.[13]

The previous five years had been a period of recession, leading to a number of failures in the mercantile community. Charles's trading house had remained profitable but, by 1820, two of his brothers had been declared bankrupt.

The first to become insolvent was Edward Lyne, a wine merchant in Plymouth. Edward had diversified on the outbreak of war, setting up in partnership with his cousin, Benjamin Tucker, to run a prize agency for cargoes seized from the enemy. This was a lucrative activity and Benjamin (as secretary to Lord St Vincent) was able to direct many captured vessels to Edward in Plymouth. But over the years, the cousins lost respect for each other and, when Edward failed to obtain money owed to him by Benjamin, he was unable to pay his debts. He was bankrupted in June 1818, less than two years before Joseph Lyne was also declared bankrupt.[14]

Joseph had been in financial difficulties for some time, mainly because of over-enthusiastic trade with South America. "The opening of South American states to direct commerce with this country," explained Charles in one of his pamphlets, "opened a new extended market for the sale of our manufactures. Our merchants eagerly availed themselves of this new field and, as their early shipments were sold to great profits and quick returns, an immense over-trading took place. The markets soon became overstocked, and ruinous prices in some instances and total want of sales in others were the consequences. There are more of our manufactures lying there a dead weight than can be consumed for years, and more than the produce of those states can pay for for several years to come."[15]

After his possessions were taken by the bailiffs, Joseph left his house in Highgate and moved to a cottage in east London where his second wife died six months later, leaving him with two small daughters as well as the youngest children from his first marriage.[16] He and his family then settled in Liskeard, where they were looked after by his three unmarried sisters. His brother Edward had also returned to Liskeard and his presence allowed Joseph to discuss the problems of financial distress, as well as the difficulty of raising children in straitened circumstances.

Four of Joseph's sons had already left home: the eldest (an epileptic young man with bouts of mental instability) had been living in Cornwall for some years, two were working as merchants in South America, and his third son, Francis, was about to set up in business on his own account. Francis, now aged twenty, was the only son available to woo John James in Lisbon – to try and ensure a place in the old man's will – and although Joseph was broken down in health and spirits, he spent the next few months making plans for his son to visit Portugal.

17

A Mild and Placid Spirit

1820–1826

"Mr Stephens, an Englishman by birth who has passed his life in this country, is now in the enjoyment of a green old age, blest with the smiles of fortune in a superlative degree for his wealth is immense."
Marianne Baillie, November 1821

"I will sell to you for half-a-crown all that I get from the Stephenses."
Charles Lyne to William Doherty (Lewis Stephens's book-keeper), 1794

Dom João learnt of the revolution in November. An absolute monarch by tradition, he loathed the idea of constitutional government but his instincts led him to be cautious and he took no action. It was not until February that he made the decision to return to Portugal, leaving his elder son Pedro to act as regent of Brazil. In April 1821, a squadron of ships set sail for Lisbon, carrying the king, his wife and younger son, the body of his mother, and numerous courtiers, priests and officials.

The squadron arrived in the Tagus after a voyage of ten weeks. "The flagship is surrounded by small boats crowded with people," wrote an Englishwoman viewing the proceedings through a telescope. "An English frigate is covered with flags of the gayest variety of colour, its crew attired in gala costume. They are swarming amid the rigging like clustering bees and I can perceive some officers stationed at the same giddy height."[1]

The king went ashore the following day and was taken to parliament where, with "a wild and distrustful expression," he swore to uphold a constitutional government.[2] He moved into a palace in Lisbon and did his best to act fairly to the new regime, while his wife, Dona Carlota, made her home in Queluz where she lived in retirement, plotting the downfall of the constitutionalists and instilling in her younger son, Miguel, a belief in the absolute power of monarchy. Carlota had total control over Miguel. He was, unlike his father (and giving rise to rumours about his paternity), good-looking, athletic and charming, and Carlota would use him as a puppet, a figurehead for her plans to control the country.

The following spring, the body of Dona Maria was interred in a church she had built in Buenos Aires. The coffin was opened and it was the job of her unfortunate daughters to dress the corpse in new clothes, so that courtiers could pay their respects to the dead queen and kiss her freshly-gloved hand. The ceremonies lasted for three days, "during which period," wrote a visitor to the city, "the great guns on sea and land, and the bells of every steeple in Lisbon, thundered and pealed without intermission. It is a great hardship for us little people that a queen cannot be interred without rendering many of her subjects distracted."[3]

John James was seventy-five years old at the time of Maria's interment and described as "enjoying a green old age, surrounded by numerous friends and blest with the smiles of fortune in a superlative degree for his wealth is immense."[4] He rarely left the Largo dos Stephens but kept an open table for members of the English community. Every day, his servants laid on a banquet for those who wished to attend, "but the special favourites alone were invited to coffee in another room and, when John James arose and bowed and left the table, the others that remained took their departure."[5]

In 1823, he was visited by Joseph's son, Francis, sent by his father to win his way into the old man's affections. "An extraordinary feeling possessed my mind when I first saw Mr Stephens," wrote Francis in his memoirs. "I could arrive at no settled feeling just by looking at him. I felt he made me welcome, although the pressure of his hand was scarcely enough to make me happy. His words were few but kind, and

I dined with him every day, sitting on his left at the head of the table.

"His mode of life was very singular and very strange. A daily public dinner was the order of the house, and those of his acquaintance who liked it would meet in his reception room about twenty minutes before the dinner hour. In this room was a table covered with newspapers and, at the proper time, the butler appeared at the door and, with an extended finger, counted heads and then prepared the table. When dinner was announced, Mr Stephens would make his appearance through a door of another room, bow to us, say nothing, and lead the way to the dinner table, more as a listener and a thinker than a talker. He spoke when politeness required, very rarely otherwise, but his face was always beaming with kindness as if he was happy because he saw others so. There was a mystic something that made everyone like and respect him, but he was strange to a degree. Every now and then, he would give proof that he had a store of trite sayings and, to check a vulgarity or too much freedom, he had a way of his own."[6]

John James delegated all matters of household administration to his butler and the quality of housekeeping had deteriorated to an extraordinary degree. "Mr Stephens's chairs had long been in use," explained Francis, "and some curious specimens were about the room. One day, I arrived late in the reception room and had to balance myself on the corner of a chair as its cane bottom was entirely gone. And when I joined the dinner table, I was surprised to see with what ease the servants handed me mustard in a broken wine glass, and to see the tablecloth darned to a great degree. I never discovered any want of common sense in anything Mr John James Stephens said or did. He merely wanted to live without the bother of servants and had found out the way to do it: allow them so much a year and be content with a nominal mastery."

John James was equally uninterested in dress (his valet had died four years earlier and not been replaced).[7] "Men of the very highest class used to dine with Mr Stephens," continued Francis, "and they came with diamonds attached to their knees and their shoes, but Mr Stephens's own clothes were drab knee-breeches, white cotton stockings, and a coat like the old-fashioned court dress, all very tidy and very clean. But I knew him more than once to come into dinner with only one string to his shoes, as if he could only afford one, and his shoes took it by turns to appear in proper order."

The English community suspected that John James would leave the bulk of his fortune to Charles Lyne, the cousin with whom he maintained a regular and affectionate correspondence, but there was much talk about the bequests he would leave to friends in Lisbon. Francis was accosted one day by an elderly merchant, who was concerned that the Stephens fortune would not be distributed widely enough. "I fancy," he said in a low voice, "that Charles Lyne will get all the old gentleman's money." The merchant also approached John James about the matter. "I believe, Sir," he said at the dinner table on more than one occasion, "there is no doubt that Mr Charles Lyne is a *very* rich man." John James never varied his reply, "I can't say, I've never counted his money."[8]

Francis remained in Lisbon for several weeks but failed to impress his elderly cousin, although John James lent him the capital required to establish a merchant house of his own. After a final dinner in the Largo dos Stephens, he embarked on the return voyage to Falmouth, spent a few days with his father in Liskeard, then travelled to London to set up his new trading company.

Meanwhile, in a coup planned by Dona Carlota, the constitution had been overthrown and absolute power returned to the king. On 27 May 1823, Miguel left Lisbon for Vila Franca with the declared purpose of restoring "the inalienable rights of the crown."[9] He was followed by a troop of cavalry and part of the Lisbon garrison, and soon large numbers of people travelled the road to Vila Franca. Riding on horses and mules, carried in chaises and bullock-carts, the exodus from Lisbon showed the strength of popular feeling against the constitutionalists who (as political theorists) had done little to improve conditions in the country.

The king was urged to follow public opinion and declare an absolute monarchy but, for three days, he remained loyal to the constitution. On 29 May, he walked in the Corpus Christi procession, unnerved by shouts of "*Viva el rei absoluto!*" Troops were still deserting the city and soon the regiment guarding the palace changed allegiance. As João heard the familiar chant from soldiers outside his windows, he realised that he could hold out no longer. He joined his son in Vila Franca and issued a proclamation restoring absolute power to the monarchy.

He returned to Lisbon on 5 June, the mob dragging his carriage through the streets. He formed a new government and began to repeal the laws brought in by parliament, but his wife continued to plot against him. On 29 April 1824, the British envoy held a ball to celebrate the birthday of George IV, an occasion attended by John James who drove in his chaise to the envoy's house in Buenos Aires. His return home in the early hours of the morning was disturbed by conspirators who were out in force that night, horses cantering through the streets, soldiers marching down narrow lanes. "Long live the queen!" proclaimed posters pasted on the walls of the city. "Let João abdicate or die!"[10]

Next day, Lisbon was in uproar. Under his mother's instructions, Miguel ordered troops to assemble in the central square, he arrested several hundred people, and took command of his father's palace where he forbade all access to the king. Foreign diplomats forced an entry and found Dom João almost catatonic with fear. Miguel was summoned and, after consultation with his father, agreed to disperse the troops and release his prisoners. But he had no intention of honouring these promises and, for the next eight days, he and his men terrorised the city until the king sought safety on a British warship. Miguel, ordered once more into his father's presence, was taken prisoner and João agreed to send him into exile. "It is possible," wrote the British envoy, "that the sight of more polished and cultivated manners in England, France or Germany may have some effect on his Highness's mind. I own I fear the contrary."[11]

Miguel sailed from Lisbon on 13 May and the king returned to his palace. Ministers were aware of the queen's part in the conspiracy; they hoped to send her into exile too but, when Carlota refused to leave the country, she was kept prisoner in the palace of Queluz.

A few weeks earlier, John James had received depressing news from Christ's Hospital. For almost seven years, James Palmer's daughters had taken care of Philadelphia whose mind was destroyed by dementia. She recognised no-one, not even her closest friends. The Palmer sisters fed her, comforted her, brought her home when she was found wandering, and dealt with her incontinence. Palmer had retired in January, but he and his daughters remained in the Treasurer's House for another three months as Philadelphia's life came slowly to an end.[12]

John James was expecting the news, but it still came as a shock and his first thought was to write to Sousa in Marinha Grande: "I have this instant learnt of the death of my dear sister. We always lived together in perfect union and good friendship, and there never was, nor will be, a kinship stronger in social virtues. The next packet boat will bring me details of her funeral. We must all obey the will of God."[13]

Philadelphia had died intestate and, since Palmer was elderly and frail, John James sent powers of attorney to his friend's three daughters who valued her assets at £180,000.[14] Because he was sole beneficiary, John James had now inherited all the wealth made by his three brothers in Portugal. The shares left by Lewis to his brothers and sister had reverted to him; he had inherited William's fortune in 1803, half of Jedediah's in 1804, and, at Philadelphia's death, he inherited her share of Jedediah's estate as well as the substantial legacy left her by William. Meanwhile, his financial assets were divided between Lisbon and London, where (through the agency of Samuel Aislabie) he had become a member of the United Company of Merchants of England trading to the East Indies and held a number of stocks, including Bank of England annuities.

Early the following year, more depressing news arrived in the Largo dos Stephens as the Palmer sisters informed John James of the death of his great friend in London.[15] Eight years earlier, he had nominated Palmer as his chief executor, so it was time to write a new will. His main consideration was the glassworks which (despite Sousa's threat of closure) continued in full production. William had suggested that the factory be sold to the Portuguese nation, but crown revenues had declined since then and the state coffers were empty. Dona Maria's decree of 1780 was still in force. The factory had to remain in single ownership; John James was unable to pass it on to a consortium of businessmen and no individual would have been willing to accept such an unprofitable concern.

After mulling over the problem for several weeks, John James decided to leave the glassworks to the state. "As a monument of my esteem and gratitude for the favours and protection afforded me in this country," he wrote on the first page of his will, "I bequeath to the Portuguese nation the buildings, mansion, and all houses, farms, lands, orchards, vineyards, gardens, water-courses, etc, at Marinha Grande that may be called the fixed capital of my glass concern, beseeching the government to appoint an authority to administer the same. Thus I firmly hope that prosperity, stability and permanency may afford this useful and beautiful fabric in benefit of Marinha Grande in particular, and the advantage of this kingdom in general, and for ever."[16]

Next, he left charitable donations totalling £14,500, including £3000 for Christ's Hospital ("to whom I am indebted for my civil and moral education, being left an orphan at a tender age"), the interest to be paid to the Palmer sisters who had taken such good care of Philadelphia. He gave 150 legacies and annuities (£60,000), and bequeathed three months' earnings to all his workers at Marinha Grande, two years' salary to his clerks in Lisbon, and one year's wages to his servants in the Largo dos Stephens.

Charles's son, Stephens ("son of Wilhelmina, whose memory I revere"), was left several items, including the Stephens family jewellery. By contrast, the only mention of Joseph's children (including Francis who had visited Lisbon two years earlier) was in a long list of legacies to "my paternal relations, descendants from my grandfather, Lewis Stephens, vicar of Menheniot."

Finally, as the English community had expected, John James appointed his cousin in London as chief executor and residuary legatee. "The Largo dos Stephens," he wrote, "together with the furniture here and at Marinha, and glass in store, I bequeath to my much esteemed and respected cousin, Charles Lyne, who, after discharging my debts and fulfilling my legacies and bequests, I appoint my residuary legatee to liquidate my concerns and mitigate trouble and anxiety to my survivors. That no responsibility may disturb the remainder of his days, I am sure he will with pleasure religiously comply with all my bequests."

On 24 May 1825, John James dated the papers and wrapped them in the same sheet he had used for his previous will, crossing out the name of James Palmer and adding that of Charles Lyne. Under the names, he had already written the words: "The last will and testament of me, John James Stephens of Lisbon, in case of my death to be opened by the vice-consul and read by him in an audible voice before witnesses." He then locked the papers in the drawer of his bedroom wardrobe, the key to which he kept in his waistcoat pocket.[17]

John James was seventy-seven years old and feeling the infirmities of age. Although he was visited by friends in the city, he rarely attended the banquets which his servants continued to provide for the English community. As the heat of summer invaded the Largo dos Stephens, he became increasingly frail, a decline mirrored in the palace of Bemposta where the king's life was also drawing to a close.

Dom João died in March 1826, leaving a country split between liberals and absolutists. On his deathbed, he appointed his daughter, Isabel, to act as regent for her elder brother Pedro, a man with liberal sympathies who had declared himself emperor of an independent Brazil. Pedro drew up a constitution for Portugal and, since it would damage the independence of Brazil if he wore both crowns, he abdicated the Portuguese throne in favour of his seven-year-old daughter, Maria da Glória. Maria would inherit the crown on condition that she marry her uncle Miguel, who had to swear to the constitution before he could return to Portugal to act as regent for his child bride.

Pedro's constitution arrived in Lisbon in July and, a few weeks later, an absolutist rebellion broke out in the north of the country. Throughout the summer, there were plots and counter-plots, and John James wrote to Sousa about the worsening political situation. He wrote at least three times a week. He ordered 800 sheets of window glass for the palace of Ajuda, sympathised with Sousa's difficulties with drought and disease, and congratulated him on the completion of yet another warehouse (which contained 1000 crates of glass previously stored in the open air).[18]

John James had not seen Marinha Grande for twenty-five years, not since he made the journey in 1801 to ask for William's approval of his marriage plans. At that time, the glassworks were highly profitable but John James's later management was disastrous. In his efforts to preserve the factory as it was in William's lifetime, he had plunged it into loss, producing large quantities of glass that failed to sell and forcing him to build additional warehouses almost every year. Competition had recently increased with the opening of new factories and many of his craftsmen left Marinha Grande to work for these new employers. Although this was beneficial under the circumstances (reducing production as well as cutting the wage bill), John James chose to perceive it as ingratitude. In his many letters to Sousa, he never mentioned the lack of profitability, referring only to practical detail. He managed the glassworks as he managed his household: with little thought and total delegation.

Not a reflective man, he was untroubled by such matters during his final weeks of life. He had suffered from attacks of breathlessness in the spring, when the doctor treated him with poultices and purges, after which his health improved for a few months. The attacks returned in October. His handwriting became shaky and difficult to read, and he wrote his last letter to Sousa on 11 November.[19] That night, he suffered another, more serious attack and he died at three o'clock the following afternoon.

A servant was sent to summon the vice-consul, Jeremiah Meagher, who arrived in the early evening. Directed by the butler, he withdrew a key from the waistcoat pocket and unlocked the wardrobe drawer. Five of John James's closest friends had attended his death-bed and they listened with close attention as Meagher read aloud the sixteen pages of the will.[20] It came as little surprise that John James had left his fortune to Charles Lyne, nor that he had left the glassworks to the Portuguese nation; of greater interest was the long list of friends and acquaintances who would receive financial bequests.

The body was taken on a carriage shaft to the English burial ground in Buenos Aires and placed in the mortuary chapel. On 14 November, it was carried into the newly-built church in the centre of the cemetery.[21] No steeple or tower had been permitted by the authorities and the exterior was designed "to resemble a private dwelling house."[22] No bells could be tolled, no music played during services, so it was a simple ceremony that was read over the coffin before it was carried down the path towards the gates and turned left towards the final resting place of the Stephens family.

"When the soul is departed," John James had written in his will, "how detestable is the body. But in consideration of its having been the abode of a mild and placid spirit, I recommend that the corpse is decently interred in the same grave with my much revered brother, William Stephens, showing by this union in death our intellectual harmony during life."[23]

Interlude

London

1826–1827

In 1826, Charles was preoccupied by the commercial crisis which started in December the previous year. With a high degree of optimism in the economy, many new businesses had been set up, their share prices rising dramatically until the collapse of several companies led to a general panic.

He published another pamphlet in March, this time addressed to the lord high chancellor and written in his usual confrontational style: "From what has been said in and out of the Houses of Parliament, it appears evident that neither the causes and extent of the distress, nor the means of correcting it, are well understood. Nor are the remedies proposed at all calculated to meet the evil; they are, on the contrary, more calculated to continue and extend it."

He listed several causes of the crisis, including the return to the gold standard ("I am at a loss to conceive upon what grounds the government could so encourage the Bank of England, and still more astonished to conceive how the directors, as practical men, could suffer themselves to be so seduced"). As for the proposed remedies, "I don't know that it would well become me to deprecate the plans the chancellor of the exchequer has so confidently put forward but, if asked for my opinion, I should say that he has not understood the cause of the distress, nor its effects. His plan will not work well, or will not work at all; and the holding out of any plan in a matter of this kind, which does not eventually succeed, will create disappointment, dismay and distress."[1]

The merchant house set up by Francis Lyne was one of the casualties. As Francis wrote in his memoirs, "The great panic of 1826 ruined hundreds of commercial establishments, including merchants, bankers, and traders, and my young house failed at the end of the year. My letter going to Lisbon, telling Mr Stephens of my misfortune, crossed with the letter which brought news of his death to my uncle."[2]

Charles was sixty-two years old and already a rich man (since retiring from business, he had speculated wisely in stocks and shares, and his personal wealth stood at half a million pounds).[3] Although he was expecting the letter from Lisbon, he was stunned when he read the contents and realised the magnitude of John James's bequest. His inheritance from Portugal was described by the British consul as "a princely fortune of above £700,000," to which was added the value of John James's assets in London.[4] He proved the will on 13 December and, "in grateful and affectionate regard for the memory of his kinsman from whom he derives considerable property," obtained royal licence to take the name of Stephens, a licence which allowed him to create a Lyne Stephens coat of arms.[5] At the same time, he began to administer the will.

There were a hundred legacies to pay in England and Portugal, together with charitable bequests for which capital had to be transferred: Christ's Hospital (£3000 East India Stock), the City of Exeter (£1000), and the British consul in Lisbon (£10,500 in Bank of England annuities). The most important matter was the glassworks, a bequest the Portuguese government seemed in no hurry to accept. John James had appointed two other executors (both merchants in Lisbon), and Charles employed a Portuguese attorney to act on his behalf.[6] It was in his interest that the hand-over be completed as soon as possible for, in the meantime, he was having to subsidise the operating costs of the factory.

Another difficulty was that John James had left him his stocks of finished glass. These were packed in 12,000 crates and were, according to the *provedor* of Leiria, "sufficient to supply the consumption of Portugal for ten years, even if no other glass is imported from abroad."[7] The stocks were valued at the equivalent of £5 million in today's values, although much of the glass was broken, having been moved from one warehouse to another, the crates piled on top of each other to save space.[8] Meanwhile, the factory remained in production and further crates were entering the warehouses on a daily basis.

Charles instructed his attorney to sell the glass at a thirty percent discount[9] and, on 30 January, he wrote to the secretary of state for finance, Barão do Sobral Hermano, referring to the "urgent necessity of finalising the necessary measures so the government can take possession of the factory."[10] A few days later, he learnt of the death of José de Sousa e Oliveira, the manager who had worked for the Stephens brothers for more than thirty years. Sousa had survived John James by just two months and was succeeded by his nephew, a man who had worked in the factory for some time (most recently as treasurer and paymaster) but who was relatively new to management.[11]

This was unfortunate timing and Charles soon realised that he had to make the journey to Portugal. His presence would ensure that Sousa's nephew operated the factory as cheaply as possible and, at the same time, he could put greater pressure on government ministers to accept John James's bequest.

There had been no improvement in the political situation since Pedro's constitution arrived in Lisbon the previous summer. Princess Isabel had addressed her parliament in October, with news that Miguel had sworn his oath to the constitution and was soon to be betrothed to his young niece, Maria da Glória. She had also asked for troops from England to keep the peace and prevent absolutist uprisings. The British government agreed to this request; 5000 soldiers embarked for Lisbon in January and Charles hoped their presence would ensure the safety of the country during his visit.

On 21 February, he attended a committee meeting at Christ's Hospital and informed the members that he had transferred £3000 East India Stock to the Hospital, the income to be paid to the Palmer sisters during their lifetimes. The stock had, the committee noted, appreciated to £7200 and Charles was thanked for his "prompt and kind attention to the interests of this institution."[12] A few days later, he set out for Cornwall, travelling on the weekly steamship between London and Falmouth. On arrival, he took a room in the best hotel and sought out the captain of the next packet boat to Lisbon. This was the *Duke of Marlborough* under the command of John Bull, the most senior and colourful of the packet boat captains. Bull was an old friend of John James's and had dined many times in the Largo dos Stephens, so Charles was assured of good company and interesting conversation on the voyage.

On 4 March, the *Duke of Marlborough* hoisted its flag and fired a gun, a signal that Bull had received orders to sail.[13] As the ship made preparations for departure, the passengers were rowed to the moorings and, almost fifty years after he left Liskeard to be apprenticed to Lewis Stephens, Charles embarked on his final voyage to Lisbon.

18

Transfer to the State

1827

"*I bequeath to the Portuguese nation all the premises and establishment at Marinha Grande. Thus I firmly hope that prosperity, stability and permanency may afford this useful and beautiful fabric in benefit of Marinha Grande in particular, and the advantage of this kingdom in general, and for ever.*"
John James Stephens, 24 May 1825

"*It is not convenient for government to be property owners (even less administrators) of industrial establishments which, in the hands of governments, almost never produce profits commensurate with capital employed. More often, they produce losses.*"
Conselho da Fazenda, 1 March 1827

Two weeks later, when the *Duke of Marlborough* sailed up the Tagus, Charles discovered that landing formalities had been tightened. "Without a moment's delay," wrote another traveller, "we were hurried into the police boat and placed under the charge of two soldiers who accompanied us to the different offices where our passports had to be countersigned. For three hours, we were bandied about from office to office, from one authority to another, until we were ushered up five flights of stairs into the chamber of an old *escrivão*, or notary public. Here we complied with all necessary formalities and, paying our fees, were conducted by the soldiers to our hotel. The customs officer had refused us permission to take on shore any part of our baggage, so we were put to the greatest inconvenience."[1]

As the police boat ferried Charles to the landing steps at the Praça do Comércio, he encountered once more the sights and sounds of the city which had been his home for twenty-five years. Passport formalities completed, his escort accompanied him to the Largo dos Stephens where he was welcomed by the servants. In his will, John James had instructed that "the usual hospitality of this house be continued for twelve months after my decease," and every day at noon, a collection of elderly merchants arrived in Rua de São Paulo, read the newspapers in the reception room, and followed the butler to John James's dinner table.

Charles hosted these dinners for the next few days as, driven by curiosity, greater numbers than usual arrived for the midday meal. He accompanied the servants on a tour of the buildings and, when the door to William's office was unlocked for the first time in twenty-four years, he found letters, bills and money orders that had remained there since the spring of 1803.[2] He made an inventory of John James's furniture, inspected the crates of glass piled up in the warehouse, and had a meeting with his co-executors who informed him that, although the council of the exchequer considered the matter in February, the government had made no decision on John James's bequest.

The regent had instructed her ministers to "allow for the continued working of the factory and the people employed therein who depend upon it for their livelihood,"[3] but the exchequer was short of funds and unable to subsidise the losses. The council had examined the options of selling the glassworks and closing them down, but both ran counter to the specific wording of John James's will (and closure would result in unemployment). Its preferred course of action was to lease the factory. If rent was charged, this would bring some profit to the exchequer and, if not, would at least save the state from financing the operating costs.[4]

By the time the council issued its report on 1 March, the regent's health had broken down under stress. Her brother in Brazil had sent a constitution which she was obliged to uphold, her mother was plotting for the return of an absolute monarchy, the unstable Miguel would soon be returning to

Portugal, and the country was split between absolutists and liberals. It is hardly surprising that Isabel took to her sickbed, suffering from a variety of symptoms including epileptic fits. "Each day diminishes the moral strength of the government," wrote a politician on 10 March. "Her Highness's illness prevents the employment of measures which are of urgent necessity, and to these inconveniences must be added the cessation of all acts which require the royal signature. This puts a stop to many measures of general interest and impedes the progress of private business."[5]

Irritated at the weakness and inefficiency of the government, Charles made arrangements for the journey to Marinha Grande, a journey which was uncomfortable and dangerous. "Are you not afraid," a traveller was asked a few weeks earlier, "to be alone and unarmed now the country is so unsettled and the robbers have been so daring?"[6] Thieves had spies in many places and were often forewarned of a journey. "It is necessary," explained a young woman who travelled to Leiria in January, "to procure carriages and mules from particular individuals in Lisbon or the towns on the road. The driver of the carriage is in correspondence with the band; and the spies, who are in ambush by the roadside, know the signal of their comrade and do not leave their lurking-places. While the traveller continues under the charge of this man, he is as safe as though he were seated at his own hearth."[7]

The public highway from Lisbon to Coimbra had not been repaired since the French invasions and was in an appalling state. "The distance between Lisbon and Leiria," wrote the Lisbon correspondent of *The Times* on 13 April, "is about eighty miles. To traverse such a space on English roads and with English post-horses would be an affair of eight or nine hours but, in Portugal, it becomes a toilsome march of two days, not unaccompanied with danger and hardship. The road is more rugged and formidable than an English imagination can conceive. In some places, the traveller is obliged to abandon it altogether and find a new track for himself, picking his steps over bare rocks or treading knee-deep in barren sands. The jolting of a carriage among loose stones, or over roots of trees from which torrents have washed away the earth, requires considerable skill to avoid broken bones."[8]

On leaving the city, Charles took river transport to Vila Franca where he hired a driver, carriage and mules. "The road from Vila Franca to Leiria," the correspondent continued, "passes through a district thickly covered with olive groves. A little further on, the country becomes an extensive bed of sand. A solitary church, with the drifted sand piled high against its grey stone walls and only one roofless house in view, is the resort of robbers, where the erection of crosses attests the occurrence of bloody deeds."[9]

Charles was unaware of the precautions required when hiring transport and it was here, in the sandy wasteland, that he was attacked by thieves. "A few weeks ago," explained the correspondent, "an English gentleman who directs the glassworks at Marinha Grande was assaulted and robbed by armed men. Since then, carriages which pass this way obtain an escort to the town of Alcoentre. And between this place and Rio Maior, the British consul at Figueira was robbed and murdered two years ago, the atrocity committed with perfect impunity at midday and within fifty yards of a village."[10]

One of John James's friends had been killed by thieves on a journey from Marinha Grande to Lisbon, and Charles was lucky to have escaped with his life.[11] Appalled and distressed, he made his way to the inn at Alcoentre. The following morning, he moved on to Rio Maior, the road passing through a pine forest where "the deep sand buried the feet of our horses to the fetlock and nearly blinded us whenever a gust of wind swept through the trees."[12] From Rio Maior, he travelled to Alcobaça and, after a comfortable night in the monastery, took the road to Marinha Grande where he was welcomed by Sousa's nephew and namesake (who was known in the village as Sousa *Sobrinho*).

He found the factory in a state of profound unease. The workers knew the government was unwilling to accept John James's bequest; they also knew that Charles would not subsidise the losses indefinitely. The threat of closure hung over the glassworks and, as he interviewed the clerks and studied the account books, Charles became aware of the extent to which John James had squandered his brother's fortune. The weekly operating costs were estimated at 600 *milreis* (the equivalent of £400,000 a year in today's values), and John James had been subsidising the glassworks by this amount for twelve years.[13] Meanwhile, his glass continued to be of poor quality. "The glass manufactured here," explained Sousa *Sobrinho*, "is of lower quality than English crystal but Mr Stephens chose not to make improvements because of the lack of sales."[14] As a result, Charles's stocks were proving difficult to sell (despite the discount), particularly since there were plentiful supplies of imported glass on the market.

Charles stayed at Marinha Grande for five weeks. On 26 April, he received a copy of a decree bearing the stamp of the regent but not her signature (she remained too ill to meet her ministers or sign her name). The government had agreed to the recommendations made by the council of the exchequer; the state would accept John James's bequest on condition that the factory was advertised for public auction and leased to the highest bidder.[15] Aware that no entrepreneur would be willing to pay rent for such an unprofitable factory, Charles made arrangements to return to Lisbon where he hoped to persuade ministers to take a more realistic view of the situation.

Sousa accompanied him on the journey, leaving the factory in the care of the book-keeper. They hired transport from a safer source and, on arrival, found the city in a state of paralysis. The regent was thought to be on her deathbed and government business was at a standstill. "It was generally believed," wrote *The Times* correspondent on 3 May, "that her Highness had already expired or could not long support the alarming attacks to which she had been subjected. She was a little better in the afternoon but, having had a relapse in the evening, I am afraid it is all over. The foreign ambassadors have couriers in readiness to despatch the news to their respective courts."[16]

Isabel's eighty-one-year-old aunt, a sister of Dona Maria, was poised to take over the regency but the princess survived and, as soon as the crisis was over, the council of the exchequer began to seek a tenant. The government went ahead with the auction; advertisements were prepared for publication in the *Gazeta de Lisboa* and arrangements made for public announcements in Marinha Grande on three days in mid-May.[17]

Charles, who had failed to persuade ministers that these formalities were a waste of time, now resolved to close the factory.[18] Five hundred people were employed in the glassworks, 2000 dependent on them for their living, and this in a region which had no other industry except a resin factory and a sawmill.[19] John James had been prepared to subsidise the area but Charles was not so generous. It was the state's problem and, if the government wished to maintain employment in Marinha Grande, then the government must fund the losses.

Sousa informed the book-keeper that the glassworks would close on 23 May, the *Gazeta de Lisboa* advertised the factory for letting and, on 17, 18 and 19 May, public announcements were made in the main square at Marinha Grande. As Charles had expected, no bidders came forward.[20] He had already booked a cabin on the *Magnet* packet to Falmouth (which was due to sail on 20 May) and, postponing the deadline by a week, he ordered Sousa to close the factory at the end of the month.[21]

A few days later, Sousa wrote again to the book-keeper: "Mr Lyne has left and the last order he gave me was to close the factory on 31 May. Can you imagine how I felt? I begged and pleaded and carried on, for myself and all the workers. He told me that it was pointless saying anything but, with much effort, I managed to get the date changed to 2 June.

Imagine what a state I have been in, what bad news, what arguments I have had to put up with!"[22]

Sousa approached the minister responsible, Barão do Sobral Hermano, and was granted an interview on 25 May. "I explained the need to take prompt action," he wrote to the book-keeper, "and told him there was no alternative to the government taking over the factory. To this he replied (with a wry face), 'I know how assiduous you have been in trying to achieve this, but it is easier to close it down if need be.' He asked me to take over the leasehold myself but, as I explained, I do not have the funds and I would not find partners because the conditions put forward are unsuitable, having been written without full knowledge of the facts. I shall speak to him again tomorrow; I shall beg and beseech and carry on as I did before and, if I fail to achieve results, I shall seek an audience with her Highness, the regent."[23]

The minister was moved by Sousa's distress and it was fortunate that the regent (who was now in Benfica on the outskirts of Lisbon) had recovered sufficiently to meet with her ministers. As the correspondent of *The Times* wrote on 28 May, "The princess regent has been at Benfica since the twenty-fourth and feels the benefit of the country air in the gradual improvement of her health. She now sees her ministers on the business of their respective departments and, though still weak, inspires no fears of a relapse."[24]

Sobral Hermano attended the regent after his meetings with Sousa, and perhaps Sousa also made the journey to Benfica. Isabel wished to maintain employment in Marinha Grande; she put additional pressure on the minister and, on 28 May, the government made another attempt to lease the factory. It published a set of accounts covering the fourteen years between 1813 and 1826, although the figures were amalgamated and only gave totals for the entire period (income: 1004 *contos* of *reis*; expenditure: 590 *contos;* profits: 414 *contos*).[25]

Publication of these accounts without further elaboration was an act of desperation (the figure for income included the value of the stockpiled glass which, at 400 *contos*, was roughly equal to the profits for the entire period), but the strategy proved successful. A consortium of businessmen arranged a meeting with Sobral Hermano and offered to lease the glassworks rent-free. With the factory due to be closed a few days later, there was little time to be wasted; the decree that the glassworks should remain in single ownership was repealed and the consortium took over the administration on 1 June.[26]

Charles, meanwhile, was already in England, the *Magnet* having dropped anchor at Falmouth on 28 May.[27] During his last days in Lisbon, he had presided over the daily dinners, left money for the hospitality to continue until November, and given instructions for the sale of the Largo dos Stephens at the end of the year. He held discussions with his co-executors and attorney, and directed that his stocks of glass be offered for sale at an even greater discount. He arranged for John James's financial assets to be transferred to London, and visited the Protestant cemetery in Buenos Aires to pay his respects to his cousin and benefactor. Finally, he ordered a monument to be erected over the grave.

He instructed the masons to copy the neo-classical memorial built for Lewis Stephens more than thirty years before, an ornate sarcophagus set on a shoulder-high plinth. He gave much thought to the inscription: "Sacred to the memory of John James Stephens Esq. Always unostentatious but ever conspicuous for honour and integrity, benevolence, hospitality and affability, and for the most extraordinary equability and placidity of temper. For these he may be equalled, he cannot be excelled. This token of love and esteem was erected by his devoted and faithful cousin and companion for many years, Charles Lyne Stephens."

He ordered the servants to pack up John James's possessions and the trunks were sent to the quayside to be taken aboard the *Magnet*. A little later, he embarked himself and, as the vessel slipped its moorings, he watched the open space of the Praça do Comércio slide into the distance, the statue of Dom José disappear behind the buildings of the waterfront. He was relieved to be on his way home, not least because of the worsening political situation. While Lisbon appeared calm on the surface (held in check by the presence of British troops), underneath it was seething with hatred. The government was weak and unstable, the conflict between absolutists and liberals driving a wedge through Portuguese society. "The atmosphere is dark and gloomy," wrote another visitor as he sailed for England, "the signs of the times portentous and alarming. At such a critical moment for Portugal, it is impossible not to have apprehensions about the future."[28]

During the voyage, Charles walked the decks of the packet boat aware that he was returning to a different life. Nine years earlier, he had retired from business with a small fortune of his own; now he would take his place amongst the richest men in England. As the *Magnet* sailed north through the Bay of Biscay, he thought of the vagaries of fate, the decision he had taken so lightly in his father's study. "Which will you be," his father had asked, "a poor clergyman or a rich merchant?" His brother Richard had made the first choice and remained a poor clergyman all his life. Charles had taken the second option; Lisbon had become his home for twenty-five years, he had forged a friendship with John James Stephens, and inherited more wealth than his parents in Cornwall could ever have imagined.

His mind also returned to the cemetery in Buenos Aires where his four cousins lay buried. But when he visited John James's grave, he forgot that William was interred in the same patch of ground (the headstone having been removed six months earlier when the grave was opened). There had been so much for Charles to think about in Lisbon, so much for him to do. Perhaps it is not surprising that he failed to remember John James's burial instructions, as well as the day in 1803 when he stood in the same spot, watching William's body descend into the ground, his cousin standing beside him inconsolable with grief.

The masons took time to carve John James's memorial and it was not until several months later that it was taken to the cemetery and assembled above the double grave, close to the monument from which it was copied. John James had lived his life in William's shadow, but the memorial which extolled his virtues had erased the name of the brother he had worshipped, the brother whose death he had never truly acknowledged.

"The spot of interment is so beautiful," wrote an English visitor to the burial ground. "Everything around is calm, silent and cool; shrubs adorn the avenues and the fairest and sweetest flowers are placed upon the graves."[29] And a clergyman who strolled through the cemetery shortly after Charles sailed for England referred to the Judas and magnolia trees which, "mingling their rich deep foliage, create a welcome shade for those who have hearts to pause here."[30]

PART FIVE

Charles
The Years of Wealth

19

Consolidation

1827–1830

"I was never to attend a gambling club – no, no, it must never be said that I was even seen at such a place. And it was bad custom too – which many young men had – of lounging away their evenings at playhouses."
Charles Lyne to William Gibbs, April 1812

"Chicksands is let to Mr Lyne Stephens who certainly has a million of money. He married his daughter last week and only gave her £200,000!"
Frances Ongley, 10 June 1830

By the time Charles returned to London in early June, all society had learnt of his inheritance. To his own assets of half a million pounds, he had added the Stephens wealth of several times that amount, giving him one of the largest fortunes in England (about £70 million in today's values). He and his children were in demand by high society and several young aristocrats came to the house in Devonshire Place. "Among the many offers of marriage made to my daughters," Charles boasted to his brother in Little Petherick, "a number have been from young noblemen, one of them an earl for Louisa which, if she had fancied, she might have been a countess at this moment. And this besides other noblemen who have offered for her and also for her sister, among whom are some of the first families of rank."[1]

Charles had hoped to be a peer himself by this time, hopes dashed a few days before he sailed for Lisbon when the prime minister, Lord Liverpool, suffered a massive stroke and was found paralysed and unconscious on the floor. Liverpool had admired Charles's intellect (despite his criticisms of government policy) and, as news of his inheritance spread through

London society, he had offered him a peerage. "Before Lord
Liverpool was seized with the violent attack with which he
lays so dangerously ill," Charles explained to his brother, "I
had the offer of being made a peer and Stephens a baronet. I
refused the offer without hesitation and left it to my son to
accept the baronetcy or not as he might like. He also refused
the offer and my daughters appeared well pleased that we
had declined, observing that ostentatious honours were of no
good."²

Charles was making the best of the situation. He would
have loved a peerage but had declined with a show of
humility, assuming that Liverpool would remain in power
and make the offer for a second time. This was unwise for the
prime minister never regained his faculties. He was replaced
by George Canning (who had acted as special ambassador to
Lisbon twelve years earlier) and, in January 1828, by the
Duke of Wellington, men with whom Charles had little
acquaintance.

He had always been generous to his family, helping those
who were in financial difficulty, and two months after his
return from Portugal, another brother was declared bankrupt
(the third in nine years). William Lyne had worked for
Charles for two decades, first as an apprentice in Lisbon, then
as manager of the Liverpool office of Lyne, Hathorn &
Roberts. His own trading house, set up after Charles retired
from business, failed in the commercial crisis of 1826 and,
losing his home in Liverpool, he moved to a cottage on the
Cumberland coast which his brother had bought for him.³

Charles, meanwhile, was looking for a grander house in
London and, in January 1828, he took a lease on a mansion
in Portman Square.⁴ And as he and his family settled into
their new home, depressing news was arriving from Portugal.
Negotiations were underway to allow Miguel to return to his
country; his brother in Brazil had granted him powers of
regent and, in Queluz, Dona Carlota celebrated with her
priests and attendants. "If you are coming back disposed to
govern according to that vile constitution," she wrote to

Miguel, " you might as well bury a knife in your mother's heart."[5]

Miguel arrived in Lisbon in February and, under instructions from Carlota, instigated a campaign of terror against the liberals. Frightened refugees packed their bags and went into hiding, fleeing during hours of darkness to ships anchored in the Tagus. Parliament was dissolved and British troops ordered to re-embark for England. At last the old queen could wreak her vengeance on the constitutionalists, and also on foreigners. Gangs were hired to abuse and throw stones at British merchants, and shouts of "Death to the English!" echoed through the streets of Lisbon.

Large numbers of liberal refugees fled to England, some of them to Marylebone where they met the beneficiary of a vast Portuguese fortune. Short of money and with no way of making a living, they relied on the charity of friends and acquaintances, and perhaps Charles did his best to help them although, as a supporter of the Duke of Wellington (whose government was pro-Miguel), he had little sympathy for their political beliefs.

At the end of June, Miguel declared himself king of Portugal since the death of his father, ousting the rights of his brother in Brazil and his young niece, Maria da Glória. The Largo dos Stephens had been sold by this time, but Charles's attorney was still trying to market the glass stored in Marinha Grande, Lisbon, São Martinho and Vila Franca. In time, Charles would write off the value of the stocks, for looting destroyed much of the glass during the next few years and, when civil war broke out in 1832, there was fighting in areas where the remaining crates were stored.

Over the years, Charles had used profits from his merchant business to give his son an entrée into society. Stephens was two years old when his family returned from Lisbon and his early memories were of the tall thin house in Devonshire Place, a house where male influence was missing as his father spent long hours in his counting-house or was away on business trips abroad. An only son in a family of four daughters, he had been brought up by nurses and maidservants, and was unaccustomed to the rough and tumble of normal boyhood.

At the age of eight, his father sent him to a private school, Fulham Park House, in Parson's Green Lane to the west of London.[6] "Oh, that first night, when my mother was gone and I was alone with the mocking fiends to whom my anguish was such glee," wrote a pupil with a similar background. "I was a singular diversion to them, not having been brought up with other boys. Scarcely had I cried myself into an unquiet doze when I was seized, dragged from bed and carried away in the dark, gagged and bound. I was borne into the open air and two of my tormentors laying hold of my arms and two of my legs, I was swung against a tree in the playground, to undergo the operation termed bumping."[7]

Stephens was equally shocked when he was bumped during his first night at school, but he survived the ceremony and remained at Fulham Park for five years. He then returned to Devonshire Place to be educated at home by private tutors. In May 1819, he was admitted to Trinity College, Cambridge, where he took five years to complete what was normally a three (at most four) year course of study.[8] Stephens was acting the young man-about-town, spending more days at Newmarket races than at his studies. "Cambridge," explained a commentator of the time, "is but a short distance from that place of sporting notoriety, Newmarket, so it is next to impossible but that a youth of an inspiring mind should be up to all the manoeuvres of a racecourse."[9]

In the spring of 1825, his father purchased a commission in the Tenth Hussars. This cost £840 (£34,000 in today's values) and a year later, at even greater expense, he purchased promotion to the rank of lieutenant.[10] The regiment was based in Leicestershire when Stephens received news of his father's inheritance and, as he obtained leave and hurried home to London, the government was arranging for troops to be sent to Portugal. The Tenth Hussars formed the cavalry brigade, two squadrons sailing for Lisbon, the third stationed in Ipswich as a depot. Overlooked for the service squadrons because of his absence in London, Stephens was the only lieutenant to remain in England. He travelled to Ipswich in January and remained there until February 1828, when the depot marched to Brighton to welcome the service squadrons home from Portugal.[11]

A few weeks later, Charles and his daughters joined him in Brighton, renting the most expensive house on the seafront. Stephens invited his fellow officers to dine with the family and his father, recently returned from Portugal himself, listened with interest to the stories they had to tell, particularly since the cavalry had been based in Leiria, just a few miles from Marinha Grande.[12] Charles enjoyed these military evenings, but they soon came to an end for Stephens sold his commission in the early summer, preferring to enjoy his father's fortune in a life of leisure.

The family remained in Brighton for the rest of the season; the town was the most fashionable resort in the country and the Lyne Stephens name was opening many doors. There were dinners and entertainments hosted by ladies of society, where Stephens was wooed by mothers of unmarried daughters and his sisters received attentions from young bucks eager to improve their fortunes. The season ended sadly for Charles's younger daughter died in October, her body taken to London and interred in a private vault under St Marylebone church.[13] Charles's second daughter had died in 1824, so the vaults now contained his wife and three of his four daughters (all of whom had died before the age of twenty).[14]

Three days after the funeral, Charles wrote to his brother in Little Petherick: "I have been blessed with the very best of wives and children, but the Almighty, while he thought proper to give me so many angels, has in his wisdom also thought proper to take the greater part (now four of them) to Himself, and the only consolation we have is the firm and unshaken belief that they are removed to regions of the blessed. My dear little angel was not only the delight of all at home, but was so to all with whom she came in contact. Her goodness, her worth, her amiability of manners, her intellectual powers, indeed her every quality shined, if I may say so, brilliantly in every society."[15]

Five months later, Richard left Cornwall for the first time since he was a student at Oxford. He was bound for London, where he would stay with Charles in Portman Square before visiting a number of his children. It was so unusual for the rector to leave his parish that the villagers gathered to watch him depart; and as the carriage rattled over the narrow bridge in the valley, they called out "God bless you, Sir, and a happy voyage!"[16]

After a journey of several days, Richard arrived in Portman Square to find himself waited on by a retinue of servants, an experience vastly different from his humble life in Cornwall. For Richard was, as one of his grandchildren remembered, "a very learned scholar; he read St John Chrysostom's hard Greek as easily as we read a newspaper. His manners were courtly and belonged to an age gone by. Well do I remember his clerical hat, knee-breeches and silk stockings, and every night I kneeled to ask his blessing, which he gave simply and earnestly, his hand on my bended head."[17]

This learned but simple parson felt uncomfortable in the glamorous milieu of Portman Square and, although he was pleased to see Charles again, the two men had little in common. After a brief visit, he moved across London to stay with one of his sons in Hoxton, taking with him a Portuguese gold coin as a parting gift.[18]

Two months after Richard's visit (when the mourning period for his daughter was over), Charles opened his mansion to society. "The Portman Square house soon had a name for good dinners," wrote Francis Lyne. "The Duke of Cambridge considered the cook 'not bad,' Lord Eldon found no fault, and the newspapers announced when the Lyne Stephens dinners for the London season had commenced."[19]

At the same time, Stephens frequented the theatre, became a founder member of the Garrick Club,[20] and sought election to Crockford's, the gambling house in St James's Street which had opened the previous year.

The club, explained a member, "included all the celebrities of England, from the Duke of Wellington to the youngest ensign of the Guards. At the gay and festive board, which was constantly replenished from midnight to early dawn, the most brilliant sallies of wit, the most agreeable conversation, the most interesting anecdotes, interspersed with political discussions and logical reasoning on every conceivable subject, proceeded from the soldiers, scholars, statesmen, poets and men of pleasure who, when balls and parties were at an end, finished their evening with a little supper and a good deal of hazard at old Crocky's."[21]

Fortunes were won and lost at Crockford's (during the first two seasons, a total of £300,000 changed hands, much of it into the pockets of Crockford himself who had started life as a London fishmonger). "Who can forget," continued the member, "the large green table, the croupiers with their suave manners, sleek appearance and stiff white neckcloths, and the almost miraculous dexterity with which they swept away the money of the unfortunate punters."[22]

As Stephens mingled with the dandies and gambled on the hazard table where stakes of £1000 were placed on the fall of the dice, Charles was looking for a country estate suitable for a man of fortune. He sold the house in Weymouth and, after his son accompanied his new friends to Melton Mowbray for the hunting season, signed a tenancy agreement for Chicksands Priory in Bedfordshire. A religious house of the Gilbertine order, the Priory dated from the twelfth century. It was extended over the years and, after the dissolution of the monasteries, was acquired by the Osborn family who converted the building and landscaped the grounds. The present baronet had been in financial difficulties for some time; he had been forced to let the Priory and, in late 1829,

Chicksands was vacated by its tenant and became available for rent.[23]

The house was furnished with old master paintings and antique furniture, and Charles soon began to redecorate the building and plan a new stable block. At the same time, he made arrangements for the marriage of Louisa, his only surviving daughter, to Captain Charles Bulkeley of the Life Guards. The Bulkeleys were an extended family of American merchants who had lived in Lisbon for many years. Lewis Stephens married into the family in 1779 and his brother-in-law, Thomas Bulkeley, accompanied Philadelphia to London in the autumn of 1810. Thomas and his family settled in Montagu Square and, after her father inherited the Stephens fortune, Louisa rejected several aristocratic suitors, preferring the company of Thomas's second son.

Louisa married her cavalry officer on 1 June 1830 and a grand reception was held in Portman Square.[24] Charles Bulkeley was a rich young man and, as he departed on honeymoon, his wealth was increased by a handsome dowry (£8.5 million in today's values). As an elderly lady in Bedfordshire wrote a few days after the wedding, "Chicksands is let to Mr Lyne Stephens who is building stables and otherwise doing a great deal to the house. He certainly has a million of money. He married his daughter last week and *only* gave her £200,000."[25]

Four weeks later, the death of George IV gave Charles an opportunity to buy Stephens a seat in parliament, another rung up the social ladder. Despite the changes of the industrial revolution, parliament remained in the hands of the land-owning classes and there was growing demand for reform. Charles's home county of Cornwall returned forty-four members, while the industrial towns of England had no members at all and the little town of Looe, where Stephens was born, had as many members as London. In the boroughs of England, seats were bought and voters bribed, while the growing middle classes had no voice in electing their representatives.

The king's death increased the clamour for change and it was feared there would be revolution if parliament remained unreformed for much longer, fears fostered by the July revolution in France which toppled the Bourbon monarchy. The prime minister, the Duke of Wellington, opposed reform of any kind, but the mood of the people soon led to a general election and Charles encouraged his son to stand for Barnstaple in north Devon. As Stephens travelled to Barnstaple to involve himself in the campaign, his uncle Richard's family was stirred into action. From his rectory in Little Petherick, Richard mustered support from anyone acquainted with a voter in the town; his son-in-law, Peter Glubb (a lawyer in Liskeard), acted as Stephens's agent; and Glubb's partner, Benjamin Lyne (Richard's third son), took the coach to Barnstaple to support his cousin.

The election was held on 2 August and at half past ten that night, Benjamin sent a note to his father in Cornwall. "The poll has closed," he wrote, "and it stands thus: Stephens 370, Tudor 332, Campbell 243."[26] Barnstaple returned two members, so Stephens and George Tudor were elected, the first time for them both.

The government survived the election but the cost of the campaign was high, with Charles paying over £5000 (£235,000 in today's values) for his son to enter parliament. Half the men who voted for Stephens lived outside Barnstaple, most of them in London, and their expenses amounted to £2200; those who lived in the town were entertained at an additional cost of £1730; the election dinner cost £500; lodgings for Stephens and his valet were estimated at £200; and a further £500 was spent on agents and managers. As one of the electioneers wrote to Peter Glubb, "I ask you, Sir, is it not high time to have reform in parliament when it is known that many of the freemen have received their travelling expenses in London and, when come to the poll, have voted contrary to what they promised?"[27]

20

Reform and Litigation

1830–1837

*"We will not lend our support to any individual who has opposed the
Reform Bill, and we will frustrate all attempts to continue those infamous
and fraudulent practices which have hitherto stigmatised this borough as
the nest of fraud and corruption."*
Barnstaple flyer, July 1832

*"It does not do to rush into chancery on one's own
unsupported convictions."*
Charlotte Hawkey, 1871

A few days after the election, Charles received a letter from
Robert Matthews, British consul in Lisbon at the time of his
visit to Portugal. John James had bequeathed £10,500 in
Bank of England stock to the consul (and treasurer of the
British Contribution Fund) to pay annuities to the poorer
women of his acquaintance and, after their deaths, "for the
consul, merchants and factors to bestow on such widows and
orphans as may apply for relief to be granted." In July 1825,
the passing of the Consular Act had abolished the Society of
British Merchants & Factors, together with the Contribution
Fund, but John James had made no amendments to his
will.

Charles had contacted Matthews in May 1827, shortly
after returning to Lisbon from Marinha Grande. He had
offered to hand over the £10,500, but the consul was unable
to accept the money as the Contribution Fund no longer
existed. Charles had therefore retained the capital in John
James's name and, as his executor, distributed dividends to
the annuitants named in the will.[1] In 1830, a new consul

began to chase the money, concerned that, as annuitants died off, the dividends would revert to Charles instead of the widows and orphans in Lisbon. He instructed his predecessor to accompany Charles to the Bank of England, "where steps are to be taken for payment of the dividends according to the will, whereby remittances will be made to the consul here in Lisbon."[2]

Matthews's letter arrived in Portman Square on 13 August and Charles replied the following day. "An Act of Parliament having done away with the Society of Merchants & Factors at Lisbon," he explained, "I was prevented from transferring the stock to the consul and treasurer of the British Contribution Fund, the latter being extinct. I have taken the best counsel opinions on the matter, and these were that the only way I could be relieved from the trust that has indirectly fallen upon me was by putting it into chancery."[3]

This was the infamous court of chancery, where even friendly suits could drag on for decades and lawyers took their costs from the funds year-by-year until, in some cases, little or nothing was left for the beneficiaries. "There is a suit before the court which was commenced nearly twenty years ago," wrote Charles Dickens in 1853, "in which from thirty to forty counsel have been known to appear at one time, in which costs have been incurred to the amount of £70,000, and which is a *friendly suit*. There is another well-known suit in chancery which was commenced before the close of the last century, in which more than double the amount of £70,000 has been swallowed up in costs."[4]

"Such an action would," Charles's letter continued, "incur considerable expense and considerable delay and, as many of the annuitants are in great want (some in a state of misery), the delay and expense of putting it into chancery would be almost fatal to them. It is under that consideration alone that I have been induced to take upon myself the trouble of receiving the dividends and distributing them to the annuitants, a trouble irksome at all times to a person of my advanced age, and particularly so to me as I have many concerns of my own that fully occupy my time."[5]

Matthews, who had spent most of his life abroad, was unaware of the inefficiencies and expense of the court. As British consul at the time of John James's death, he filed a friendly suit against Charles, after which the funds were administered in chancery and declined in value over the years as legal fees and court costs were taken from them.

Towards the end of August, Charles left Portman Square for his first autumn season at Chicksands, and Louisa and her husband joined him on their return from honeymoon in Europe.[6] Stephens remained in London as parliament had been summoned to meet on 14 September; it was then prorogued and he was driven to Chicksands where he and Charles Bulkeley hosted a shooting party for their friends. Towards the end of October, he returned to London, was sworn in as member of parliament, and attended the House on 2 November when the Commons began to debate the King's Speech.

The political situation deteriorated during the next two weeks. Wellington declared that he would resist all attempts at parliamentary reform, an uncompromising attitude that led to a fall in public confidence. On 15 November, when a number of ultra right-wing Tories (including Stephens and George Tudor) voted against the government in a division on the Civil List, the Tories were defeated by twenty-nine votes.[7] Wellington resigned the following morning, the leader of the Whig party took over as prime minister and, during the winter, the Whigs worked in secret on their plans to reform the representation of the country.

Meanwhile, Stephens had set out for Melton Mowbray to spend the winter riding to hounds over the Leicestershire countryside. He remained there for three months, returning to the Commons on 1 March when Lord John Russell rose to introduce the Reform Bill. "The great day at length arrived," wrote a political diarist, "and to describe the curiosity, the intensity of expectation and excitement, would be impossible. The secret had been so well kept that not a soul knew what the measure was till they heard it."[8]

It was six o'clock in the evening. The chamber was packed and the atmosphere electric. How widely would the Bill extend the franchise? How many boroughs would be purged as land-owning peers lost their rights to control seats in parliament? Soon the Tories learnt that sixty boroughs were to be abolished, while a further forty-six were to lose one of their members. As Russell announced the names of the condemned boroughs, he was greeted by shouts of laughter from men unable to believe that such huge change was possible. "More yet," said Russell, smiling, before listing the boroughs which would have reduced representation.[9]

The vote on the Reform Bill was taken on 23 March, shortly before three o'clock in the morning.[10] When the speaker announced the numbers, it was learnt that the Bill had been passed by just one vote, 302 to 301, the fullest House in parliamentary history. "The tellers scarcely got through the crowd," wrote a pro-reform member, "for the House was thronged up to the table and the floor was fluctuating with heads like the pit of a theatre. But you might have heard a pin drop as the speaker read the numbers. Then the shouts broke out and many of us shed tears. We shook hands, and clapped each other on the back, and went out laughing, crying, and huzzaing into the lobby."[11]

By five o'clock, most of the members had made their way to Crockford's. Charles gambled at whist there (he was an excellent player)[12] and he went to the club to wait for his son. He was not alone. "I went to Crocky's after the opera," wrote a retired politician, "being determined to await the result, and there were quantities of people in the same mind, friends and foes, but we were all as amicable and merry as could be. A little before five, our minds were relieved by the arrival of the members and the same good temper and fun were visible on both sides."[13]

A day or two later, Stephens took the fast mail coach to Melton Mowbray to enjoy the last few days of the hunting season and attend a banquet given by Lord Wilton.[14] He returned to London as parliament reassembled on 18 April and the Reform Bill went into committee. The following day, when the government was defeated on a motion affecting the Bill,[15] the prime minister asked the king to dissolve parliament and allow him to obtain a larger majority in a general election. Initially, the king refused but, on 21 April, he changed his mind; and next morning, when he learnt that a Tory peer planned to pre-empt his right of dissolution by proposing a motion against it, he ordered the royal robes to be prepared and the crown sent over from the Tower of London. Appropriately dressed, he set out for Westminster in the early afternoon, cannons firing to signal his approach.

Parliament had been forewarned of the king's intentions and the Commons was in uproar. "The speaker was agitated," wrote a political commentator, "and several members were not collected enough to receive his decisions with the usual deference. Honourable members turned upon each other, growling contradictions. The spokesman of the opposition gained a hearing but, as soon as he was in full flow, boom! came the cannon which told that the king was on his way, and the roar drowned the conclusion of his sentence. Not a word more was heard for the cheers, cries and shouts of laughter, all put down at regular intervals by discharges of artillery."[16]

On entering the Lords, the king asked that the Commons be summoned and members accompanied the speaker, rushing in "very tumultuously."[17] Flushed by the drama, his crown sitting awry on his head, the king read his speech, then he drove back to his palace while the lords and members returned to their homes. As the country prepared for another election (on the single issue of "The Bill, the whole Bill, and nothing but the Bill"), Stephens decided not to defend his seat. He was no more committed to parliament than he had been to his regiment, while Charles regretted the huge expense of the campaign that had elected his son for a mere seven months. Opinion in the country was overwhelmingly in favour of reform and Stephens had no hope of re-election. "We will not lend our support," proclaimed a flyer in Barnstaple, "to any individual who has opposed the progress of the Reform Bill, and we will frustrate all attempts to continue those infamous and fraudulent practices which have hitherto stigmatised this borough as the nest of fraud and corruption."[18]

In the spring of 1831, Louisa Bulkeley was expecting her first child. To protect her baby from the jolting of a carriage journey to Chicksands, the family remained in Portman Square until her daughter was born in October. The child was baptised in St Mary's, Bryanston Square, but celebrations were short-lived for Louisa was infected by the birth and, on 28 November, weighed down by loss and grief, Charles attended the funeral of his last-remaining daughter.[19]

He employed a nurse to care for his infant grand-daughter but, of his five children, only Stephens remained to him. He loved his son for his high spirits and gentle nature, but wished he would spend his time on more intelligent pursuits than hunting, gambling and the theatre, occupations of which he had always disapproved. That summer, when a London gossip sheet summed up the betting season at Crockford's, Stephens was listed as one of the main losers, having incurred significant debts which were subsidised by his father.[20]

Meanwhile, friends and relatives enjoyed the hospitality provided in Chicksands Priory and Portman Square. One visitor was Charles's niece, Charlotte Todd (grand-daughter of William Tonkin of Lisbon), and he soon became aware of a growing intimacy between Charlotte and his son-in-law, who had retired from the Life Guards in 1832. The couple were married the following December and returned from honeymoon to live with Charles in London and Bedfordshire.[21]

Eighteen months later, Charles received news of his brother's death in Little Petherick. Richard's health had deteriorated since his visit to London and he was fearful that his children would grow envious of their wealthy cousin. "Whereas in families," he wrote in 1831, "the most wise and sovereign Lord does almost always, without respect to age or merit, give to some of the branches more and to some less of this world's goods – and is now doing so in my family – I pray my children to whom less has been given not to envy their brethren who have more. I charge them to be afraid of the riches of this world because, if not used according to the will of God, they make it impossible to be honest here or happy hereafter."[22]

Richard died in September 1834, having penned a final letter to his children. "Farewell," he wrote in Latin, the language in which he felt most comfortable, "I take my flight, not on the wings of death, but of love; not to a gloomy wilderness, but to the bright and joyful presence of God and Christ; and with their likeness I shall be satisfied for ever and ever. Weep not, my dearly beloved, but rejoice and follow me."[23]

Charles was distressed at the news. He and Richard had met only a few times since boyhood, but they had written to each other and shared a logical intelligence inherited from their father. Charles used his intellect on mercantile matters and economic pamphlets; Richard spent his time on theology. "It was difficult to say," wrote one of his daughters, "which predominated most, the simple-minded father of his flock or the studious and learned divine. His life was one of thought, a continuous exercise of mind in all its faculties, companionship with doctrines and high imaginings."[24] And Richard had a reputation in academic circles. "I have heard," wrote his niece, "that his opinions on the most abstruse questions in theology are held in respect at Oxford."[25]

Meanwhile, the country was preparing for a general election and it was suggested that Stephens should stand for his father's home town of Liskeard. After the Reform Bill received royal assent in 1832, a radical politician, Charles Buller, had replaced Lord Eliot as member for the town. Two years later, when Peter Glubb was seeking a candidate to regain the seat for the Tories, he proposed the former member for Barnstaple. "I have no doubt," he wrote to Eliot, "that Mr Lyne Stephens will come forth as a candidate and, under his banner, I hope to fight the radicals and their radical monster, Mr Buller."[26]

Stephens agreed to Glubb's proposal and, on 25 November, he drafted his election address. He was known to have voted against the Reform Bill, so the address was worded carefully. "I am firmly attached to our unrivalled constitution," he wrote, "and therefore opposed to any sudden or incautious changes while, at the same time, I am not one of those who think that all improvement is impossible or who would resist the reformation of acknowledged evils. Such legislation would receive my most cordial support as would have for its object the protection of those great interests from which spring the prosperity of our country. I mean the agricultural and commercial, both of which are endangered from the efforts of those who can see no safety but in perpetual change."[27]

Although Stephens concluded his address with the words, "it is my intention very shortly to pay my personal respects to you," he never made the journey to Liskeard. On 6 December, Peter Glubb wrote to a new candidate: "I take the earliest opportunity of informing you that Mr Lyne Stephens has withdrawn from the contest as to the representation of this borough. My vote and any little influence I have you may command."[28] This was a rapid change of mind for Stephens withdrew his candidacy just a few days after his election address was printed. He had little chance of success and, rather than waste his time electioneering, he preferred to be in Melton Mowbray with his friends and his horses.

Charles and the Bulkeleys were in Chicksands when Stephens set out for Leicestershire and they remained there for most of the following year. In September, Charlotte gave birth to a daughter, and the infant was taken to London and baptised at St Mary's, Bryanston Square.[29] The family then returned to Chicksands where Stephens and Charles Bulkeley hosted their annual shooting party. The brothers-in-law had little in common; there had been several disagreements over the years and in November 1835, when the house was full of guests, they had an angry confrontation. According to Francis Lyne, "Captain Bulkeley quarrelled with my cousin Stephens and challenged him. Two officers of the Guards acted as seconds. As men of honour and gentlemen, they did the best they could and there was no fighting. But the commotion in the house was very great and, when it reached my uncle's ears, he said that a man who would seek to take the life of his son should not rest under his roof. Early next morning, Charles Bulkeley, with his wife and children, left the house to know my uncle's face no more."[30]

A few days after the Bulkeleys drove away from Chicksands to take a house in Mayfair,[31] Charles learnt that a ruling by the court of chancery had increased his wealth by more than £30,000. Lewis Stephens's bequest to endow a school in Exeter had failed under laws of mortmain (which ruled that land could not be transferred into the "dead hand" of churches or corporations), so the capital remained invested in bank stocks. Lewis's widow had enjoyed the interest and dividends but, after her death in July 1827, the stocks reverted to her husband's estate and to Charles as the only surviving legatee of Lewis's will. And since that time, another relative of the Stephens family, believing he had greater claim to the money, had gone to great lengths to obtain it.

Thomas White Cogan was the son of Thomas Cogan of Cornhill who had befriended John James and Philadelphia when they were children. Because his mother was first cousin to Lewis Stephens, Cogan believed himself to be Lewis's heir-at-law and therefore entitled to the money (held in new four percent annuities and now worth £30,996). He had approached Charles as soon as Mary's will was proved; he had "frequently and in a friendly manner applied to Mr Lyne Stephens as the surviving trustee of the new four percent annuities, and requested him to transfer the same to him and to pay him the interest and dividends which have accrued thereon. But this Mr Lyne Stephens absolutely refused to do."[32] Charles had explained to Cogan that, although he might legally be Lewis's heir-at-law, the money was still due to Charles as the sole surviving legatee, but his explanation fell on deaf ears.

In 1828, Cogan instigated legal proceedings in chancery. His bill was filed in December and Charles was ordered to pay the funds into court.[33] As usual, the wheels of chancery turned exceedingly slowly and it was not until three years later that advertisements were placed in a number of journals requesting that claimants to the money, as possible heirs-at-law, should make themselves known to the court. No sensible claims were received and, in June 1834, the judge ruled that Thomas Cogan was Lewis Stephens's heir-at-law, although he made no mention of his eligibility to receive the money.[34] Finally, in November 1835, the judge declared that, "Charles Lyne Stephens, as next of kin of the testator Lewis Stephens, is absolutely entitled to the £30,996 in new four percent annuities, and to the interest and dividends which have accrued since the death of Mary Stephens, and that Thomas Cogan's bill stands dismissed out of court without costs."[35]

The case had dragged on for seven years. Researchers had been employed to examine the genealogy of all Lewis Stephens's relatives and affidavits obtained from anyone who remembered the family. Each side had been ordered to pay their own costs but, whereas Charles had responded to Cogan's bill with the words "he is a stranger to all and singular the several matters and things mentioned and leaves Thomas Cogan to make such proof as he shall be enabled,"[36]

Cogan had tied himself in knots to prove himself the heir-at-law and received not a penny. Meanwhile, the cost of litigation had greatly exceeded the value of his legacy from John James. "It does not do," wrote one of Charles's nieces, "to rush into chancery on one's own unsupported convictions."[37]

Charles was lonely after the departure of the Bulkeleys and saddened by the loss of his grand-daughter (who was to grow up in London and Plymouth having no contact with her mother's family). In the summer of 1836, he decided to give up Chicksands Priory, the ancient Gothic building in which he had invested so much time and money. Chicksands had given him status, but it was remote and secluded and a solitary place for an elderly man to live alone. After Stephens hosted his final shooting party in November, Charles left the Priory for the last time and returned to London to spend the winter alone in Portman Square.[38]

A few weeks later, he was once more embroiled in litigation, this time with the assignees of his bankrupt brother Joseph. Since Joseph had received one-fifteenth of Lewis's residual estate, his assignees felt entitled to one-fifteenth of the £30,996 which Charles had just received, together with a similar proportion of the interest and dividends. Charles had believed that the matter was finished, that he was free from the lengthy lawsuits which had plagued him since John James's death ten years before. The grounds for this latest request were thin (Charles had won his case against Cogan because he was the surviving legatee, whereas Joseph had been dead for almost seventeen years) but, tired of litigation, he chose not to contest the case. In an indenture signed in February, he denied the right of the assignees but, "in consideration of Joseph Lyne having been his brother, with respect for his memory, and being unwilling to be involved in litigation with his representatives," he agreed to hand over the sum of £2690. This was used to give a final dividend to Joseph's creditors.[39]

Having rid himself of the lawyers, Charles was free to enjoy his fortune but, apart from throwing expensive dinner parties and playing whist at Crockford's, there was little on which he could spend his money. He was accustomed to subsidising his son's hunting activities and gambling debts but, in the spring of 1837, he was astonished when Stephens asked for money for a different purpose. He wanted £10,000 (almost half a million in today's values) to persuade a French ballerina to become his mistress.

21

The Fair Brimstone

1831–1837

"Duvernay was one of the most ravishing women you could wish to see. She was twenty years old, had charming eyes, an admirably turned leg, and a figure of perfect elegance. As for her dancing, she was full of fire and grace."
C-P Séchan, 1883

"Many things can be done with a foreign dancer if you commence operations with a dinner and end them with a diamond."
Alfred Bunn, manager of the Theatre Royal, 1840

The future beneficiary of the Lyne Stephens fortune made her début in the Paris Opéra House in April 1831. She was almost overcome by stage-fright but, after five more performances increased her confidence, she was engaged as a soloist and given her first leading role at the end of the year. She was, wrote one of the Paris journals, "very young and very pretty, dances to perfection, and her miming is full of fascination. This young virtuoso is making rapid progress."[1]

Yolande Duvernay was born in Versailles in December 1812. Her father was an actor and her mother, who had been on stage herself as a young woman, was to become a formidable presence in her daughter's life at the Opéra. When Yolande was six years old, the family moved to Paris, to a little house in the Passage Saulnier near the School of Dance where she was to study for the next twelve years.[2]

"If you only knew," wrote another pupil, "the courage, patience, resignation and hard work that was needed, the terrible tortures that had to be endured. Every morning, the teacher imprisoned my feet in a grooved box; heel to heel, with knees pointing outwards, my martyred feet remained in a parallel line by themselves. They called this turning out. After half an hour of the box, I had to endure another form of torture; placing my foot on a *barre* which I had to hold with the opposite hand. This was called breaking in. After being turned out and broken in, we were forced to study *assemblés, jetés, balancés, pirouettes sur le cou-de-pied, sauts de basque, pas de bourrée* and, finally, *entrechats quatre, six and huit*. And do not imagine that such brutal fatigues last only for a short time. They must continue for ever and be constantly renewed."[3]

The pupils came from poor families and the younger girls were known as *petits rats*. "It is because she is a child of the building," explained an aficionado, "because she nibbles, chatters and plays there, that she has received the name of *rat*. She is a little girl between six and fourteen, a ballet pupil who wears cast-off shoes, faded shawls and soot-coloured hats, who warms herself over smoky oil-lamps, has bread sticking out of her pockets, and begs you for ten sous to buy sweets. The *rat* makes holes in the scenery, rushes about behind the backcloths, and plays in the wings. She is supposed to earn twenty sous a night but, with the fines which her pranks entail, receives only eight to ten francs a month and thirty kicks from her mother."[4]

Pupils who showed promise were transferred to *classes de perfectionnement* taught by the ballet-masters, Auguste Vestris and Jean-François Coulon. Vestris was an elderly man (he had made his début as far back as 1772) and Yolande joined his class in November 1829 when she was sixteen years old. She was not accepted on merit alone; her parents had written several letters to the director of the Opéra before their ambition was accomplished.[5] Vestris understood his audience. "He was a sensualist," explained the director, "he demanded provocative smiles, poses and attitudes, almost without decency or modesty. I often heard him say to his pupils, 'be charming and coquettish, display the most captivating freedom in all your movements; you must inspire passion so that men in the audience desire to sleep with you.'"[6]

In early 1831, a new director took charge of the Opéra. In his early thirties, Louis Véron was unattractive in appearance, having thick features and a heavy build, but Yolande's mother did all she could to encourage his interest in her daughter. On the rare occasions when Yolande came to class alone, Vestris would rush off to the Opéra House. "He would run up all excited," wrote Véron, "his hair flying, his feet turned out, and say to me, 'she is there without her mother.'" The director found Yolande extremely desirable in her practice costume, but she was often in tears and Vestris would sprinkle the floor with a watering-can. "Look," he would say to Véron, "she's been crying again."[7]

After the revolution of July 1830, Véron foresaw the rise of the bourgeoisie and he indulged the tastes of this new fashionable class. The doors of the *foyer de la danse* (the room where dancers stretched their limbs before going on stage) were opened to select members of the audience and young men-about-town began to treat the backstage as their private seraglio. He also introduced the star system, providing a sequence of "young and beautiful dancers who perform better and differently from those who preceded them. If one is aiming neither at the intelligence nor at the heart, one must appeal to the senses and most particularly to the eyes."[8] He attended the *classes de perfectionnement*, to select pupils whose beauty and talent would appeal to his audience, and his first rising star was Yolande (who had taken the stage name of Pauline Duvernay).

The persistence of her mother had been rewarded. Scheming, ambitious and domineering, Madame Duvernay's sole desire was to gain power in the Opéra House through the advancement of her daughter.[9] Now she decided that Yolande should leave Vestris and enrol with Filippo Taglioni, who taught a more fluid and expressive style of dancing. Taglioni found his new pupil exasperating and expelled her from class on more than one occasion, although her tears always softened his heart. As Véron wrote in his memoirs, "this young dancer, lifted to prominence by a skilful mother, had above all studied the power of weeping."[10]

One evening, when Yolande was about to perform a *pas de deux* with Lise Noblet, Véron found her sobbing backstage. "When I asked the cause of her sorrow," he remembered, "my curiosity was received with the most obstinate silence. Her mother took me aside. 'I will tell you,' she said. 'She is dancing this evening with Mlle Noblet who has the most beautiful jewels to wear, while my daughter has none.' Despite my long experience, a woman's tears always affect me and I sent to the jewellers for the remedy for such poignant sorrow."[11]

Duvernay's first leading role was the abbess in *Robert le Diable*, a role previously danced by the star of the Opéra, Marie Taglioni. The curtain rose with lapsed nuns being summoned from their tombs by a young man, while the abbess encourages them to give in to pleasure. She dances before the boy, luring him towards the grave, but he escapes and the nuns sink back into their tombs. It was a role which Vestris had prepared her for, in which she displayed the sensuality of her dancing. The seduction scene had proved difficult for Marie Taglioni, but it presented no problems for Yolande.

Véron, meanwhile, had commissioned a new ballet, *La Tentation*, to exploit the talents of his protégé who had now become his mistress. Duvernay danced the role of Miranda, a woman shaped by a demon to be more alluring than any woman on earth, and she appeared on stage rising from a cauldron, dressed in white, her dark hair loose around her shoulders. Although the ballet (which opened in June 1832) was overlong and not a success, Duvernay's spirited dancing was received with enthusiasm. "She is a pretty woman," wrote one critic, "and a talented one."[12]

Yolande was the new star of the Opéra. "Each evening," wrote one of her admirers, "the name of Duvernay was acclaimed by a thousand voices."[13] A stage painter was equally smitten, describing her as: "one of the most ravishing women you could wish to see; she was twenty years old, had charming eyes, an admirably turned leg, and a figure of perfect elegance."[14] She was also an excellent mime. In one ballet, a group of female warriors formed a council of war on stage; while the other dancers simulated a few gestures of communication, Yolande, "by means of the funniest miming and the most expressive and passionate gestures, conveyed all the phases of a lively discussion. Universal laughter and applause greeted these gay and animated scenes."[15]

One evening in the autumn of 1832, bored by long performances in La Tentation, she failed to appear at the Opéra House. Her apartment was empty, Véron and her mother searched the city and, fearing she had drowned in the Seine, they inspected all female corpses in the morgue. Her disappearance was the talk of society and it was several days before the composer of La Tentation received an anonymous note with details of her whereabouts. Calling for a carriage, he hurried through the streets and found Yolande in a convent. She had, she told him, felt a sudden desire to become a nun.[16]

The publicity did her no harm and she reappeared on stage to the delight of her admirers. Renowned for the spontaneity of her conversation and her witty replies to potential suitors, stories began to circulate about her mischief with the men who tried to woo her.[17] "You say you love me," she said to an elderly Russian, "but do you love me as much as 100,000 francs?" Next day, she returned from class to find the Russian installed in her apartment, reclining on the sofa. "My dear," he said, "you asked me yesterday how much I loved you. Here is my answer." And he opened a box which contained the money in gold pieces. "Take your feet off my sofa," Yolande replied, "and take away that scrap-iron. I was only joking."[18]

As news of this rebuff spread through society, another admirer (a young diplomat) made his way to the dancer's apartment. "*I* shall not offer you gold," he told her. "It is my life I would sacrifice for you." Yolande laughed. "You men are all the same. You offer me things I either do not want or cannot take." But after listening to his protestations, she appeared to relent, "Very well," she said, "bring me one of your front teeth." An hour later, the young man returned with a handkerchief held to his mouth and a pill-box in his hand. As Yolande opened the box, he removed the handkerchief and pointed to a bloody gap. "You poor man!" she cried, "I asked for a bottom tooth and you've brought me a top one."[19]

The fame of Duvernay had now reached London where two theatres (King's Theatre in the Haymarket and Theatre Royal in Drury Lane) functioned as opera houses on a seasonal basis, engaging members of the Paris Opéra on short-term contracts. In the autumn of 1832, the manager of the Theatre Royal approached Véron with a request that Yolande should appear there for the first six weeks of the 1833 season. "Her mother does her more harm than good," wrote Marie Taglioni a few days later. "She was offered a London engagement, but Madame Duvernay gave it out that it would be difficult to accept as she has had offers from all the foreign courts."[20]

Despite her mother's intrigues, Yolande accepted the engagement at a salary of £750 and, in early February, she and her parents crossed the channel and took lodgings in Cecil Street near the Strand.[21] Her first performances (in *The Sleeping Beauty*) were a disappointment; audiences were unenthusiastic and reviews were mixed. She had greater success in March when she appeared in *The Maid of Cashmere (Le Dieu et la Bayadère)*, a performance which had a powerful effect on the young William Makepiece Thackeray. "When I think of Duvernay prancing in as the Bayadère," he wrote, "I say it was a vision of loveliness such as mortal eyes can't see nowadays. How well I remember the tune to which she used to appear! Kaled said to the Sultan, 'my Lord, a troop of those dancing and singing girls called Bayadères approaches' and, to the clash of cymbals and the thumping of my heart, in she used to dance! There has never been anything like it, never."[22]

"*The Maid of Cashmere* has made a regular hit," wrote a theatre critic, "and those who have not seen Mlle Duvernay in the part have no idea of the extent of her talents. It is a great pity she did not make her first appearance in this piece, for then she would much earlier have done the trick. Now she is within a day or two of her departure from London, the people are beginning to flock after her. Her benefit performance is on 30 March and we understand that she posts off to Dover the moment the curtain falls, for she is under heavy penalty to be in Paris by 1 April as she dances there the following night."[23]

Meanwhile, the men-about-town were clustering around the new celebrity. The manager of the Theatre Royal "declared his attachment by some tender but understood expression of the eye," and Lord Ranelagh was so smitten that he followed Yolande to Paris where she flirted with him for a few weeks before sending him home to England. "Although I play the sleeping beauty in public," she told him, "I cannot perform it in private without first passing through the ordeal of the church."[24]

Yolande had another successful year in Paris, happy in the continued affections of Louis Véron. In early 1834, she returned to London, this time engaged by the King's Theatre for the first three months of the season. In the ballet *Sire Huon*, she danced a *pas de deux* with Marie Taglioni. "The greatest charm of this ballet," wrote *The Times*, "is in the exquisite movements of the exquisite Taglioni. Mlle Duvernay, whom a party has set up as a rival to Taglioni, came in for her full share of approbation. She deserved it, for she dances with much spirit and elegance, but she will never equal Taglioni."[25]

Yolande achieved a greater triumph during this London season than she had the year before, although Taglioni felt the need to qualify her success. "She has had here," she wrote, "what we call a *succès d'estime* only but, as a beauty she has enjoyed enormous success."[26] And Duvernay had conquered the fashionable set in a way the plainer Taglioni never could. The King's Theatre was the centre of high fashion and, just as the Paris Opéra opened the backstage to members of the audience, the King's Theatre opened a green room where performers mingled with their admirers. Men of fashion watched the ballet from omnibus boxes which abutted the stage, then strolled into the green room to make assignments with the dancers of their choice.

Towards the end of her contract, Yolande accepted a proposition from Edward Ellice (known as "the Bear"), the son of a cabinet minister. "Ellice, being an aspiring young man of fashion," wrote a retired politician in early May, "has formed a connection with Duvernay, the opera dancer, to whom he has paid £2000 down and contracted to pay £800 a year. The dear young creatures were seen going down in a chaise and four to Richmond. Captain Gronow, the MP and duellist, negotiated for the young Bear with the dancer's parents."[27] A gossip sheet also learnt of the visit to Richmond: "The ratification dinner given by Ned Ellice to his darling Duvernay at the Star and Garter has excited much remark amongst the admirers of that fascinating *danseuse*. Lord Allen is perfectly out of his wits and Lord Tullamore is stark staring mad with vexation and envy."[28]

Yolande's engagement at the King's Theatre ended a few days later, after which she was expected to return to France. "So attached is Ned Ellice to the fair and affectionate Duvernay," wrote the gossip sheet on 11 May, "that it is more than probable the liaison will terminate in marriage. Duvernay was to leave London for Paris last night, and there was every reason to believe her ardent lover would accompany her or follow in the course of a few days. Papa Ellice protests strongly and firmly against anything bordering on a match with the 'Fair Brimstone,' as he styles her."[29]

A week later, Yolande was still in London. "Duvernay was to have left for Paris on Saturday last," explained *The Satirist* on 18 May, "but at the pressing solicitation of the Duke of Devonshire, she was induced to prolong her stay and, on Monday, by special invitation, she accompanied Ned Ellice to the duke's villa at Chiswick where a splendid fork luncheon was prepared. The duke enjoyed himself in unrestricted delight, and a jealous schism has arisen between the duke and young Ned on the subject of the fair *danseuse*."[30]

Ellice believed the duke would supplant him in Yolande's affections. He began to behave jealously and Yolande, resentful of all attempts to curtail her freedom, rejected her English lover. "Young Ellice is inconsolable for the loss of Duvernay," wrote the gossip sheet on 1 June, "and what adds to his affliction is that his rival, the Duke of Devonshire, has made a proposition so liberal in its provisions that no doubt can arise as to its immediate acceptance."[31] But Yolande was warned that the middle-aged duke was only playing with her affections, and she returned to Paris and Louis Véron. "Duvernay complains bitterly of the young Bear," commented *The Satirist*, "and congratulates herself that she has escaped from his claws. Véron is quite delighted and gives it out that he is safe in the affection of the charming *danseuse*."[32]

Yolande was fond of Véron, who had done so much to advance her career, but their relationship was threatened by the scheming of her mother. Shortly after their return from London, Madame Duvernay attempted to trap Véron into marrying her daughter, a plot discovered by the concierge at the Opéra House.[33] Then she tried to belittle his influence on Yolande's career. "My daughter's talent has no need of your help," she said to him one afternoon. Véron did not reply, but he sent for the leader of the *claque* (a group of men who led the applause in the Opéra House) and instructed him to ensure that Yolande received no ovation that evening, "not a single hand-clap." That night, after finishing a pirouette, Yolande smiled at the audience in anticipation of applause from the *claque*, but the theatre remained totally silent. Fleeing from the stage, she collapsed sobbing in the wings while her mother demanded an interview with Véron. "You see?" the director told her. "Your daughter's talent does need help."[34]

During the summer, as Duvernay rehearsed the principal role in a new ballet, Véron tired of his mistress. He transferred his favour to a new protégé, Fanny Elssler, and decided to substitute Elssler in the role. Yolande used all her guile to persuade him to change his mind; she had already learnt the part and Véron (moved by her tears) had the scenario rewritten to include leading roles for both women. A few weeks later, he openly displayed the change in his affections; attending a performance at another theatre, he booked separate boxes for Duvernay and Taglioni, but sat close to Fanny Elssler in the most conspicuous box of all.[35]

Overshadowed by the talents of Taglioni and Elssler, exasperated by her mother, and grieving for the loss of Véron whose influence had done so much for her career, Yolande tried to poison herself. Alone in her apartment, she swallowed a glass of vinegar in which she had soaked some copper coins. Hearing her groans, the neighbours broke down the door and, with the help of a doctor, she soon recovered from the effects of this strange concoction.[36] She also recovered her spirits for her mother found her another protector, a man to whom Yolande was already attracted. The Marquis de La Valette was a charming, elegant and good-looking young man who was to make a name for himself in the diplomatic service. The natural son of an actress, he had become a familiar presence in the Opéra House and, after a liaison with another dancer (who had borne him a child), his eye fell on the beautiful and spirited Duvernay.[37]

Rumours were spread that her mother sold her to La Valette for 40,000 francs, infusing a sleeping potion in

Yolande's drink so that, despite her misgivings, she woke up next morning in the arms of the handsome marquis.[38] Whatever the truth of this story, Yolande was happy with her new lover. He was younger and better looking than Louis Véron, his adventurous personality was a match for her own, and he treated her with kindness and affection. There was much laughter in her apartment when she starred in a new ballet in which dancers shot arrows into the wings. One evening, she aimed her bow in the wrong direction; the arrow sped into the auditorium and missed the heir to the throne, the Duc d'Orléans, by just a few feet.[39]

La Valette had friends in high society and, in May 1835, Yolande was devastated to learn that he was to marry a young woman from a wealthy family. This prompted an overdose of opium.[40] "The ending of an intimacy," wrote a Paris journal, "was denoted by the announcement of the marriage of one of the parties. The banns had been published, the contract signed. On hearing the news, our young artiste lost her reason, gave way to despair and, when she thought she had but little time to live, called on her former lover to whom she uttered these words: 'you are about to marry and I am about to die.'"[41]

Yolande had taken too little opium to kill herself but the marriage was called off, partly because of the scandal and partly because La Valette was genuinely fond of his mistress.[42] She returned to the stage on 17 June but, after dancing in a new ballet in early October, disappeared again from public view. "Pretty women," explained a Paris journal, "are prone to more indispositions than others."[43]

Yolande miscarried her baby a few months later. She returned to class in January,[44] danced in several productions during the spring and summer, and on 29 September, the entire company of the Opéra travelled to the palace of Compiègne where the army was carrying out manoeuvres in the presence of the royal family. The performance was held in a small pink and gold theatre; Yolande danced a *pas de trois* and, after the show, was introduced to the king and queen, and "received the most amiable attentions from senior officers."[45] She also met the Duc d'Orléans, who teased her about her marksmanship and the evening, eighteen months before, when she had almost impaled him with an arrow.

Two weeks later, shortly before La Valette accepted a diplomatic appointment in Stockholm, Yolande returned to England for a third London season, engaged by the Theatre Royal, Drury Lane, at a salary of £600 a month. Her first performance was postponed because of rough weather in the channel, and the men of society awaited her arrival with anticipation.[46] "The competition for an opera dancer of celebrity is immense," wrote *Town* magazine. "No sooner does she land and her address become known than a regular bevy attend her dwelling, and envied indeed is the favoured one whom she first honours with her notice. But the nobs have singular ideas of mutual accommodation in this respect. It is not uncommon to see the lady driven to the theatre in the carriage of one swell and back in another. She may take the air with a lord in the morning and a duke in the afternoon."[47]

Having flirted with the men who besieged her apartment, Duvernay opened her London season on 3 November. A month later, she appeared in the first London production of *Le Diable Boiteux* in which she performed a Spanish dance, the *cachucha*. Wearing pink satin trimmed with black, she stood on stage, "her figure arched back, her leg gleaming through her silk stocking. How charming she is with a rose at her ear, fire in her eyes and her sparkling smile. At the tips of her fingers, the ebony castanets are acquiver. Now she springs forward and the clatter of her castanets breaks out. How she twists! How she bends! Her swooning arms flutter about her drooping head, her body curves back and her white shoulders almost brush the floor."[48]

The *cachucha* was a huge success and Duvernay's sensual performance became the talk of London. The dance was particularly appreciated by the men in the audience, one critic referring to, "those movements of the hips, those provocative gestures, those arms which seek to embrace an absent lover, that mouth crying out for a kiss, that thrilling, quivering, twisting body, that costume with its low-cut, half-open bodice, that sensual grace and lascivious abandon."[49] Fanny Elssler, who created the *cachucha* in Paris, may have danced it with more elegance but Yolande infused it with sexuality. She teased the men of society who sat in the omnibus boxes, well aware of the effect she was having on their blood pressure.

The season at Drury Lane ended on 2 February, but Yolande's popularity was so great that she was offered a further two-month engagement at the King's Theatre.[50] A few weeks later, her role in a new ballet included a *pas seul* danced in a nightdress before a mirror. "The bedroom scene," wrote *The Satirist*, "is rendered by her quite as warm, to say nothing further, as the frequenters even of the stalls can desire. The fashion in which she reclines on the bed we must not attempt to describe, but it inspires the bald-pated part of the audience (those whose brains are too ardent for the continued existence of hair above the ears) with intense delight."[51]

On 13 April, Duvernay gave her benefit performance which included the *cachucha* and the *pas seul* before the mirror. Her contract ended two days later but, on 24 April, the manager of the King's Theatre announced that, "in compliance with the numerous wishes of the subscribers, he had succeeded with much difficulty and great expense in effecting an arrangement with the director of the Paris Opéra."[52] Yolande would remain in London until the season ended in August.

"There is much of originality about Duvernay," concluded *The Times*. "Her style is far removed from the poetical one of Taglioni and may be called the naïve school of dancing. She bounds about in the most playful manner, and falls into her various attitudes as if by accident and with a general air of good humour that is highly pleasing."[53]

22

Amongst the Dandies

1836–1845

My Lord Tomnoddy he raised his head
And thus to Tiger Tim he said
"Malibran's dead, Duvernay's fled,
Taglioni has not yet arrived in her stead;
Tiger Tim, come tell me true,
What may a Nobleman find to do?"
R H Barham, *The Ingoldsby Legends*, c.1840[1]

"Several of my dancers have made rich and brilliant marriages, which they
gained by their talents, their spirit and their beauty. Some did not accept
the offer of marriage without a certain resistance; others only arrived at
their goal with much perseverance."
Louis Véron, 1854

Stephens left Chicksands for Melton Mowbray a few days
before Yolande arrived in England for her third London
engagement. He and his friends gathered for the opening
dinner of the season on the first Sunday in November, the
Quorn hounds meeting for the first time the following
morning.

The country around Melton was ideal for hunting. "A
winter in Leicestershire," wrote Nimrod, a sporting journalist, "is the *passe-partout* that leads to the best society in the
world. When turned out of the hands of his valet, the
Meltonian fox-hunter presents the very *beau-ideal* of his
caste. The exact fit of his coat, his superlatively well-cleaned
leather breeches and boots, and the high breeding of the man
can seldom be matched elsewhere."[2] Another sporting writer
had a different opinion of the aristocrats and wealthy

commoners who made their way to Melton every winter. The town, he wrote, "draws a lot of noisy, perfumed, chattering coxcombs who have no idea of hunting and no real pleasure in the thing."[3]

Stephens had learnt to enjoy the sport in 1826 when the Tenth Hussars was based in Leicestershire ("the Tenth has placed fox-hunting above all sports," wrote a fellow officer; "it gives a quick eye, knowledge of terrain, the requisite dash and *going straight*").[4] But he had little style on horseback. His balance was poor and he was known as one of the weakest riders in Melton.[5]

During his first three seasons in the town, he stayed with his valet in the George Hotel, which offered high standards of comfort and had an excellent cook, and he also dined at the Old Club which held banquets several nights a week. In the autumn of 1832, he teamed up with three other men to form the New Club in premises opposite the George. Here the four sportsmen lived together and, as they employed one of the best chefs in the country (Francatelli, who later became chef at Crockford's), the club became renowned for its dinners.[6]

Six months later, he persuaded his father to build him a house in Melton, together with a stable block which alone cost £2000 and boasted the Lyne Stephens coat of arms above the hayloft. The buildings were completed in October 1833 and, as his servants organised the house, and the grooms and stable boys transferred his horses to their new accommodation, Stephens visited the dealers to increase his stock of thoroughbreds. Soon his stables contained fourteen horses and, with mahogany partitions and a livery of green blankets embroidered in gold, they were known as the most luxurious in the town.[7]

Later that winter, he sat for the artist, Francis Grant, who was working on a painting set in the breakfast room of the Old Club. *The Melton Breakfast* portrayed a number of notable Meltonians. Stephens was depicted at the back of the group, sitting eagerly but unobtrusively on a sofa, while several men of title were engaged in various activities in the foreground. Studying the painting as it was displayed in the Royal Academy in the summer of 1834, Stephens regretted turning down Lord Liverpool's offer of a baronetcy, an offer he had declined seven years earlier in deference to his father. In time, he would inherit the Lyne Stephens fortune, but titles had greater status than wealth and a baronetcy would have given him prestige in the town.

Every year, the season ended with a race meeting held during the first week of April. The races in 1837 attracted particularly large crowds ("there were more strangers of rank and fashion than usual," reported a London newspaper, "and large dinner parties most evenings at the New Club").[8] During the previous winter, several sportsmen had arrived in Melton with news of Duvernay and her *cachucha*, and as soon as the race meeting was over, Stephens hurried home to London and took his box at the King's Theatre for her benefit performance.

He was enchanted; and as he watched Yolande's provocative *cachucha*, followed by her slower, more seductive dancing in the *pas seul* before the mirror, an idea began to take shape in his mind. Duvernay was the most celebrated dancer in London, and also the most beautiful. It was a great accomplishment, as one of his acquaintances put it, "to cultivate intimate relations with the reigning *favorita*. The protector of the beautiful *danseuse* was certain of exciting the envy of his less fortunate associates. This was so expensive a luxury that only a theatre-goer with a handsome income could venture to indulge in it, but it was so fashionable that married men and even elderly men were proud of the distinction."[9]

Perceived as a parvenu, Stephens had made little impact on the fashionable set; he had inherited his father's lack of stature and his personality failed to impress. Hoping he would be regarded more favourably if he persuaded Yolande to become his mistress, he spent the next few weeks waiting in the green room, inviting her to dinners, delivering gifts of expensive jewellery. Initially, Yolande was not attracted to her new admirer, being accustomed to men of greater sophistication and wit, but Stephens was wise; he also targeted her mother, a woman who was happy to be paid for her daughter's favours. Madame Duvernay put increasing pressure on Yolande to accept his offer and, as Stephens persisted in his attentions, ignoring every rebuff and showing a touching desire to please, Yolande began to change her mind. He was a kind man, she realised, as well as a rich one.

She knew she was not the brightest star of the Opéra. She was the most beautiful, the most sensual and the most witty, but the dancing skills of Marie Taglioni and Fanny Elssler were more fluid and controlled. Taglioni had recently departed to spend three years in St Petersburg but Elssler remained in Paris, a city to which Yolande must soon return. She had been in England for six months and remembered the lukewarm reviews she received after returning from her first London season. Now, after a long absence, the critics might find fault again and compare her unfavourably with Elssler.

As soon as Stephens became aware of her change of mind, he called on an acquaintance, Count d'Orsay. Over six feet tall, strikingly handsome and always most exquisitely turned out, d'Orsay was king of the dandies, driving around London in a green coach, its white wheels striped with green and crimson. "When I saw him driving in his tilbury," wrote one of his friends, "he looked like some gorgeous dragonfly skimming through the air."[10]

Stephens had known d'Orsay for several years (they had helped to found the Garrick Club, as well as being fellow members of Crockford's) and the count was acquainted with Yolande; he was an *habitué* of the theatre and entertained the stars of the Paris Opéra during their London seasons. Stephens hoped that d'Orsay, a French aristocrat, was the right man to negotiate with Yolande's mother, and d'Orsay took on the task with pleasure (being a little in love with Fanny Elssler). A settlement was agreed by the end of May. Yolande's mother received £8000 and her daughter would be paid an allowance of £2000 a year, to convert into a life annuity from January 1840 on condition she remained faithful in the meantime.[11]

A few weeks later, when the Marquis de La Valette arrived in London on his way from Sweden to Paris, he made his way to the King's Theatre and found himself barred from Yolande's dressing-room. He sought out his friend, the dancer Antoine Coulon, who told him about the Lyne Stephens fortune and asked him to relinquish his hold on Yolande's affections and return to Paris. She would, he said, "always remember your love for her and the sacrifice she asks you to make to ensure her happiness."[12]

The marquis had little money of his own, but he was still in love with Yolande and he sent his seconds to Portman Square to issue a challenge. This took Stephens by surprise; he had not expected La Valette's arrival and was alarmed at the prospect of fighting for his mistress. Hoping to defuse the situation, he agreed to meet his rival on Putney Heath but asked that La Valette should first talk with Yolande. The meeting took place in her dressing-room, while Stephens waited outside, his seconds beside him armed with combat pistols. After fifteen minutes, the door opened and La Valette emerged. "Now, sir," said Stephens, standing to attention, "I am at your service." "The honours of a double triumph are yours," replied the marquis. "With your permission, I shall return to France."[13]

Stephens had bought Yolande's fidelity but he had to watch as she was wooed by other men during the final weeks of her contract. She was naturally flirtatious and, although she had no intention of risking her life annuity, she teased Stephens about his competitors. In early June, a gossip sheet published a conversation between them: "'Dat Lord Lowther,' observed Duvernay to Lyne Stephens, 'vat you call de leetle son of de dog?' 'Puppy.' 'Oui, poppy, he ver great poppy, he make love to me every night.' 'Does he!' exclaimed the parvenu, 'then it is time for me to cease making love by day.'"[14] Two months later, it was reported that Yolande had rejected his proposal of marriage. She had, she told him, "no objection to be transported for a few months or even years, but I love liberty too well to be a prisoner for life."[15]

Duvernay completed her London season on 19 August, the last time she appeared on stage. In September, she and Stephens travelled to Paris where she informed the new director of the Opéra, Henri Duponchel, that she was breaking her contract which still had seven months to run. She was too valuable a star to lose at such short notice and Duponchel threatened to sue.[16] But with her lover prepared to pay any fine the courts might impose, the couple returned to London where Stephens took a lease on a house in Kensington.

He provided Yolande with a cook, housekeeper and lady's maid, as well as a carriage with a coachman and two horses. "She had a fine mansion," wrote a French periodical, "and entertained each week a dozen of the wittiest and most distinguished men in town."[17] Stephens spent much of his time in Kensington, but he continued to live with his father in Portman Square and Yolande was often alone. With time to remember her years of celebrity, the roars of applause from the auditorium, the many men who begged for her favours, she sometimes felt nostalgic for the stage. "One cannot renounce this life of excitement and triumph without pain," explained one of her admirers. "It is a sacrifice which only the heart can understand but which all the money in England is not enough to repay."[18]

Two months after their return from Paris, before Yolande had become accustomed to her new life in London, Stephens set off again for Melton Mowbray. He hunted there for three more seasons but, in 1840, he sold his horses and let his house and stables.[19] Thirty-nine years old, he had put on weight from years of good living and, with a taste for expensive food and wine, he found it hard to follow the diet recommended for men in the hunting field. "A rich repast with an abundance of wine or spirits," wrote a sporting journalist, "occasions indigestion, headache and nervous debility, in which state no man is in a comfortable condition to ride over a country."[20]

Yolande had become entitled to her life annuity in January 1840 (whether or not she remained faithful) and, since she was free to travel, she began to visit Paris to see her friends and family. Soon there were rumours that she had rekindled her relationship with the Marquis de La Valette. "Duvernay is now in Paris," wrote a gossip sheet in November 1841, "and unknown to Lyne Stephens, constantly sees La Valette with whom her former intimacy is renewed. Again does he press that fair creature in his arms; again does her voluptuous bosom heave against his throbbing breast; again are her lips glued to his in all the tender dalliance of love's delights."[21]

This was a false report for La Valette was now involved with another star of the Opéra (Duvernay's old rival, Fanny Elssler). When Stephens confronted her about the rumours, Yolande accused him of lack of trust and, playing on his sense of guilt, she achieved an important concession. Four weeks later, another gossip sheet reported that "Lyne Stephens Snr, Lyne Stephens Jnr and *Mistress* Stephens are, after the present winter, to occupy one house, *the* one in Portman Square."[22]

Charles, meanwhile, was tiring of city life. Seventy-eight years old, he had little in common with his son's mistress, who insisted on conversing in French, and he missed Chicksands Priory and the tranquillity of a house surrounded by gardens, woods and fields. In June 1843, he purchased the Roehampton Grove estate: a mansion house with views over Richmond Park (Grove House), a smaller dwelling house (Lower Grove House) and a farm.[23]

Stephens and Yolande remained in London. Alone in Portman Square, they led a glamorous life, attending the theatre and entertaining the fashionable set. Yolande was mistress of the house, but she was not a wife and attitudes were changing as Victorian morality tightened its grip on society. Hoping to salvage her reputation, she devised a strategy to persuade Stephens to propose for a second time. "Several of my dancers have made rich and brilliant marriages," wrote Louis Véron. "They carry honourable names and live in the lap of luxury. Some did not accept the offer of marriage without a certain resistance; others only arrived at their goal with much perseverance. Here is how one of my dancers transformed her little household into a regular union."[24]

A titled Englishwoman had died, he explained, and her lady's maid (a woman known for her strict morals) was in need of a new position. Yolande employed her in Portman Square and, one evening, as guests were arriving for dinner, the maid approached Stephens and told him that her mistress was unable to leave the bedroom. He made his way there and found Yolande sobbing on the bed. "I can no longer live in such public contempt," she cried. "My maid has learnt that we are not married and has resigned from my service. I cannot bear this insult. I shall return to Paris tomorrow if you think so little of me as to allow this situation to continue." Stephens, moved by Yolande's tears (as Véron had been before him), immediately proposed marriage.[25]

Yolande, who was becoming increasingly religious, insisted on a Catholic service, while Stephens was equally determined on an Anglican ceremony. This led to a compromise. Catholic marriages had been legal for only sixteen years; previously, couples attended two services: Anglican for legality and Catholic for their faith. Now Stephens and Yolande resurrected the custom. Charles would have preferred his son to marry a Protestant girl from a good family but, always indulgent to Stephens, he not only gave his permission and agreed to be a witness, he also provided a dowry of £10,000.[26]

On the afternoon of 14 July 1845, the wedding party left Grove House for St Mary's church in Putney. After the service, the couple made their way to the Catholic chapel in Chelsea, before returning to Grove House where Charles and their guests awaited them.[27] The following day, they departed for Europe, travelling through France and Italy, and discovering the pleasures of paintings and sculpture, antique furniture and *objets d'art*.

28 Stephens Lyne Stephens, 1858/9. He is holding a wad of banknotes to indicate his status as England's richest commoner

29 Grove House, Roehampton, photographed c.1920

30 Grove House, Roehampton, rear view showing the façade and terrace added by Stephens Lyne Stephens in the 1850s

31   Edward Claremont, military attaché in Paris, lithograph by
C W Walton, c.1868

32   Yolande Lyne Stephens in
mourning dress, 1860

33   Frances Claremont with
her youngest daughter,
c.1859

34 Lynford Hall north front, photographed a few months after Yolande's death

35 Lynford Hall from the south-west, photographed by *Country Life*, 1903

36 Yolande's barouche in Paris (with Jones the coachman), late 1860s. The horses travelled with Yolande, crossing the channel at least twice a year

37 Church of Our Lady and the English Martyrs, Cambridge, photographed before the opening ceremony in October 1890

38　Edward Claremont, photographed in Paris in the late 1880s

39　Yolande Lyne Stephens, painted in Paris by Carolus Duran, spring
1888. She is wearing the rope of pearls that she gave to the church in
Cambridge later that year

40 Lyne Stephens mausoleum, Grove House, Roehampton. Stephens and
    Yolande are interred in a sarcophagus inside the building. Edward
    and Frances Claremont, and their son Harry, are buried outside, close
    to the steps leading up to the main entrance

23

The Richest Commoner

1845–1864

*"Stephens Lyne Stephens became, on his father's death, a millionaire but
no miser, spreading his money by thousands, literally so. He was one of the
noblest-minded and kindest of men."*
Mary Chudleigh, April 1860

*"There is always something melancholy in contemplating the building of a
house by one who has looked forward to dwelling therein, and to find him
cut off before his hope is realised."*
Country Life, November 1903

They returned from honeymoon to divide their time between
Portman Square and Lower Grove House in Roehampton,
which Stephens had occupied as a country residence the
previous year. Despite Yolande's hopes, their marriage had
shocked society and done nothing to improve her reputation.
It was acceptable (if improper) for a man to keep a mistress
with a sexual history; to marry her was social disaster. As one
of their neighbours explained, "Because Mrs Lyne Stephens's
character had not been spotless, it was natural that the
matrons of Roehampton refused to call upon her."[1]
Stephens's lifestyle changed after his marriage and, while
this was partly due to social ostracism, it was also because he
himself had changed. In his mid-forties, he had grown out of
his pleasure-loving youth and was mixing with more serious-
minded men such as Sir John Lubbock, son of the banker
who held the accounts of Lyne, Hathorn & Roberts.
Lubbock, a fellow student at Trinity College, Cambridge,
was an astronomer and mathematician. He was treasurer and
vice-president of the Royal Society and vice-chancellor of

271

London University, although he spent most of his time on his estate in Kent, a friend and neighbour to Charles Darwin.

Having ceased to entertain the fashionable set and preferring to live more quietly in Roehampton, Stephens gave up the Portman Square house in the spring of 1846.[2] He commissioned an architect to improve and enlarge Lower Grove House, and he and Yolande began to acquire an art collection. They were attentive to Charles, who lived just a short distance away, but they maintained a separate establishment and the old man was often alone. When Francis Lyne's wife visited Roehampton and was shown around Grove House by the butler, she saw the long dinner table laid with a single place setting. "Oh! what a melancholy sight," she said. "Ah, Madam, it *is*," the butler replied.[3]

Charles reached his eighty-fifth birthday in March 1849, and Stephens and Yolande moved into Grove House to keep him company. Two years later, at the invitation of Sir John Lubbock (one of the treasurers), Stephens travelled to London to spend several days at the Great Industrial Exhibition. Works of industry from all nations were displayed in the huge glass structure in Hyde Park and, at his father's suggestion, he made his way to the exhibit of crystal glassware from Marinha Grande. The quality of glassmaking had improved since John James's death and the display received an honourable mention from the official jury. "We congratulate the manufacturer of crystal at Marinha," wrote Georges Bontemps, the most eminent glass technician of the time, "for having the courage to send samples of his products to the centre of excellence for crystal. His designs are well executed, his glass well made. Only the colour lacks that extra quality desired by a well-trained eye."[4]

Although his father had been unwell for several months, Stephens felt no sense of danger when he left Roehampton for the Great Exhibition. But Charles's condition deteriorated during his absence and he died on 9 May, with only his butler, George Fisher, at his bedside.[5] A servant took the news to London and Stephens hurried home to pay his last respects to the father who had loved him, indulged him, and never criticised him, despite disapproving of his lifestyle. During the next few days, as he involved himself in funeral arrangements, grief mingled with guilt and remorse as he blamed himself for being absent when the old man had needed him most, when he should have been sitting by his father's side, comforting him on his final journey and saying his last farewell.

Charles had asked to be buried with his family and, although interments were no longer permitted in London churches, exceptions were made for those with private vaults. Stephens contacted the authorities and, on 15 May, the cortège made its way to Marylebone where Charles was interred beneath his old parish church, close to the bodies of his wife and four daughters.[6]

Meanwhile, his lawyer, Meaburn Tatham, had opened the will which Charles had written in his own handwriting nine years before. He had left £50,000 in trust for his grand-daughter, and bequeathed legacies and annuities to many members of the Lyne family. He had given mourning rings to seventeen of his closest friends and left a year's wages to his household servants, together with the sum of £1000 "to my old, faithful, and very excellent servant, George Fisher."[7]

Finally, he had left the residue of his estate, "to my very dear and much beloved and most excellent son, Stephens Lyne Stephens, who is my only son and the only child of mine now living." Having come to the conclusion that Stephens might never marry, he had added a proviso: "The property I leave to him will be his absolutely and he, of course, may do with it whatever he may think proper. But should he die unmarried, it is my wish and most earnest desire that he should leave the bulk of the property to his and my near relations, the Lynes, that is to say to such of them as he may think proper and in such proportions as he may think proper."

Charles had been generous with his fortune. According to one of his nieces, "he distributed his wealth by thousands

every year, to relatives, friends and depressed merchants,"
and after his death, Stephens matched him for benevolence.[8]
He helped many members of the Lyne family and gave large
sums to charity, including £3000 to the Crimean Army
Fund.[9] And responding to Yolande's growing devotion to the
church, he also gave to Catholic institutions.

"On looking over our annals and reports, we find many
notes referring to the goodness of this worthy gentleman,"
wrote the mother superior of a convent in Hammersmith.
"He gave £500 towards the building of Nazareth House and,
on many occasions when driving by, he would stop the
carriage and hand the sister who opened the door a five or ten
pound note for coal or something else needful for the aged
poor or orphan children, always with the injunction, 'Mind,
you are not to say anything of this to Mrs Lyne Stephens. She
has her charities, I have mine.' Twice or three times a week,
he would leave at the door bouquets of the choicest flowers
from the hot-house, with the request that they be put on the
altar for him. On one occasion, when two sisters were
returning from Roehampton laden with cans of milk, Mr
Lyne Stephens overtook them, stopped the carriage, and
insisted on the sisters getting in with their cans, much to their
discomfiture for the milk spilled over the carriage. Mr Lyne
Stephens possessed that rare quality which makes the giving
of charity so pleasing to those who give as well as those who
receive, he never had to be asked."[10]

During their early years in Roehampton, while Stephens
worshipped in the Anglican chapel near the gates of Grove
House, Yolande travelled further afield to attend mass. In
1850, when nuns from a French teaching order bought a
property on Roehampton Lane to found the Convent of the
Sacred Heart, Yolande made contact with the mother
superior. Stephens contributed £500 towards the construction of a chapel and, when the building was completed, she
attended services in the convent, sitting in a side chapel for
lay members of the congregation.[11]

Stephens and Yolande had settled into a marriage of companionship and genuine affection. He adored her beauty, elegance and wit; she appreciated his kindness, gentle nature and sense of humour. He made up for the time he had wasted at Cambridge, stocking his library with books on history, literature, music and art, and they travelled in Europe, attending sales of art collections and enriching Grove House with old master paintings and French antique furniture.[12]

His father's fortune having made him the richest commoner in England (with an annual income of £2.6 million in today's values),[13] Stephens set out to become a man of property. In the summer of 1851, he employed the architect William Burn to design extensive alterations to the back of Grove House, remodelling the elevation and adding a new wing and an Italian-style terrace.[14] Three years later, he made further improvements to the estate (including the building of a new lodge)[15] and to satisfy Yolande's desire to spend time in her home city, he purchased a house in Paris.

"One of the historic mansions of Rue du Faubourg St-Honoré has just been sold," wrote a Paris periodical in March 1857. "It conjures up memories of Comte Molé, minister of King Louis Philippe, but the new owner will be a celebrity of quite a different sort. She made her début as a dancer at the Opéra in 1831; she had an adorable figure, slim, supple and elegant, with magnificent eyes and perfect legs."[16] Stephens equipped the Hôtel Molé with servants, horses and carriages, and every year, he and Yolande spent the spring and early summer in Paris, enjoying the opulent lifestyle of the Second Empire. They mingled with Parisian society and attended the Opéra to watch the new generation of dancers, where Yolande, grown into respectable middle age, was heard to murmur "how shocking!" at the amount of leg displayed on stage.[17]

Meanwhile, Meaburn Tatham had told him of land in Norfolk which his legal firm was handling and which was due to be auctioned in the summer of 1856. The Lynford Hall estate consisted of 8000 acres, its mansion house surrounded by "a beautiful park, through which flows a branch of the River Wissey, intersecting the pleasure grounds and plantations and terminating in an expensive lake."[18] Stephens travelled to Norfolk to inspect the property, which was situated in an area of sandy soil planted with pine trees (similar to Marinha Grande, the source of so much of his fortune). He liked what he saw and, at midday on 2 July, he attended the auction and bought the estate for £133,500.[19]

The existing house at Lynford was not sufficiently grand for his purposes, so he planned to replace it with a larger, more opulent mansion. He re-employed William Burn and asked him to study Hatfield House before working on his plans, for he had passed this Jacobean mansion many times on his journeys to and from Melton Mowbray and been impressed by its domes and towers and magnificent windows.[20]

Burn had the largest country house practice in Britain and Lynford Hall was one of his biggest houses. The plans included a grand entrance hall and staircase, six large reception rooms and several smaller rooms for private use, together with a total of fifty bedrooms and dressing rooms. The house was to be plumbed with running water, lit by gas from a private gasworks, and ancillary accommodation included a servants' wing, extensive stable block and three entrance lodges.[21]

Building work started in 1857 and, the following year, Stephens was appointed sheriff of Norfolk. In celebration, he commissioned a full-sized portrait of himself, an unflattering likeness for he had become grossly overweight and was depicted with a wad of banknotes in his hand, a symbol of his status as England's richest commoner. He was in poor health when the portrait was painted; he had taken little exercise since giving up hunting, he smoked constantly, drank too much and enjoyed the rich food prepared by his French chef. By the time he was appointed sheriff, he was suffering the effects of prolonged high blood pressure. He felt sick and lethargic, his eyesight was poor and he had constant headaches.[22] His symptoms worsened in January 1860, but he had no sense of danger and was astonished when the doctor told him he had little time to live. "Are you not surprised?" he asked him. "No," replied the doctor, "but I am very sorry."[23]

Stephens died on 28 February, five months after his fifty-eighth birthday. In his will dated December 1851 and a codicil written eight years later, he bequeathed Grove House and his art collection to Yolande absolutely, and Lynford Hall to Yolande for her lifetime (after which it would fall into his residuary estate). Following his father's wishes, he had left the Lyne Stephens fortune in trust for his widow and, after her death, to the living descendants of his four Lyne uncles, most of whom had little or no money of their own. Yolande was sole executor and Stephens had appointed three trustees: two of his friends and contemporaries, Sir John Lubbock and Sir Richard Williams-Bulkeley, and a younger man, Lubbock's eldest son.[24]

News of the will spread through the Lyne family and, on 6 March, as the cortège made its way from Roehampton to Kensal Green cemetery, it was followed by many potential beneficiaries, including Francis Lyne who had visited John James in Lisbon almost forty years before, hoping to obtain some of the Stephens fortune for himself.[25] After the funeral, Yolande shut herself away and the servants watched her small figure dressed in black as she took solitary walks around the lake in the gardens. She was mourning her husband. She had chosen him for money and kindness but had grown to love him during fifteen years of marriage. Finding Roehampton too full of memories, she decided to travel to Paris as soon as the will was proved; she would go to the Hôtel Molé where she would be comforted by friends and relatives in the city.

Meaburn Tatham proved the will on 29 March and, a few days later, Yolande crossed the channel to France. Stephens had made no mention of the Paris property in his codicil, so she searched his papers in the Hôtel Molé and found a document dated May 1857: "I give and bequeath to Madame Lyne Stephens, my wife, my house and messuage situate at Paris, 85 Rue du Faubourg St-Honoré, together with the household furniture, horses and carriages found there at the time of my decease for her own absolute use and benefit."[26]

After her return to England, Yolande produced this paper which was, she informed the trustees, a valid will under French law, so the Hôtel Molé was hers absolutely and not part of Stephens's estate in which she only had a life interest. The trustees thought differently. They sought legal advice on the matter and were advised that, because Stephens was domiciled in England, his property in France should fall under his English will, in which case the mansion would be treated as part of his residuary estate.[27]

At the same time, they were daunted by the size and complexity of the administration. To relieve themselves of responsibility, they applied to have the will administered as a friendly suit in the court of chancery, the court renowned for its inefficiency, the court known to swallow up whole fortunes in legal charges. The plaintiffs were the three trustees, and the defendants named as Yolande and the "issue" of the four uncles (represented collectively by Francis Lyne and two of Richard Lyne's sons who lived in London).

The trustees approached the court in July 1860 with a bill of complaint filed by Meaburn Tatham. "The plaintiffs are advised," explained Tatham, "that they ought to convert the testator's residuary estate and invest the proceeds according to the trusts of his will and that, owing to its extent and magnitude, such conversion is attended with difficulty and risk. They therefore pray that the residuary real and personal estate may be administered by this court and that the rights of all parties therein may be ascertained and declared."[28]

Other issues brought up by the bill of complaint were the legal situation regarding the Hôtel Molé and the amount of interest and dividends that should be paid to Yolande.[29] Stephens's will was clear on this point (the income from his residuary estate was to be paid "into the hands of my dear wife, to the intent that such interest, dividends and annual produce may be for the sole and separate use of my wife, independent of any future husband"),[30] but the trustees asked the court to vary this provision. The widow, they wrote, "claims to be entitled to the income of the residuary estate from the day of the testator's death but the plaintiffs are advised that, having regard to the nature of such estate, she is not entitled to receive such large benefits and it is doubtful what amount of income she ought to receive."[31]

Several motives were involved in this attempt to pay Yolande less than her due, motives in which jealousy, bigotry and snobbery all played a part. Her command of English was poor and she found it difficult to communicate with the lawyers and trustees who were giving such little credence to her rights.[32] They felt it inappropriate that such a large fortune should have fallen into the hands of a former ballerina, a woman who was not only foreign but also a Catholic. They hoped the court would grant her an allowance and order the balance of the income to be reinvested, increasing the value of Stephens's estate during her lifetime and providing a larger pay-out to the English beneficiaries.

A few months later, the trustees tried to sell Lynford Hall (despite the fact that Stephens had left it to Yolande "for her own use and benefit" during her lifetime). Learning that Queen Victoria was looking for a country estate for the Prince of Wales who was approaching his twentieth birthday, they suggested that Lynford might be suitable for his purposes. The queen considered the offer but, in early 1862, she chose the larger Sandringham estate.[33] Only then did the trustees give permission for Yolande to take possession of the mansion which had been completed the previous year.

"There is always something melancholy," wrote *Country Life*, "in contemplating the building of a house by one who has looked forward to dwelling therein, and to find him cut off before his hope is realised."[34] Stephens had longed to occupy Lynford Hall. He had planned to host shooting parties for his friends and show off his great wealth but, in the autumn of 1862, Yolande moved alone into her new house where she felt even more isolated than she did in Roehampton. From the windows of the mansion, she looked out over the wide expanse of formal garden, beyond which lay the park, its glades and woods receding into the distance as far as the eye could see.

More than three years after her husband's estate was placed in chancery, the court met to consider the money which had been spent on completion of the house. Nineteen barristers attended the session in November 1863 when the judge ruled that all sums should be paid from the residuary estate, except the claim for furniture which Yolande should settle on her own account. Finally, in a decision typical of the court of chancery, the judge "directed a reference to chambers to inquire whether the pulling down of the old house at Lynford was for the benefit of the testator's estate and what had been done with the materials."[35] Although the value of these materials might (possibly) have added a tiny proportion to the value of Stephens's estate, this would have been more than offset by the cost of lawyers investigating the matter.

The trustees failed to reduce Yolande's income, for the court granted her sole benefit from the Lyne Stephens fortune. In her late-forties, she had retained her good looks: her slim figure, the fine bone structure of her face, her large grey eyes. Men still found her attractive and many longed to share the wealth in which she had a life interest. A year after her husband's death, it was rumoured that she was to marry the Duc de Richelieu (with whom Stephens had been acquainted for some years, Richelieu having hunted from time to time at Melton Mowbray).[36]

But Yolande turned down all offers of marriage and, as the months passed, she became concerned about her immortal soul. She worried about her years as a dancer, the years when she had shown more of her body than Victorian morality deemed proper, the years when she had slept with powerful men in exchange for influence and financial protection. Most of all, she remembered her miscarriage in 1835 and came to believe that her childless marriage was punishment from God for failing to protect her baby. She was aware, too, of the snobbery and religious intolerance of the period and, with no-one to advise or protect her, she retreated into the arms of the church.

She talked to her priest and the mother superior of the convent in Roehampton, and with their advice, resolved to remain a widow and dedicate herself to charitable works. In this way, she hoped to save her soul. And to commemorate the man who had rescued her from the stage, she decided to build a mausoleum in the grounds of Grove House. Stephens's body would be re-interred here in a sarcophagus large enough to hold two coffins. During her lifetime, she would visit the building and pray by his tomb; after her death, she and her husband would lie side-by-side for eternity.

She commissioned William Burn to design the mausoleum and the building was consecrated (in an Anglican ceremony) in August 1864.[37] Two weeks later, Stephens's body was disinterred from Kensal Green.[38] It was brought home to Roehampton and, as the clergy read prayers for the dead, the coffin was lowered into a white stone sarcophagus in the centre of the building, its four sides decorated with the Lyne Stephens coat of arms.

PART SIX

Yolande
The Years of Regret

Interlude

Australia

1861

At the time of Stephens's death, one of the beneficiaries of his fortune, Lewis Jedediah Lyne (youngest son of Joseph Lyne), was living at a goldmine in South Australia. He was not the only oddity amongst Joseph's children, many of whom were in some way peculiar, but Lewis Jedediah was the strangest of them all, partly because he was stone-deaf.

Born in Lisbon in 1806, he sailed for Australia as a young man and thereafter avoided all contact with his family.[1] He found employment in various merchant companies, but "was very obstinate and determined and would not work one minute (literally) after the clock struck the appointed hour."[2] By the mid-1850s, he was reduced to working as a stable-hand in the Burra mine at Kooringa. He became ill in 1860 and, for the first time in thirty years, wrote to Richard Benjamin, one of his brothers in England, who sent him £50, told him of the death of his wealthy cousin and explained that, under the terms of the will, he was entitled to a share in the Lyne Stephens fortune. Lying in the makeshift hospital at the mine, Lewis communicated with the medical officer and, after he died in January 1861, the doctor sent a letter to Richard Benjamin in London.[3]

Lewis had been unable to work for many months, he explained, "but when he came under my care, he was put on the benefit club and received fourteen shillings a week sick pay. When he became worse, I made enquiries as to his

285

comforts but he always replied that he required none. One could get nothing out of him. He associated with no-one. He could not fraternise with ignorant labouring men and he was not in a position (had he the desire which I question) to mix in society. He spent his evenings in the Mechanics' Institute reading and, I am happy to say, never spent any time in the public house, a too frequent occurrence here with men of education like him and in his circumstances. He was very deaf indeed and this may have had a great deal to do with his almost misanthropic disposition.

"I became interested in him and treated him as a friend. I felt so distressed at his miserable existence that I proposed he should enter the hospital here, but he was so proud that it was difficult to get him to consent. He died very quietly and was kept up for a long time before his dissolution by brandy alone. I must mention, to be faithful, that he believed in brandy and took more than was good for him.

"He left no will. He drew a sketch of a will which I sent to a lawyer to be properly drawn, but I could never get him to sign it. But I can tell you what his intentions were. He informed me that, on the death of a lady, a cousin of his named Mrs Lyne Stephens, he would become possessed of several thousand pounds and he wished it to be divided equally between his brothers and sister."

The doctor's letter took three months to reach Richard Benjamin in London. "The accounts you sent me about my brother Lewis are indeed *triste*," he wrote in reply. "Poor fellow! I have no doubt that early and continued disappointments in life had gradually weakened his mind and produced a morbid feeling which prevented him appealing to his family for help. The law will distribute the property as he would have wished, and I feel much obliged for your great kindness."[4]

24

A Lawyer's Will

1860–1890

"The lawyers must make more than they ought out of this will and the Lyne family must very largely suffer. Elaborate wills from a lawyer do sometimes more confuse than explain."
Francis Lyne, 1883

On 22 March 1860, a report titled "Unexpected Legacies, Plymouth" was published in *The Times*: "The gossips of this neighbourhood have been discussing the will of a rich Englishman who has recently died on the continent. More than a quarter of a century since, there was landed at Plymouth the body of a gentleman in a rough ship coffin covered most closely with tarred stuff. Deceased was a native of Cornwall who had made a princely fortune in Portugal and, when returning home in a sailing vessel, died on board. His will required that the two millions which he left should become the property of a poor nephew, provided he took his name, Lyne Stephens. These terms the nephew accepted and, for some unexpected reason, he quitted England and went to Italy where, like his uncle, he became prosperous in trade, dealing chiefly in wines. His fortune was doubled and, having died recently childless, the entire of his property, said to be four millions, falls (after the death of his wife) in equal proportions to the blood relations, most of whom are called Lyne, Glubb and Stephens. They reside chiefly in this vicinity and are in number about eighty; each receives at the present time £1000 and it is estimated that, hereafter, every one of them will obtain £50,000 in addition."[1]

This extraordinary report was taken up by a number of local newspapers,[2] prompting one of Richard Lyne's daughters, Mary Chudleigh, to write to the editor of the *Royal Cornwall Gazette*. "Having heard of the many absurd stories now circulating in different newspapers respecting the family of Stephens," she explained, "I beg the favour of you to insert, firstly, what I know to be true and, secondly, what I believe to be the origin of the mysterious stories which have spread about, as such marvellous tales are wont to do."[3]

Having told the story of the fortune (somewhat inaccurately), Mary referred to Stephens as "one of the noblest-minded and kindest of men." "He had no children," she explained, "but leaving his wife more than handsomely provided for, he willed, at her decease, the whole of his residuary property to the issue of his four uncles, thereby blessing about eighty claimants who will not fail to bless him for the largeness of his heart in this great outspread of benevolence, giving a joyous independence which may extend downwards through generations."[4]

Mary herself was a beneficiary, as were her two sons, but Stephens's motives were not as altruistic as she supposed. He had prepared his will seven months after his father's death, instructing Meaburn Tatham to draft a clause that followed Charles's expressed desire that his son should "leave the bulk of the property to his and my near relations, the Lynes." Tatham had worked for Charles and his son for many years but, whereas Charles had written his will in his own clear and unequivocal language, Stephens had relied on Tatham to draft it for him. And since he had no business or legal experience, he had simply signed the will that Tatham placed before him. This stated that his residuary estate, after the death of his widow, should be divided amongst "such issue" of his four uncles (Richard Lyne of Little Petherick and his three bankrupt brothers) "as shall be living at my decease, share and share alike."[5]

In February 1861, when the court of chancery ruled that those entitled to a share of the fortune should provide proof of their claims, Meaburn Tatham contacted the potential beneficiaries. "Amongst other enquiries which are to be made," he wrote, "the first is as to who were the issue at the time of the testator's death of the uncles named in his will. When the proper time arrives, I am directed to take in the claims of a great number of those who represent themselves as such issue, and I shall be glad to hear from you if it is your wish that I should carry in your claim also."[6]

This was a smart move, for the beneficiaries were compelled to employ lawyers to prove their claims and many of them did instruct him to act on their behalf. As Francis Lyne explained, "My cousin was not equal to his father in knowing the value of a word. The lawyer who made his will left out some words, which my cousin did not notice, hence it became what is called a lawyer's will and very materially frustrated the intention of my uncle and, of course, my cousin. The lawyer did much injury to the Lyne family and, not long after my cousin's death, he told me that he already had sixty of my relations as clients. The lawyers must make more than they ought out of this will and the Lyne family must very largely suffer."[7]

The problem was that Tatham had failed to define the word "issue." Stephens had intended it to mean the children and grandchildren of his four uncles but, because the word had not been defined, the court gave it the widest possible interpretation. Since every beneficiary had to prove his or her pedigree, it was not until 1863 that a definitive list was drawn up with eighty-nine names. Later that year, after several families had queried the term "living at my decease," the definition was enlarged to include infants still in the womb at the time of Stephens's death. This added another four (born between June and November 1860) and there were rumours of lawyers attending childbirth to certify the safe arrival of a beneficiary.

The person who did most to help Tatham prepare the claims was Richard Lyne's eldest son who supplied information for a family tree several yards long. "It was at Mr

Tatham's special request," he wrote to his brother in December 1863, "that I undertook to procure the necessary information as to births, marriages, deaths, christenings, etc. It not only occasioned me much trouble but also subjected me to much expense and, despite Mr Tatham's repeated request, I refused all remuneration."[8]

The beneficiaries on Tatham's pedigree were a diverse bunch, differing in age when Stephens died from a few-days-old foetus to an elderly widow in Liskeard. They varied from establishment figures (General Sir Frederick Glubb) to the eccentric (Joseph Leycester Lyne, the self-styled Father Ignatius who tried to re-establish monasticism in the Anglican church); from the misanthropic (Lewis Jedediah Lyne) to the charitable. They included clergymen, lawyers, stockbrokers and ship-owners, as well as farmers, poets and novelists, several of whom had moved to the colonies.

But the will split families, the difference of a few weeks in the presumed date of conception or a few hours in the time of death determining whether an individual became a beneficiary or was excluded from all interest in the estate. Many beneficiaries sold their reversionary interest, although shares sold in the 1860s, when Yolande was relatively young, achieved less than a third of their full value.[9] Francis Lyne was incensed. "As soon as the contents of the will were known," he wrote, "every son and every daughter throughout the Lyne family were set free of their parents' control, and thousands upon thousands of pounds have been lost to the family by the sale of reversions."[10]

Over the years, thirty-nine beneficiaries sold their interest in the will, occasionally to relatives but mostly to assurance companies. The first share was auctioned less than a year after Stephens's death. "The absolute reversion to one ninety-third part of the residue of the estate of the late Stephens Lyne Stephens Esq," announced an agent in December 1860, "receivable on the decease of a widow lady, now in her forty-eighth year. To be sold by auction at the Mart, Bartholomew Lane, on Thursday 3 January at twelve o'clock."[11]

Most of the beneficiaries who retained their interest died during Yolande's lifetime, their shares becoming part of their estates to be passed on to further beneficiaries. Lewis Jedediah was the first to die, and Meaburn Tatham distributed his share amongst his brothers and sister and advised on the matter of legacy duty. He recommended immediate payment. "The present value of a share may be roughly taken at £3000," he explained, "and the duty payable thereon, at three percent, would be £90 if paid now. The share when it falls into possession will be worth (say) £9000 and the duty payable, at three percent, would be £270, supposing it *not* to have been already paid. If the course I have suggested be adopted, there will be a saving of much trouble bye and bye, and of some expense. I am of the opinion that, in order to keep matters clear, the duty should be cleared whenever a share devolves by death on others."[12]

Each time a reversionary interest changed hands, lawyers were employed to draw up the documents. An example of this absurdity was the short life of Frances Nicholas, one of the beneficiaries still in the womb at the time of Stephens's death. The court accepted her claim on the grounds that she was born eight months and three weeks later, although she lived for less than a year. She died in August 1861 and her one ninety-third share in Stephens's will passed to her father as next of kin; and when he died two years later, it was bequeathed to his wife, herself a beneficiary, who then became entitled to two ninety-third shares.

It was not only beneficiaries who became involved in complicated genealogy; because the money was placed in chancery, fraudsters had taken up the matter and were persuading large numbers of people to make erroneous claims to the fortune. Normally, when estates were put into chancery, it was because the heirs could not be found. Lists of estates held by the court were published in the *London Gazette*, allowing fraudsters to circulate local newspapers with exaggerated reports of fortunes waiting for heirs to claim them. Most editors believed these stories to be true and published the details, whereupon the fraudsters advertised in the same newspapers, offering to claim the fortunes on a fee basis. Whole families were deceived in this way and lost large sums of money trying to prove their claims.

"No public office causes more heartbreak among the ignorant public, or raises more unfounded hopes, than this branch of the Supreme Court," said a member of parliament when the matter was raised in the House of Commons. "It is believed by many persons that the amount of unclaimed funds in chancery reaches something like £100 million. There exist, not only in London but also in the provinces, flourishing agencies which lay themselves out to deceive the public. One adventurer has been spending as much as £350 a week in advertisements, suggesting that people apply to him for information which will lead them to realise fortunes in reference to those funds."[13]

So while the genuine beneficiaries proved their claims, numerous families in Cornwall were being defrauded by the con-men, a situation that continued throughout the period the Lyne Stephens fortune remained in chancery, a total of forty-eight years. Families with the name of Stephens invented ancestors who had gone to Portugal and built glass factories; and even today, there are puzzled family historians whose pedigrees contain the names of Oliver and Jane Stephens and their five children, dropped fraudulently but hopefully into unconnected family trees.

In January 1862, a William Philp of Liskeard contacted a family in St German's. "As a Christian," he wrote, "I feel it my duty to inform you that there has been a meeting held at Liskeard concerning the money which was supposed the late Stephens Lyne, by some unlawful means, had defrauded the Stephens family of. Their family connections are now making their claims and, since your late husband's mother was called Nanny Stephens previous to her marriage, you will do the same by getting your husband's register and his mother's. From what I can hear, there is every probability that you will get the money and their counsel informs them that it will be settled in March."[14]

In February, he wrote again: "From making further enquiry into your business, I am informed that this gentleman who accumulated such amount of money was called Stephens and died at Lisbon some thirty years since, leaving Stephens Lyne a certain amount of his property and the sum of £700,000 to the nearest relation he had. Where this money has been during this time, I do not know but, at present, it is in chancery for the nearest in kin who will make claim for it. I have not the least doubt that you and your family connections are the nearest in kin to that Mr Stephens. I hope you will lose no time in making it known to your family, and also that the Lord will incline the heart of some gentleman to take up your case by putting it in some wonderful counsellor's hands on condition that you make amends for their trouble. I believe an influential gentleman would be a strong tower to you and delight at the idea of doing good to the poor."[15]

Philp suggested that an ancestor of the family, John Kellow, had been the second husband of Jane Stephens (daughter of Lewis Stephens, vicar of Menheniot) who married Charles Lyne's grandfather in 1720 and was widowed fourteen years later. He informed the family that, if they could find an entry in a marriage register for Jane Lyne and John Kellow, they would be sure to receive some of the Stephens fortune. He had obtained a copy of Jane's baptism from the Menheniot register (16 January 1694) and the baptism of a child he believed to be the daughter of Jane and John Kellow (27 July 1753), but failed to conclude that Jane was unlikely to have given birth at the age of fifty-nine.[16]

"All my spare time since I saw you last," he wrote in April, "has been taken up in making a diligent search concerning your affairs. They now find from the will that John James Stephens left his grandfather Lewis Stephens's descendants £30,000. Granny Tucker's mother must have been his aunt and therefore Granny Tucker and John James Stephens, the last brother that died at Lisbon, must have been first cousins. I trust that you will be able to work up Granny's claim and send it in before the fifteenth of this month as the chancery business will then again commence. Bless the Lord, there is hope for all of you now."[17]

Nine days later, he learnt that the family was becoming disheartened by the lack of progress. "I am sorry to find you are getting discouraged about the will," he wrote. "If I was my own master and could afford it, I would search all the churches that was necessary and send in your claims in a fortnight. A poor man by the name of Stephens, at a place called Burnt House about five miles from here, has sent in his claim. He came in through one of the vicar's sons who had a daughter called Jane Stephens after his mother. If so, this Jane Stephens, vicar's daughter of Menheniot, must have been a sister to him whose daughter you come in by."[18]

For almost fifty years, this poor and ill-educated family would live in hope that some of the Stephens fortune would be theirs. "My father died twenty-two years ago," wrote a Margaret Dymond to her cousin in 1887, "and I have been trying to find out the mystery ever since. What is the information you are in want of? I understand it is not much and that you have a lawyer working for you. What I know might be of service to some branches of the family, if they would only try to link the family and make a claim. There would be no mistake then, as information is in the court who the family is that the money belongs to. So if we could not find everything, the court might make up the deficiency and the right parties would have the money."[19]

William Philp still believed that proof lay in the marriage registers. "I have always understood that John Kellow married Jane Stephens," he wrote in March 1887, "and it appears very clear to me that, if you can get their marriage certificate, your claim is good. I have been given to understand that several thousand pounds were given or left to Jane Stephens by the grandfather, in addition to what was left by John James Stephens which is now in chancery."[20]

These letters relate to just one family, but the fraudsters persuaded most Cornish families with the name of Stephens to consider a claim on the fortune, money to which they were not entitled (even if they had been descended from Lewis Stephens of Menheniot, which none of them were). There had never been any doubt that the three wills in the case, those of John James, Charles and Stephens, were all valid and clear in their intentions.

25

Dolls' Eyes for Idols

1864–1890

"General Claremont made himself so indispensable to her that he obtained the management of her property and, with his wife and children, became permanent members of her family."
Mrs Smith of Mount Clare, Roehampton, 1912

"I can well imagine your happiness at being a mother. Many years of my life were passed in expectations, and as many in regrets, till I became resigned to the will of God."
Yolande Lyne Stephens to Katharine Claremont, May 1883

By the time her husband's body was interred in the mausoleum, Yolande had become a lonely and deeply pious widow. She never spoke of her years on the stage and was grateful to the few people prepared to offer genuine friendship. This had become a rare pleasure in England. The social ostracism resulting from her marriage had increased after Stephens's death, for those who had stayed on friendly terms with the richest commoner in England felt less inclined to maintain relations with his French Catholic widow. Meanwhile, the matrons of Roehampton continued to ignore her, and the gentry in Norfolk made no attempt to befriend the solitary woman who spent several months each year at Lynford Hall.

Yolande was ill-equipped to handle her financial affairs, or deal with the lawyers and trustees who were treating her with so little respect. When Sir John Lubbock died in 1865, his eldest son joined Sir Richard Williams-Bulkeley on the administration of the Lyne Stephens fortune. These men patronised Yolande, but matters improved in 1870 when

Horace Pym entered into partnership with Meaburn Tatham and took over the legal management. Pym was a young man with a gift for friendship and hard work. "Invited to a party in the evening," wrote one of his descendants, "he often appeared in the office next day, rubbing his hands, with a new job in his pocket. He was once reputed to have sprung up from a dinner table and hurried away without hesitation when word came that a client required his help."[1]

Yolande had no access to the capital in her husband's estate but, since the income on his wealth was more than she could possibly spend, the money in her own name began to accumulate and she soon amassed a fortune of her own. Dividing her time between her three houses, she spent the spring and early summer in the Hôtel Molé, the next few months in Grove House, and the winter in Lynford Hall. As she moved from one place to another, her household travelled with her (her Italian butler and French under-butler, her housekeeper, French chef and lady's maid, her footmen, housemaids, coachman and grooms).[2] When she crossed the channel, her carriage horses and pet poodles crossed the channel too, and she bought her dresses from Worth, the English couturier, at his premises in Rue de la Paix.[3]

She was accepted in Parisian society, and it was here she met the man who offered her the emotional support she missed so much after the death of her husband. Edward Claremont was military attaché at the British embassy in Rue du Faubourg St-Honoré, close to the Hôtel Molé. Six years younger than Yolande, he was the natural son of an English general and a French actress, and had spent his childhood in Paris before moving to live with his father in England. He was commissioned into the army and, as he rose through the ranks, he served in Canada and the Crimea before being attached to the diplomatic service. He and Yolande shared childhood memories of theatrical Paris, as well as an interest in art and antiques, and with his help, she expanded the art collection she had inherited from her husband. From auction rooms and sales of great European collections, she adorned her properties with old master paintings, French antique furniture, Sèvres porcelain, Gobelins tapestries, and Chinese dragons from the Summer Palace in Peking.[4]

Yolande's friendship with Claremont matured during the 1860s. He managed her affairs, took leave from the embassy to attend shooting parties at Lynford and, by the end of the decade, he and his family had moved into the Hôtel Molé. She accompanied him to banquets and balls and, in the spring of 1867, they enjoyed the Great Exhibition as the city filled with dignitaries from all corners of the globe. There were dances several nights a week and Yolande was a guest at the Tuileries when Louis-Napoleon entertained the crowned heads of Europe, as well as the Prince of Wales who had so nearly acquired Lynford Hall as his country estate.

Yolande enjoyed her sojourns in Second Empire Paris, but this glamorous lifestyle came to an end in July 1870 when (on little provocation) Louis-Napoleon declared war on Prussia. Claremont sent his wife and children to London, and encouraged Yolande to leave a city where mobs marched through the streets singing the *Marseillaise* and shouting *"Vive la guerre!"* She returned to Grove House where she shut herself away, not only because the matrons of Roehampton ignored her presence among them, but also because the French were unpopular in England for it was believed that Prussia had no chance of victory.

But the German army was in excellent fighting form and, after several victories, they marched on Paris where the mob took to the streets and the Second Empire was overthrown. The city was surrounded in late September. Most British diplomats had left the embassy, but Edward Claremont remained at his post and Yolande fretted for news of him, as well as for her family and friends. Some news did manage to filter through for, although Paris was cut off from the outside world, communications were despatched by hot-air balloons which flew over Prussian lines into the safety of unoccupied France.

By December, food was in short supply and Claremont felt that his knowledge and abilities would be of better use elsewhere. He rode out of the city under a neutral flag and arrived in London towards the end of the month.[5] Ten days later, he accepted an invitation from Yolande to visit Lynford Hall, where he could enjoy the shooting as well as ample dinners prepared by her French chef. He had little reassurance for her. "Members of the Red or Republican party are the only advocates for a serious resistance," he had written in a despatch from Paris, "and the government is obliged to yield to them for fear of having civil war raging in the streets. Altogether it is a most painful and unprecedented position, and I am afraid we shall have to witness dreadful scenes."[6]

On 19 January, he was instructed to join the British ambassador in Bordeaux, to act as observer in the French Army of the East (commanded by General Bourbaki). The instructions were sent to his London address and did not reach him in Norfolk until the beginning of February.[7] Bourbaki's army had been defeated by this time and Claremont's reply was brusque. "I hope you will excuse my not answering your despatch sooner," he wrote from Lynford Hall. "I suppose the fate which has befallen the army of General Bourbaki precludes the necessity of my complying with the instructions you conveyed to me, and I shall therefore await further orders."[8]

Claremont was disillusioned about his diplomatic appointment, not only because of conditions in Paris, but also because of the overthrow of the French emperor. He had been on friendly terms with Louis-Napoleon. He had accompanied him on his Italian campaign in 1859 and advised him on military strategy during the battles of Magenta and Solferino. Indeed, the emperor had liked Claremont so much that he wished to have no other British officer as military attaché at his court.[9] Now, with Louis-

Napoleon in exile and his friends in the French army soon to be conquered by the Prussians, Claremont had little desire to remain at his post in a defeated city – and one which he believed to be on the brink of civil war.

He spoke of these matters to Yolande, who suggested that he leave the embassy. If he resigned his appointment, he could act as her land agent, he and his family could accompany her as she moved houses between Lynford, Roehampton and Paris, and every winter he would have the pleasure of shooting pheasants in Norfolk.

When he rode out of Paris in December, Claremont left the embassy in the care of an English banker who (in his capacity as temporary consul) officiated at the marriage of one of Yolande's acquaintances, Richard Wallace, to the former *parfumerie* assistant with whom he had been living for more than thirty years.[10] Wallace was the natural son of the Marquis of Hertford and had recently inherited his father's fortune. He had spent most of his life in Paris, he was a collector of art and furniture, and was well-known to art lovers in the city. He had met Yolande through Claremont as the two men were friends; they attended sales of art collections and advised her on her purchases.[11] A generous man, Wallace provided ambulances and money during the siege, but he was unable to feed the people and, by early January, there was almost no food left in the city.

It was a cold winter. The river was frozen, gas supplies were exhausted, trees in the parks had been cut down and burnt, and there was little coal or wood remaining for warmth or for cooking the meagre amounts of food available. Crowds attacked the homes of the wealthy to obtain fuel, pulling down fences and trellises, and felling garden trees. To avoid an insurrection, the authorities agreed to an armistice at the end of January. Peace was signed a few weeks later but, when Claremont returned to the embassy, he wrote that "even good people are so exasperated by the way their affairs have been mismanaged that they trust and respect no-one."[12] In mid-March, the Reds took control of the city. A week later, they won a majority in municipal elections and, as the Commune of Paris installed itself in the Hôtel de Ville, Parisians gathered in their thousands, wearing red scarves and shouting "*Vive la Commune!*" while cannons were fired in salute and massed bands played the *Marseillaise*.

Claremont, meanwhile, had acted on Yolande's suggestion and resigned his appointment as military attaché. Doubts had been expressed in the House of Commons about his departure during the siege and, angry that his motives had been questioned, he gave notice on 16 March.[13] He remained in Paris and wrote to Yolande about conditions in Rue du Faubourg St-Honoré. The battle to reclaim the city was underway, the army was bombarding the centre, and shells were falling on the nearby Champs-Elysées. "This is not intended," explained the new military attaché, "but as most artillery men are prisoners in Germany, the gunners are very young and their fire is often wild."[14]

On 21 May, soldiers entered the city, the people of Paris were called to the barricades, and streets became a battlefield as Frenchman fought against Frenchman. The Reds set fire to buildings in the city centre, fires which – fanned by hot weather and strong winds – consumed entire streets. "The state of Paris is heartbreaking," wrote the British ambassador, "fires in all directions, the air oppressive with smoke and unpleasant odours, the incessant roar of cannon and musketry, and all kinds of strange sounds."[15] Soldiers were executing all the Reds they could find, as well as those suspected of harbouring them; and when there were no more barricades to defend, surviving Reds were lined up against walls and shot, their corpses burnt on funeral pyres or thrown into mass graves.

The carnage ended in early June. The government took control of the city and order returned to the streets. Yolande crossed the channel and, accompanied by Claremont, returned to the Hôtel Molé. The trellis and fences of her mansion were gone, the trees cut down and uprooted. The house had been looted during the Commune, its roof and masonry damaged in the battle to reclaim Paris. Her family and friends were tired and malnourished, and much of the city centre was in ruins. It was a sad homecoming.

There was one benefit from the events in Paris: Edward Claremont was free to take charge of Yolande's business affairs. As a neighbour in Roehampton explained, "he made himself so indispensable to her that he obtained the management of her property and, with his wife and children, became permanent members of her family." His friendship with Yolande was genuine but he also had his eye on her fortune for he was, in the neighbour's opinion, "not a man of good character and his unhappy wife, who was an excellent person, disliked and resented the dependent position bitterly. But she had to submit and we used to see her Sunday after Sunday in Roehampton church with her handsome daughters."[16]

Claremont advised Yolande to give up the Hôtel Molé (now ruled to be part of Stephens's estate) and helped her acquire a more manageable property, a large first floor apartment in the Champs-Elysées. In London, he accompanied her to meetings with the lawyers and trustees and, in October 1876, he was appointed trustee of the Lyne Stephens estate in place of Sir Richard Williams-Bulkeley who had died the previous summer.[17]

Yolande adored Claremont, although she was too pious to take him as a lover. He had saved her from loneliness and, in gratitude, she showered him with gifts and jewels. Together, they attended auctions of art and antiques, and during the winter months, held shooting parties at Lynford. Indeed, it was because of his love of shooting that the trustees refused all offers for Lynford Hall, including one from the Duke of Clarence, eldest son of the Prince of Wales.[18]

Social ostracism mattered less now the Claremonts lived with her and shared her life. There were celebrations to attend when their children were married and, in June 1882, their youngest son, Harry, took his wife on honeymoon to Yolande's flat in Paris. "The apartment is too lovely," the bride wrote to her mother. "The rooms are a dream, all opening out of each other, full of curios: china, pictures, and tapestry. My room is very pretty. The walls are covered with copper-coloured brocade and the furnishings are pale blue. General Claremont is going to take seats for the opera and theatres, and Mrs Lyne Stephens says she has lots of jewels for me to choose from."[19]

In the summer of 1872, an English nun arrived at the convent in Roehampton to take over the duties of mother superior. Mabel Digby was a convert to Catholicism and a woman of great moral purpose. She had spent many years in France; she was fluent in the language and, during the recent war, had converted her convent into a hospital for wounded soldiers.[20] Yolande called on the new mother superior and was impressed by the nun's achievements, as well as her religious convictions. The two women formed a friendship and Yolande often visited the convent during her months at Grove House.

Meanwhile, she was generous with her fortune. She subsidised her relatives in Paris, gave money to members of the Lyne family who approached her with tales of woe, and paid for an ornate fountain with drinking troughs to be installed in the centre of Roehampton.[21] She gave presents at Christmas to her servants and estate workers, and made donations to lay institutions, including £20,000 to the Middlesex Hospital.[22] She contributed to religious foundations in Paris, as well as the convent in Roehampton, but the main recipient of her generosity was the Catholic diocese of Northampton. This was the largest diocese in the country but contained the fewest Catholics, so it was continually short of funds at a time when many charitable institutions were being founded.

Her first endowment was to build a chapel on her estate in Norfolk. The nearest Catholic church was ten miles away in

Thetford and it was a comment from one of her guests that first put the idea into her mind. "Why don't you build a chapel here at Lynford," he asked, when returning one Sunday from church, "and save yourself the trouble of taking your staff and guests to Thetford?"[23] The chapel was completed in 1879 and a priest from Ireland, Michael Dwane, was employed to live in a nearby farmhouse, to act as Yolande's chaplain and say masses for her soul.

She paid for many new buildings in the diocese (including a bishop's residence in Northampton and a church in Wellingborough),[24] but her crowning gift was the Church of Our Lady and the English Martyrs in Cambridge, one of the largest Catholic churches in the country. While the small church of St Andrew had served Catholics in the town for forty years, the clergy were planning to build "a new and imposing church, more worthy of the old faith of Cambridge."[25] In 1879, a plot of land was purchased near Downing College and, four years later, Canon Christopher Scott was appointed to St Andrew's with instructions to raise money for the building. He was acquainted with Yolande (he had previously worked as vicar-general of the diocese) and he discussed the matter with her on one of his visits to Lynford Hall. It was a fruitful meeting for Yolande had already formed the idea of endowing a church but had little idea where it should be sited.[26] Scott suggested Cambridge and Yolande spent several months considering the matter. On one occasion, she asked him how much it would cost. "I remember my fright," he wrote some years later, "for I had not considered it."[27]

On 15 August 1884, Yolande made the journey from Roehampton to Cambridge. It was the Feast of the Assumption and she had brought a bouquet of flowers for the altar of St Andrew's. She prayed there for a while, then visited Scott in his rectory. "Will you allow poor me to build your church?" she asked him, with no trace of irony.[28] Soon architects were selected, builders appointed, and ecclesiastical artists employed to carve the sculptures and design the stained glass windows. Work began on the rectory in 1885 and, two years later, on 30 June 1887, Yolande was guest of honour when the Bishop of Northampton laid the foundation stone of the church.

Protestants were enraged at the size of the building. "Though a generation and more had passed since Catholic emancipation," wrote a friend of Scott's, "the penal laws were still remembered and some considered that a religion so recently outlawed should avoid making itself conspicuous. Yet the new church was the most outstanding landmark in the town. Hostility was thus aroused; shoals of letters, of bigotry unthinkable, were sent to the press and the great poplar tree at the corner was white with Protestant posters and leaflets."[29] Low-church evangelicals were particularly incensed. "Dolls' eyes for idols," they chanted, aware that the "eyedollatrous church" was funded by a fortune made in a glass factory. And soon this gave rise to rumours (still widespread today) that the indolent Stephens had made his money by the invention of moveable eyes for dolls.[30]

In the summer of 1888, Yolande fell seriously ill in Paris. Anxious about her immortal soul, she talked to her priest about her years in the Opéra and, as soon as she recovered her strength, she travelled to Cambridge.[31] There are rumours that she built the church in commemoration of children she failed to conceive with her husband, but the guilt carried deep in her heart was the child of the Marquis de La Valette, the child she lost in the winter of 1835. In an act of atonement, she called on Scott in his rectory. She unclasped the rope of rare pearls she had worn every day for many years (a necklace of great value) and gave it to the church.[32]

The following May, Scott laid the capstone on the spire and, as work began on the interior, Yolande insisted that she bear the entire cost of fixtures, fittings, ornaments and vestments. She met the architect on several occasions and sometimes demanded alterations, changing the design of the altar rails and the carving on the organ case. "She knew what she liked and what she disliked," wrote a parishioner. "Scott would ask about the cost of the alterations and she would hand him a cheque before she left."[33]

In the nineteen years since Edward Claremont resigned his position as military attaché, Yolande had insinuated herself into the heart of his family. She had drawn up her will in 1887, leaving her personal fortune to Edward and, after his death, to his youngest son, Harry, her favourite amongst his children. Flattered and indulged by all members of the family, she had become spoilt and imperious. The General, as he was known, spent all his time attending to her demands, his wife Frances having a subordinate position, even with her children. The Claremonts accompanied Yolande as she moved between her three homes and, in the summer months, they spent time in grand hotels in Monaco and the French Riviera.

Although Harry spent much of his time with his parents and Yolande referred to him as "the precious boy who is heir to so much," he had no illusions about her character.[34] In April 1889, when they were staying in Paris (the party including Yolande's chaplain, Michael Dwane), he became particularly exasperated. "Madame is perfectly detestable," he wrote to his wife, "and I rarely speak to her. It is the only way to keep peace, for she turns everything round and makes a row out of nothing. She is jealous of everyone, including Dwane, and cannot bear anyone being with the General but herself. She went for Dwane this afternoon and ranted at him like a lunatic."[35]

The following spring, they returned to Paris and Claremont's health (which had been poor for several years) began to deteriorate. Yolande ignored the change. "I have better news of the General," she wrote to Harry's wife in May, "The doctors find him improved and, if his appetite would increase, I think he would get stronger. I am under the same doctor for the painful ailment of eczema."[36] Frances Claremont was more realistic. "Mrs Lyne Stephens thinks more of her own health and not enough of other people's," she wrote a few days later. "I feel very angry with her sometimes, for she must see how weak and ill he is, and how unable to put up with it."[37]

As Claremont's health continued to decline, his children gathered in Yolande's apartment and Harry sent letters every day to his wife in London. "Madame turns to me in everything," he wrote on 6 July. "As she said last night, it will be an awful blow to her after thirty years of having every wish and whim fulfilled, every trouble and anxiety taken off her shoulders. She was quite dazed. I found her standing against the wall in her dressing room almost in a faint; she says she would give anything to be able to cry."[38]

Yolande became increasingly agitated during the next few days and Harry, grieving for his father, lost all compassion. "Madame has been despicable to everyone," he wrote, "and Dwane left the house on being called a liar. Every now and then, she works herself up and fires off. No-one pays any attention to her rantings, so she is forced to shut up. We all feel for her, but her grief is purely selfish, her one refrain being what will become of *me* and *my* affairs."[39]

Claremont died on 16 July and, three days later, his wife and children accompanied the body to England.[40] Yolande stayed in Paris, unwilling to cross the channel in such unhappy circumstances. "I followed you in my mind all day during that dreary and most miserable journey," she wrote to Harry. "Consolation is impossible. And no remedy. *Je me sens bien malheureuse!*"[41] The funeral service was held in the Anglican church in Roehampton and, although his widow would have preferred a different place of interment, Claremont's coffin was carried into the grounds of Grove House and buried within the precincts of the mausoleum.

After the funeral, Frances Claremont moved back to her house in London. Three months later, on 15 October, the family gathered together to attend the opening service of the church in Cambridge. "There was a lot to do," wrote one of Scott's helpers, "and accommodation had to be found for all the bishops and abbots and others who were invited to the opening. The bishops seemed quite unable to look up their local train service and, by the time we finally got them fixed up, I could have passed an exam in Bradshaw."[42]

"The great day at length arrived," he continued, "the doors were opened and the congregation flocked in. It was a most impressive ceremony, attended by almost all the Catholic bishops and several representatives of the monastic orders. And sitting all alone on the front bench (except for her maid) was a frail little figure in black. I made the collection in the nave and started with an empty plate to where Mrs Lyne Stephens was sitting. She seemed lost in contemplation, with bowed head, and the thought 'You have done so much and I won't disturb you,' crossed my mind. I was passing on when a small hand waved and I came back. She picked up her reticule, found a little purse and, after much peering therein, placed a coin on the plate. It was a shilling."[43]

Guests at the ceremony included the Duke of Norfolk, the Claremont family, and Yolande's lawyer, Horace Pym, and his wife, all of whom attended a banquet after the service. Yolande was too miserable to join them, so a toast was drunk to "the health of Mrs Lyne Stephens who is absent on account of her recent bereavement."[44]

26

The Bitter End

1890–1894

"I cry and sob enough to break my heart. The trial is too great, too awful for anyone to bear."
Yolande Lyne Stephens, December 1890

"Conversation is impossible, so is talk. Were I the most loquacious man in the world, the constant contradictions would dry me up."
Michael Dwane, April 1892

Yolande could not bring herself to spend the winter at Lynford; it was Claremont who had enjoyed the shooting there, he who had transformed the land into one of the finest sporting estates in the country. Lynford would remind her too painfully of the man she had lost, so she returned to Grove House and the comfort of her friendship with Mabel Digby.

Two months later, one of her neighbours was surprised to find her there. Mrs Smith had been living in Roehampton for some time but had never met Yolande. "Romance and mystery hung around Grove House," she wrote, "for although Mrs Lyne Stephens had lived there for many years, no-one visited her and hardly anyone had even seen her. It was in 1890 that I at last made her acquaintance. She allowed us to skate on her lake in her habitual absence in winter but, that year, I found she was living in the house and I called to apologise for unintentional trespassing.

"I found a most beautiful house and was received by a very tiny, very slight old lady, with large eyes and the saddest face I ever saw. She was very amiable and friendly, but received my apologies with tears as she was spending the winter at

309

Roehampton because of General Claremont's death. He had liked the shooting at Lynford but now he was gone, there was no-one to enjoy it. Her broken English and her French were hard to understand, but we got on well together and parted affectionately. I saw her several times more and, on cold winter days when I went to see the children skate, her sad little form in black was constantly to be seen, taking slow solitary walks in the garden."[1]

Yolande may have controlled herself with visitors but, in private, she was hysterical, howling in anguish in what her chaplain referred to as "that tearless cry which is so painful to witness."[2] Seventy-eight years old, she was unable to cope without the emotional support of Edward Claremont and, faced with a lonely old age, she transferred her affections (and her demands) to Harry who was seriously ill with tuberculosis. "All the days I have passed have been most anxious ones," she wrote when she had not heard from him for several weeks. "I have been wishing to have a few words from you, but nothing have come. How is it, if you could not come, a line would have calmed my anxiety? I have counted the hours but all is a blank. What shall I do, waiting, waiting all the time is cruel! I cannot give you an idea of my wish to know something about you. I am most anxious."[3]

Despite his illness, Harry took over the management of Yolande's estates and succeeded his father as trustee of her husband's fortune.[4] On doctor's orders, he spent the winters in Switzerland, but he and his family often visited Yolande during the rest of the year. His visits gave her much pleasure but the winter months were lonely without him. "I have no news to give you," she wrote in February 1891. "What I could tell you of my wretched life would make you very melancholy. Solitude is not a word to express what I endure. Picture to yourself a poor woman whose mind and body is lost in this big house, having to sit alone to every meal without another soul. I had no idea I could bear so much."[5]

"Mrs Lyne Stephens's last years were very miserable," explained Mrs Smith, "and she was much neglected by her servants, so neglected that her doctor threatened to expose their conduct if they did not behave better to her."[6] The servants had cause for their behaviour, for Yolande had become a bitter, self-absorbed and bad-tempered old woman. Her butler resigned in August 1891, after which her main victims were her chaplain and lady's maid. Michael Dwane was living in Roehampton (returning to Norfolk at weekends to say mass in the chapel at Lynford) and he was treated more as a servant than a man of the church. "How kind you were to have dear Dwane with you," Yolande wrote to Harry when he was visiting Lynford to deal with business matters, "and to give him a meal of potatoes and bread and butter."[7]

Dwane expressed his anger in letters to Harry, writing of Yolande's frequent outbursts of fury, her many acts of humiliation. "I might make many a long letter out of my own too-wounded feelings," he wrote in February 1892. "Perhaps the hardest thing is the charge that I am useless, wasting my time, unable to do anything. I'm told I'm no good, I do nothing for her. When this is said with anger and violence, as you know it can, it is hard to bear in the face of a fixed determination that I shall not be trusted to do the least thing."[8]

Yolande had also become miserly with small amounts of money. She queried Dwane's expenses on his third-class rail journeys to Norfolk and, when Christopher Scott came to Roehampton to discuss the final fittings for the church in Cambridge, he was shocked by the change in her personality. Sitting in the drawing room in Grove House, he talked about the work that remained unfinished, "but he simply ceased to go on when he was treated in a way to which we are accustomed but he is not. People know little of Madame if they think they can *force* money out of her."[9]

Yolande failed to understand that the Claremont family was no longer at her beck and call. Harry was often abroad and his mother (who had spent twenty years of her life accompanying Yolande between her three houses) was irritated by the "very cross and tiresome" woman who still demanded so much of her time. Yolande visited her in London at least twice a week, driving in an open carriage from Roehampton even in the coldest weather. "I pity poor Dwane," Frances wrote to Harry. "He says from the time he comes down in the morning until ten at night when she goes to bed, she hardly lets him out of her sight and finding fault with him all the time."[10]

Although the family went through the motions with Yolande, none of them had any affection for her. They chided her for not writing more often but her letters contained little information. "I am pretty ashamed of myself," she wrote to Harry in November 1891, "to be in your debt of letters to such an extent. I can hardly tell you how it has happened, but this is a plain fact and nothing of what I can say will make it less bad. You are quite right saying that a few lines would be sufficient occasionally, but it is not so easy to give up bad habits. I ought to exert myself in getting as I should like to be but I cannot do it. People who have not seen me for some time say I look well. I think it may be to please me a bit, but why would they say that if it was out of humbug only? Of course, I am happy to hear it."[11]

"It is very true that I should write oftener and a little at a time to you," she wrote two months later, "so you should know what I am about. My saying that I have no time to write much is perfectly true, but if it is merely to let you hear what, besides business, I am able to do, well and good. My mornings are spent in a little letter writing, mixed with doing little jobs about my rooms. The short days in winter make the work very difficult, but one can have plenty of little talks and the time passes."[12]

The early months of 1892 were bitterly cold, affecting Yolande's feet which had been damaged during her years on the stage and were crippled with arthritis.[13] The pain increased her temper and irrationality, and Michael Dwane had a difficult time when she found Edward Claremont's jewel cases in one of her table drawers. In his will, Claremont had left Yolande "all the jewels and trinkets she has given me and which she is to point out, and select also the plain gold ring which I always wear."[14] The cases had been brought to Grove House for her to make the selection, but she was so overwrought that they were wrapped in paper and put away.

"I have had such a trying afternoon," Dwane wrote to Harry. "Madame was routing in the drawer of her table and found a packet at the back. She took it out impatiently and asked me to open it, saying it was doubtless papers. There were two cases and I divined at once what they were; one was the General's jewel case, the other contained his various watches. Such a scene I hope never to witness again. Madame was completely unnerved; she collapsed and began that tearless cry. Her reading of the situation, which I was quite unable to change, is that your father himself put them there, in a place which no-one had access but herself. It was so like him, she cried, so like his thoughtfulness for her in everything. And now she is alone, desolate and dreary, etc, etc."[15]

Yolande assumed that all the jewels were hers, without a thought for Claremont's wife and children. "I have suggested to Madame," Dwane continued, "that she gets you all together and either lets you choose or makes a distribution, but I am unlikely to prevail. No doubt she will tell Pym, who could disillusion her and restore the jewels to your family, although he declined to suggest such a thing last year when asked to do so."

Five days after finding these cases, Yolande sent another letter to Harry. "I know well that I do not deserve praise for my *épistolaire* work," she wrote. "I am always backward for answering letters, not that I absolutely wish to be lazy and doing nothing. Oh no, I am sometimes very angry with me, but I have not the energy to live as I used to do and I have so little to say. I do not find the least thing that would have an interest for any of you."[16]

When Yolande moved to Norfolk a few weeks later, Frances Claremont no longer had to endure her company; she suffered from liver failure and had been exhausted by the constant visits from Roehampton. Her condition deteriorated in June and Harry wrote to Lynford with news that his mother was dying. "I pray for her, it is all I can do," Yolande replied. "I want to be with you but cannot take any decision about returning to Grove House. I am always very fidgety when there is a question of moving."[17] While her companion of twenty years lay on her deathbed, Yolande fretted about the journey to Roehampton. "She wants to go and I feel sure she will go," wrote Dwane, "only she will not fix a day. She is upsetting herself and others very much owing to her nervousness about the details and *expense* of the move."[18]

She finally made the journey on 30 June and, five weeks later, the body of Frances Claremont was brought to the mausoleum to be buried alongside her husband. Yolande showed no grief as the family gathered in Grove House; she was happy to spend time with Harry and his children ("I wish I could have the dear children in my pocket," she wrote to him one winter, "to take them out for recreation and play with them till I am tired to have been pulled about").[19]

Two months later, she asked Horace Pym to draw up a codicil to her will. Yolande was grateful to Pym for his friendship over the years, especially after Claremont's death when his visits helped alleviate her loneliness. He had built a house in Kent, borrowing extensively to fund the building, and in the codicil signed on 6 October, Yolande left him a legacy of £10,000, "as a mark of my gratitude for all he has done for me during many past years of friendship, with the desire that he will use the legacy to reduce any incumbrances upon his Kent estate." The following year, she signed another codicil, leaving the fortunate lawyer her entire residuary estate in France, including her property in the Champs-Elysées.[20]

Yolande had appointed three executors: Horace Pym, Harry Claremont and Sir John Lubbock (who had been a trustee of the Lyne Stephens fortune for over thirty years). Her relationship with Lubbock had not been a happy one, but she was pleased when he brought his five-year-old son to see her in the spring of 1893. When Horace Pym next came to Roehampton, she dictated another codicil: "To Harold Lubbock, son of Sir John Lubbock, as a mark of gratitude for all his father and grandfather have done for me, the sum of £5000."[21]

She returned to Norfolk a few months later. She was suffering from heart disease and wished to die at Lynford so a requiem mass could be sung in her church in Cambridge. Horace Pym came to see her when she had settled in, making one of his regular visits to discuss legal matters. "I came here by very fast train," he wrote to his daughter, "and as I drove through the park, there were hundreds of pheasants running about and their kind old nurses, the hens under whose wings they had been hatched, were looking with surprise at their bright colours and flighty ways."[22]

Yolande's feet caused her pain during the winter and, when spring came, her heart condition confined her to the house. Apart from Horace Pym, who travelled to Lynford at least once a month, her chaplain and lady's maid were her only companions. On 5 July 1894, she put pen to paper for the last time. "I am surprised to start this letter," she wrote to Harry (in weak handwriting and in French), "as I have not written any letters since I have been here. It is such a long time since I picked up my pen that I am almost incapable of writing. I know you are easy to please and you will be happy that the first letter I have written for an infinite time is for you. In the past, I used to write without difficulty. Now slowness makes it hard for me, although it feels as if I am speaking to you. That gives me pleasure. I wish to tell you that I have become so immobile that I prefer not to go out. I am happy to embrace you because I love you. My hand wants to repeat this – I embrace you because I love you. When are you coming to see me?"[23]

A few days later, Christopher Scott came to Lynford to assure Yolande that special prayers would be read for her soul on 15 August, the Feast of the Assumption and tenth anniversary of her offer to pay for the church. That morning, while the promised prayers were intoned in Cambridge, Yolande collapsed in her bedroom and remained unconscious for several hours. The doctor offered little hope of recovery but she improved a little after Harry arrived on the train from London. "Madame is better today," he wrote to his wife on 19 August. "Her pulse is stronger and she is taking nourishment. She is having chicken broth, calf's foot jelly with brandy in it, and champagne. All this naturally, besides two injections of six ounces of beef tea. It is marvellous how she has rallied. She kicked up a row last night when her sheets were changed – quite like old times – and astonished the nurses by her strength."[24]

This burst of energy was short-lived. "She lies all day in a sort of stupor you can't call sleep," wrote Harry three days later. Sometimes she was conscious, holding Harry's hand; sometimes she slept, her breathing forced and slow.[25] Christopher Scott came to administer the last rites and, when the ritual was over, he rose from his knees and stood at the window. "From her room," he remembered, "I looked abroad upon the view without: the spacious gardens beyond the terrace with their winding well-kept walks, flowers of every hue, the marble statues, the flowing waters beyond, the long stretches of stately trees. The sun was shining and the notes of a dove the only sound which broke the stillness. But there was another sound, the laboured breathing of her to whom all that fair scene belonged."[26]

Yolande died on 2 September, her final moments shared with Harry and Michael Dwane who were praying by the bedside. Four days later, her body was taken to Cambridge where her church had been arrayed in mourning, the altar steps covered in purple cloth, the pulpit draped in black. The choir sang a funeral dirge as the coffin was placed before the altar, nuns kept watch during the night and, the following morning, a requiem mass was conducted by Scott in the presence of the bishop. And the choir of Brompton Oratory had travelled from London to sing at the mass (as they had done four years earlier for the opening of the church).[27]

"The departed benefactress whose remains lie before the altar," Scott told the congregation, "has claims upon us why she should be remembered. We have towards her a debt of gratitude for deeds on account of which she will not, we trust, be forgotten by God into whose presence she has been called. Greatly indeed was she indebted to God. Richly had she been endowed with gifts of every kind – of natural character, of special intelligence, of winning attractiveness – which compelled homage from all who came under the charm of her influence. The result was widespread renown and unbounded wealth, the possession of which too easily obtain from us an idolatrous devotion which excludes God from our hearts.

"Therefore it was that the blessing of God came in another form, by the discipline of suffering and trial. There was the trial of loneliness. Bereft of the husband whose affection we may judge by the way he laid all he possessed at her feet; French and Catholic, living amongst those who were not of her faith or nation; deprived of the surroundings of Catholic sympathy, she was thrown entirely upon herself in all that is of deepest concern. These were her crosses, destined as a corrective to the fascination of wealth, which led her to become the benefactress of our large and poverty-stricken diocese."[28]

After the service, the coffin was taken to Roehampton and, for twenty-four hours, it lay in the drawing-room of Grove House, watched over by nuns. The room was filled with flowers, mostly from the clergy of churches she had funded but also from members of the Claremont family. And there was a wreath from the widowed Lady Wallace (the French *parfumerie* assistant who married Yolande's acquaintance in Paris), a wreath from one Frenchwoman to another, both of them risen from poor backgrounds to marry Englishmen of great wealth.[29]

At noon on 8 September, a number of people gathered in Grove House: the Claremont and Pym families, Christopher Scott, Michael Dwane, two Catholic bishops, and the chaplain of the convent in Roehampton.[30] "We went to see her funeral leave the house," wrote Mrs Smith, "and while waiting were begged to go into Grove House. There were nuns kneeling by the little coffin, such a very little coffin, which lay in front of a temporary altar. Then the procession formed and, headed by the bishops, the coffin was carried across the garden. The chief mourner was General Claremont's youngest son, but he seemed too feeble to follow the funeral and sank into a chair as it left the house. There were the Claremont daughters as mourners but I saw no sign of grief, nor any tears except in the eyes of the French lady's maid who had recognised us as neighbours."[31]

The procession crossed the terrace at the back of the house, then moved through the rose garden to the mausoleum. The iron rings in the top slab of the sarcophagus were lifted, and Yolande's tiny coffin was lowered into the tomb to join the large one which held the remains of her husband.

27

Distribution

1894–1908

"To those whose memories carry them back some thirty or forty years, the announcement that the great fortune belonging to the late Mr Lyne Stephens is now to be dispersed among his heirs must revive many interesting recollections."
Cornish Times, September 1894

"To leave behind me in this sinful and wicked world so many children and grandchildren has long been a source of fear to me, lest some of them should turn after the world and not after God, after the destroyer and not their maker."
Richard Lyne, July 1831

Two weeks later, a Catholic newspaper published a mean-spirited tribute to the woman who had given so much to the church. "The operatic boards are not the exact spot to spend an apprenticeship to the great aims of existence," it read, "but when one is naturally good and desirous of obeying the commands of the church, one can work out salvation anyway."[1] The *Pall Mall Gazette* was more prosaic, referring to Yolande as "the wealthiest lady in England."[2] Her personal estate was valued at £700,000 and Stephens's residuary estate at an additional £1 million, a total of over £100 million in today's values.

She had made several bequests to charity and been generous to Horace Pym, but it was the Claremont family who received most of her fortune. There were legacies of £108,000 to Edward Claremont's six children (compared with just £7000 to the Lyne family), and Harry inherited Grove House and her entire residuary estate in England, a

319

fortune worth £425,000.³ Her will required that "any person entitled to the Roehampton estate shall take the surname and arms of Lyne Stephens" and, just as Charles Lyne had added the name Stephens after inheriting John James's fortune, so Harry Claremont changed his name in October 1894.⁴ His health had deteriorated over the previous two years and, after he proved the will, he travelled to Monte Carlo where he died on 30 December. He was forty-five years old and had outlived Yolande by less than four months.

His body was brought home to Roehampton and buried in the precincts of the mausoleum, close to the graves of his parents. "A few months after the funeral of Mrs Lyne Stephens," wrote Mrs Smith, "I was walking in Roehampton Lane when I saw a funeral procession moving towards the entrance lodge of Grove House. I enquired whose funeral it was and was told it was Mrs Lyne Stephens's heir, Mr Claremont, and I remembered how feeble and ill he had looked when chief mourner at the ceremony in September."⁵

Yolande had left her wealth in trust to Harry Claremont for his lifetime and then to his only son, Stephen. At the time of Harry's death, his son was six years old and it was he who inherited the fortune, although he would not have use of it until he reached the age of twenty-one. In the meantime, the estate was administered by Yolande's trustees, Sir John Lubbock and Horace Pym.

In her will written in 1887, Yolande bequeathed her most valuable paintings to the National Gallery and her best pieces of china, furniture and *objets d'art* to the Department of Science & Art (now the Victoria & Albert Museum). Six weeks before her death, prompted by the Finance Bill which increased the rate of death duties on large estates, she signed a codicil revoking these bequests.⁶ As a result, they fell into her residuary estate and, after the death of Harry Claremont, into the hands of her trustees who decided to sell them at auction, together with the contents of her three houses.

"The dispersal of her effects," wrote the *Pall Mall Gazette*, "which will take place at Christie's, will attract as much attention as the famous Hamilton sale a few years ago. They include historic tapestries, enamels, furniture, and china, especially Sèvres."[7] The auction in May 1895 lasted nine days and realised almost £8 million in today's values.[8] A whole day was devoted to pictures (including seventy old masters as well as paintings of horses from Melton Mowbray), and another day was allocated to the sale of silver items and jewellery.[9]

In her will, Yolande hoped that the Roehampton estate would never be sold, remaining in the family down the generations. Harry's widow lived in Grove House for sixteen years but, when her son reached the age of twenty-one, he sold the property to an American merchant.[10] Stephen was wounded in the First World War (during the third battle of Ypres)[11] and, after demobilisation in 1919, he took to drinking and gambling. He became a playboy, living the high life, buying a yacht and a fleet of expensive motor-cars, and squandering most of Yolande's fortune. When he killed himself in a car crash at the age of thirty-five, driving too fast down the country lanes of Dorset, what little remained of his inheritance passed to one of his married sisters.[12]

Meanwhile, the court of chancery had begun the slow process of winding up the Lyne Stephens estate. "To those whose memories carry them back some thirty or forty years," wrote the *Cornish Times* in September 1894, "the announcement that the great fortune belonging to the late Mr Lyne Stephens is now to be dispersed among his heirs must revive many interesting recollections. How the colossal fortune was accumulated by Mr Lyne Stephens's father when a merchant at Lisbon is an interesting story. Suffice it to say that a number of representatives of the Lyne family of Cornwall will now benefit under the will."[13]

The first action taken by the court was to authorise the sale of Lynford Hall; and while details of the auction were being prepared, a dispute arose over the garden ornaments. Did they belong to Stephens's ninety-three beneficiaries or to

Harry Claremont's infant son? The matter was referred to the court of chancery which, over thirty years earlier, had sanctioned the use of Stephens's capital to fund completion of the mansion, although Yolande herself had bought the statues and vases in the formal gardens. Now, after some deliberation, the judge ruled that the ornaments belonged to Stephens's estate (on the questionable grounds that Yolande had bought them to complete the gardens as designed by her husband).[14]

The court also had to divide the financial assets into ninety-three parts, although the wheels of chancery still turned exceedingly slowly and beneficiaries would have to wait another fourteen years before they received their full entitlement. Meanwhile, the poor families in Cornwall who believed they had claim to the money were stirred into action. Attics and cellars were scoured for papers and, for over a decade, they employed people to inspect parish registers and feed their hopes.

In October 1905, a man named Varcoe was pursuing the matter. "You will be surprised to hear from me," he wrote to his brother and sister, "but it is in reference to the case of between two and three millions of money in chancery left by a Mr Stephens who amassed it at Lisbon. Perhaps you remember the stir that has been made many times in the case? Well, I received a note from a gentleman a short time since, requesting me to call upon him. I did so, and he informed me that they have made great discoveries and there is to be a meeting of all the kindred on Wednesday next. I know you have father's certificates from registers proving our identity and relationship and, if you will let me have copies of them, I shall be glad, or any information you can supply me which will throw light on the mystery. They all seem confident they can prove themselves of the stock; so must we."[15]

A few days later, Varcoe reported on the meeting at which the families were told they had a valid claim to the money provided they could prove descent from Lewis Stephens, vicar of Menheniot. "They seemed confident all will be right in course of time," he wrote. "Two solicitors are engaged who won a case not long since. John James Stephens's will is proved to be a forgery. He died without making one."[16]

Even William Philp of Liskeard had not given up, still trying to convince a family that nothing but an entry in a marriage register prevented them from claiming the fortune. "As regards your being descended from the Lisbon Stephenses, doubtless is true," he wrote in September 1906. "In my mind, there is not the shadow of doubt, and all the registers and certificates that have been found make you the right and lawful claimants to the paternal grandfather of John James Stephens that died in Lisbon, save the marriage certificate of John Kellow to Jane Stephens. If you can find that one, your claim is at once lawful. Jane being baptised at Menheniot is true, but John Kellow and she might not have been married there. Advertising for the certificate, I think, would be useless; a diligent search would be better. Perhaps they were married in Exeter."[17]

It was not only honest families who were trying to claim the money. Less than four months after Yolande's death, the legal firm of Tathams & Pym wrote to one of the beneficiaries, an elderly man with one brother and two unmarried sisters. "A Mrs Beuce," explained the letter, "claims to be a sister of Charles Lyne of Bournemouth and therefore she would be a sister of your own. She also claims, as such sister, to be entitled to a share of the Lyne Stephens estate. Will you kindly tell us if you have ever heard of Mrs Beuce? You can understand what an enormous amount of trouble we are having with persons presuming they are claimants to this estate, and whose claims we must at once put an end to in order to prevent those who really are entitled being put to trouble and expense."[18]

Another possible beneficiary (and almost certainly a genuine one) was the illegitimate daughter of one of Joseph Lyne's sons, conceived in 1836 when he was a young merchant in Argentina. Richard Benjamin Lyne moved to Brazil less than two years after his daughter was born, but he corresponded with her throughout his life and often sent her money.[19] His family first learnt of her existence when the unmarried Richard Benjamin died in June 1899, aged ninety-six. In his will, he left an annuity to his "daughter, Carolina Lyne, born in January 1837 and now residing with her half-brother, Carlos Durand, in Buenos Aires."[20] It came as a shock to his executors (both of whom were husbands of beneficiaries) when the will was read by Tathams & Pym, together with a letter confirming that Carolina was his natural daughter. Now there might be ninety-four benefici-aries, instead of ninety-three.

Two weeks later, one of the executors, Paul Ewens, wrote to a friend in Argentina asking for further information.[21] "I have the pleasure of informing you," the friend replied from Buenos Aires, "that through the *Officia de Investigations* (Secret Police), I discovered that Carolina Lyne is still alive. One of the employees saw Dr Carlos Durand and inquired about the lady. The doctor told him that she was enjoying good health and lived near his house, but refused to give her address and said that, if anyone wanted to know about her, he should communicate directly with him. The doctor was not aware that he was speaking with a member of the Secret Police as he was disguised as a porter."[22]

The executors hoped this woman could be proved an imposter, conspiring with Carlos Durand to claim the annuity. Ignoring the difficulties faced by children born out of wedlock (Carolina had been passing herself as Durand's full-sister), they demanded that she prove her identity and, when she failed to provide evidence of her baptism, Ewens sent her a strongly-worded letter. She was, he wrote, "unable or unwilling to produce one witness, in addition to your brother, to sign the necessary documents. On the face of it, and till I am further advised, there would seem to be some mystery connected with the matter which I am unable to fathom. I shall await a proper interval after this letter but, in the event of not receiving a satisfactory reply, we shall take such steps as our solicitor shall advise."[23]

At this point, the assurance company arranging the annuity took up the matter, employing a private investigator in Buenos Aires. "Mr Carlos Durand, retired medical doctor, lives retired from all society and is little known," reported the investigator. "As to his character, he seems strange, rough and not very scrupulous. Ever since their childhood, he and his sister have lived together and she is known as Carolina Durand." In a second meeting, the doctor told a different story. "Although, in our previous conversation, he had spoken of Miss Carolina Lyne as his sister," the investigator continued, "he now declared that the Miss Carolina who lived in his house was his sister, while Miss Carolina Lyne was a different person altogether."[24]

This was enough for the assurance company to turn down the annuity, so Ewens asked another acquaintance in Buenos Aires, George Watts, to carry out further enquiries. Watts visited Durand in his house and his initial impression was favourable. "I had half an hour with Dr Durand," he wrote in January 1903, "and my conversation with the old gentleman was entirely on plants. He only speaks Spanish but I got on well with him. If you are prepared to go to some expense, I have little doubt that something can be ferreted out through undertakers, banks, municipal registers, etc."[25] Five months later, Watts had changed his mind. "From all I can gather," he wrote to Ewens, "Dr Durand is a deeply-dyed blackguard. If the woman living with him is Carolina Lyne, she is quite under his thumb. A good deal of patience is required, as no doubt Durand is on the alert. I have thought of seeing the chief of police on the subject, but great caution is necessary."[26]

Watts enclosed some notes written in Spanish which Ewens had translated. These explained that Durand had been separated from his wife for several months and inferred that he was "having marital relations with a woman whom he formerly passed as his sister."[27] This shocked the executors in England (upright members of Edwardian society) and provided them with further evidence that Carolina was an imposter. "It is likely," wrote Ewens, "that one of the reasons for Durand's separation from his wife was his relationship with the woman now living with him called Carolina. It is hardly conceivable that she can be his half-sister."[28]

For the next three years, letters were sent to and from Buenos Aires. Investigators were employed to peruse parish records, legal documents and Durand's divorce papers, while the executors wrote to the chief of police offering payment for proof of Carolina's identity. By 1905, Durand had died and Ewens was trying to obtain a copy of his will. "The consul is obtaining a copy bit by bit," wrote George Watts, "as the will is guarded and can only be got at surreptitiously. An illegitimate son has now cropped up. The case is interesting but for the time it occupies."[29]

In October 1906, when the executors learnt that Carolina Durand had died three years earlier, they prepared a deed stating that capital for the annuity would be retained in London and, if no claim was received from Argentina within the next seven years, the money would revert to the estate.[30] The deed referred only to the annuity, but the executors were more concerned about Carolina's status as a possible beneficiary of the Lyne Stephens fortune. Her heirs were three adopted daughters who would, if her identity was proved, be eligible to receive a ninety-fourth share of Stephens's residuary estate.

At no time during their correspondence had Ewens informed Carolina of her interest in the Lyne Stephens fortune but, even if her adopted daughters had been aware of the situation, they would have had little time to make a claim. In May 1906, a summons was issued by the legal firm of Robbins, Billing & Co. This requested the surviving trustee, Sir John Lubbock (now Lord Avebury), to produce a full set of accounts so that taxes and legal costs could be paid from the funds in chancery, after which the fortune could be divided into ninety-three parts and distributed to the beneficiaries, their heirs, or the assurance companies which had bought the reversions.[31]

The final distribution was made two years later. "On enquiry at the Pay Office," explained a lawyer in April 1908, "I am informed that the cheques have not yet been prepared as they are waiting for division of the fund from Messrs Robbins, Billing & Co, who have the carriage of the order. I have seen Messrs Robbins who promised to lodge the statement without delay."[32] Eight weeks later, the matter was finalised. As Tathams & Pym wrote to Paul Ewens on 25 May, "We have received out of court a further part of the one ninety-third share of Lewis Jedediah Lyne, deceased, being a final division of Stephens Lyne Stephens's estate."[33]

Although legal fees and court costs had depleted the fortune during the forty-eight years since Stephens's death, each share was still worth over £500,000 in today's values. Most of the beneficiaries who retained their interest in the estate had died, bequeathing their shares to their relatives, and in Liverpool one lucky man received (in addition to his own share) the shares of five of his deceased siblings.[34]

Two-thirds of the beneficiaries were descendants of Richard Lyne (seven of whose ten children had produced large families of their own), a situation that would have saddened the rector of Little Petherick. Richard was concerned about the moral welfare of his family and, after his brother inherited the Stephens fortune, he prepared a note which he left amongst his papers. "I adjure all my children," he wrote, "and all my children's children for ever, and every one of them to the last generation, very seriously to consider what an aggravated sacrilege theirs must be if they fall in with the injurious fashions of this infatuated age, stealing away their souls by despising God in their love of polluting pleasures, money, and the praise of men. To leave behind me in this sinful and wicked world so many children and grandchildren has long been a source of fear to me, lest some of them should turn after the world and not after God, after the destroyer and not their maker."[35]

A hundred and thirty years before the final distribution of the fortune, on a cold winter's day in his father's study, the young Richard Lyne had chosen to be a poor clergyman instead of a rich merchant. But despite his concerns, it was his descendants who inherited the fortune made by William Stephens in Marinha Grande, a fortune bequeathed to his brother Charles who preferred a different life.

Notes

Full details of works cited in short form will be found in the bibliography.

Abbreviations used

ANF	Archives Nationales, Paris
ANP	Arquivos Nacionais, Lisbon
B	Bankruptcy papers (Public Record Office)
BHSP	British Historical Society of Portugal
BN	Biblioteca Nacional, Lisbon
BO	Bibliotèque de l'Opéra, Paris
BT	Board of Trade papers (Public Record Office)
C	Chancery papers (Public Record Office)
CL	Courtney Library, Royal Institution of Cornwall
ECA	Exeter City Archives, Devon Record Office
FO	Foreign Office papers (Public Record Office)
GL	Guildhall Library
GLA	Greater London Archives
NHM	National History Museum
SP	State papers (Public Record Office)
TS	Treasury solicitor's papers (Public Record Office)
WO	War Office papers (Public Record Office)

Author's Note (pp. xi–xv)

1 Bank of England, Equivalent Contemporary Values of the Pound, an historical series 1270–2003.

Prelude (pp. 3–6)

1 Baptisms, Pillaton, 17 November 1710.
2 Polsue, II, 407.
3 Baptisms, Laneast, 20 May 1731.
4 Marriages, Stoke Damerel (Plymouth), 4 June 1707.
5 Lewis Stephens appointed prebendary, October 1731.
6 Burials, St Mary Major, 30 March 1743; marriages, St Mary Major, 11 May 1743.
7 Bush; Bradbeer.
8 Baptisms, Exeter Cathedral, 5 November 1744.

1. A Young Merchant (pp. 7–16)

1 Matthews, 4–5.
2 Petition dated April 1746 (SP 89/44, 222); Philbrick Collection on the Post Office Packet Service, February 1746 (CL).
3 Castres to Newcastle, 24 August 1746 (89/44, 243).
4 Gentleman's Magazine, 1746, 473–474.
5 Ibid.
6 Walford, The British Community in Lisbon.
7 Will of John James Stephens, London, 13 December 1826.
8 Baptisms/burials, Exeter Cathedral, December 1751.
9 Cheke, Dictator of Portugal, 50.
10 Boxer, 731.
11 British merchants to Barons, 4 February 1754 (SP 89/49, 229).
12 Castres to Holderness, 4 February 1754 (89/48, 241).
13 Walford, The British Factory, 71.
14 Tyrawley to Holderness, 9 July 1752 (89/48, 74).
15 Ibid.
16 Mawman to Tyrawley, 5 November 1752 (Walford, The British Factory, 55–56).
17 Crowle to Amyand, 5 November 1752 (89/49, 85).
18 Castres to Holderness, 4 February 1754 (89/48, 241).
19 English Factory to Holderness, 10 September 1753 (89/48, 190).
20 Crowle to Lodwick, 16 September 1753 (89/49, 133).
21 'Publicus,' 11–14.
22 English Factory to Holderness, 19 October 1753 (89/49, 166).
23 Crowle to Holderness, 29 October 1753 (89/48, 168).
24 Burials, Exeter Cathedral, 10 October 1753.
25 Christ's Hospital children's registers (GL 12818/9, 299).

Interlude (p. 17)

1 Burials, Exeter Cathedral, 1 October 1755.

2 Gentleman's Magazine, 1755, 590–591.

2. Earthquake (pp. 18–23)

1 Gentleman's Magazine, 1755, 560–562; An Account by an Eye-witness, 12.
2 Thomas Jacomb, 1 November 1755 (Macaulay, They Went to Portugal, 273–274).
3 An Account by an Eye-witness, 11.
4 Ibid, 16.
5 Ibid, 18.
6 Gentleman's Magazine, 1756, 67–68.
7 Ibid, 1813, II, 316.
8 Will of John James Stephens, London, 13 December 1826.
9 Gentleman's Magazine, 1755, 561.
10 Hay to Fox, 13 December 1755 (SP 89/50, 149).
11 Castres to Robinson, 19 November 1755 (89/50, 124).
12 Gentleman's Magazine, 1755, 592.
13 Trend, 170.
14 English Factory to Dom José, 8 November 1755 (89/50, 120).
15 Hay to Robinson, 19 November 1755 (89/50, 122).
16 Castres to Fox, 4 February 1756 (89/50, 200–203).

Interlude (pp. 24–28)

1 Keene to Robinson, 10 November 1755 (SP 94/149).
2 Kendrick, 154–155.
3 Ibid, 159.
4 Ibid, 162.
5 Christ's Hospital presentation papers, 4 May 1756 (GL 12818A/29, 111).
6 Ibid.
7 Trollope, appendix IV, cviii–cix.
8 Johnson, 100.
9 Penn, 14.
10 Christ's Hospital committee minutes, 1756–1762 (12811/12).
11 Ibid, 4 April 1759.
12 Penn, 15.
13 Trollope, 153.
14 Scargill, 133–134.

3. *Alcântara* (pp. 29–41)

1 Hay to Amyand, 8 May 1756 (SP 89/50, 242).

2 Ramecourt.

3 Petition by Stephens (Barros, 198).

4 Ibid, 3 November 1756, and royal order of same date (Barros, 192–194).

5 Accounts between Stephens and Pontes (Barros, 201).

6 Custódio, 463–464.

7 Ibid, 464; Ramecourt.

8 Dingley, affidavit, 15 February 1758 (SP 89/74, 137).

9 Dingley to Treasury, January 1758 (89/74, 131).

10 List of ships carrying culm to Lisbon (89/74, 127).

11 Dingley, affidavit, 15 February 1758 (89/74, 137).

12 Royal order, 27 October 1758 (Barros, 196).

13 Dingley to Treasury, 15 February 1758 (89/74, 135); affidavit (137); list of ships (127).

14 Dingley, letters and affidavit (89/74, 131–137); list of ships (127).

15 A chaldron is a measurement of volume and represents a little under 300 gallons.

16 Dingley to Treasury, January 1758 (89/74, 131).

17 Report by Treasury, 7 February 1758 (89/74, 133).

18 Dingley to Treasury, 15 February 1758 (89/74, 135); affidavit (137).

19 Dingley to Treasury, March 1758 (89/74, 138).

20 Notes by Stephens on passing of Culm Act (89/74, 139); Hansard, April 1758.

21 Transcription of Culm Act, April 1758 (89/74, 140).

22 List of ships (89/74, 127).

23 Custódio, 464.

24 Kendrick, 89.

25 Hervey, I, 17. The executed Marquesa de Távora was mother-in-law to the king's mistress.

26 Cheke, *Dictator of Portugal*, 203.

27 Baretti, I, 180.

28 Southey, 15 June 1800 (*Life and Correspondence*, II, 87).

29 Dingley to Treasury, 15 February 1758 (89/74, 135).

30 Carvalho to Junta do Comércio, 12 January 1758 (Barros, 196).

31 Petition by Stephens, granted on 24 July 1757 (Barros, 196).

32 Advertising leaflet for Alcântara lime (British Library).

33 A *moyo* is a measurement of volume and represents 192 gallons.

34 Junta do Comércio, 29 December 1760 (Barros, 198–199).

35 Petition by Stephens (Barros, 198); Custódio, 464.

36 Junta do Comércio, 21 July 1761 (Barros, 200).

37 Carvalho to Junta do Comércio, 19 August 1761 (Barros, 201).

38 Order for debt, 21 October 1762 (Barros, 203).

39 Christ's Hospital children's registers, 17 March 1762 (GL 12818/9, 299).

Interlude (pp. 42–43)

1 Christ's Hospital court minutes, November 1761 (GL 12806/11).

2 Christ's Hospital children's registers, 17 March 1762 (12818/9, 299).

3 Baretti, I, 63.

4. *A Family Together* (pp. 44–50)

1 Lloyds lists of shipping, April/May 1762.

2 Baretti, I, 46.

3 Ibid, I, 41–42.

4 Ibid, I, 96–97.

5 Order for debt, 21 October 1762 (Barros, 203).

6 Stephens to Carvalho (Barros, 201).

7 Stephens to Dom José (Barros, 202–203).

8 Carvalho to Junta do Comércio, 25 June 1764 (Barros, 203).

9 List of ships carrying culm to Lisbon (SP 89/74, 127).

10 Burials, Anglican chaplaincy, 26 June 1767.
11 Royal order, 27 July 1767 (Barros, 203–204).
12 Correia, 19–20.
13 Stephens adopted Campion's daughter after his death. See Chapter 8.
14 Representation by Stephens brothers, 1790 (E M Marques, 68).
15 Ibid (Marques, 68).
16 Ibid (Marques, 69).
17 Baillie, II, 5.

22 Royal orders, 14 August 1772 (Barros, 251–252).
23 Stephens brothers to Walpole, December 1772 (SP 89/74, 126).
24 Walpole to Rochford, 9 January 1773 (89/74, 123).
25 Ibid, 27 February 1773 (89/74, 170–172).
26 Ibid, 20 March 1773 (89/74, 178); Rochford to Walpole, 6 April 1773 (190); transcription of Culm Act, June 1773 (89/85, 29).

5. Marinha Grande (pp. 53–61)

1 Burials, Anglican chaplaincy, 21 April 1768.
2 Royal decree, 7 July 1769 (Barros, 37–48).
3 Junta do Comércio, 20 July 1769 (Barros, 205).
4 Beckford, Recollections of an Excursion, 37.
5 Ibid, 38.
6 M J de Sousa, 3 May 1830 (Autonomia, 3 November 1895).
7 Duarte, Os Stephens, 17–18.
8 Barros, 205–248.
9 Stephens to Mendonça, 19 October 1769 (Barros, 50).
10 M J de Sousa, 3 May 1830 (Autonomia, 3 November 1895).
11 Stephens to Mendonça, 19 October 1769 (Barros, 50).
12 Correia, 48.
13 Report by Stephens, 31 December 1770 (Marques, 33–36).
14 Royal order, 14 August 1772 (Barros, 251–252).
15 Baillie, II, 6–7.
16 Junta do Comércio to Stephens, 18 January, 14 March 1772 (Barros, 251).
17 Balsemão, V, chapter III, paragraph 4.
18 Barros, III–LII.
19 Ibid, 61.
20 Petition by Stephens, 25 June 1772 (Barros, 167–176).
21 Junta do Comércio, 13 August 1772 (Barros, 253–255).

6. A Miniature Welfare State (pp. 62–72)

1 Wraxall, I, 64.
2 Cheke, Dictator of Portugal, 77.
3 Maxwell, 106.
4 Ibid, 102.
5 Vasconcellos e Sá, Diário da Jornada (ANP, Ministeiro do Reino, livro 436, 1720).
6 Ibid.
7 Ferrão, 95.
8 Royal orders, 5, 27 January 1773 (Barros, 255–256).
9 Correia, 41.
10 Dalrymple, 132.
11 Cormatin, II, 134.
12 Similar innovations at New Lanark, Scotland, were introduced from 1799.
13 Withering, I, 336.
14 Duarte, Os Stephens, 24; A Indústria Vidreira, 312–313.
15 Petition by Stephens (Barros, 250); representation by Stephens brothers, 1790 (Marques, 69).
16 Petition by Stephens (Barros, 253).
17 Representation by Stephens brothers, 1790 (Marques, 69).
18 Balsemão, V, chapter IV, paragraph 2.
19 Stephens to Pombal, 7 April 1778 (BN, PBA 704, 89).
20 Murphy, 84; Withering, I, 314.
21 Balsemão, chapter IV, paragraph 3.
22 W Stephens, Memórias sobre a Cultura da Lucerna (MS transcription, 1803); An Account of the

Manner of Treating Bees in Portugal (Murphy, 85–88).

23 Nicolau Luís da Silva, c.1786 (Barros, 24).

24 A Gibbs, 10 December 1798 (GL 11021/5, 241–242).

25 Barros, 23; Pinto, I, 216–217.

26 Withering, I, 314.

27 A Gibbs, 10 December 1798 (11021/5, 241–243).

28 Ferro, 53.

29 Reports by Stephens, 31 December 1773, 31 December 1774 (Marques, 48–49, 54–60).

30 Report by Stephens, 31 December 1774 (Marques, 54–55).

31 Ibid.

32 Almeida, *A Fábrica de Vidros*, 311.

33 Representation by Stephens brothers, 1790 (Marques, 69–70).

7. The Fall of Pombal (pp. 73–85)

1 Cheke, *Dictator of Portugal*, 236–238.

2 Ibid, 240.

3 Ibid, 221.

4 Ibid, 254.

5 Stephens to Pombal (BN PBA 704, 27–30, 87–89).

6 Cormatin, I, 174–175, footnote.

7 Stephens to Pombal, 12, 17, 25 September 1777 (PBA 704, 27, 28, 30).

8 *Letters from Portugal on the Late and Present State of that Kingdom*, 1777.

9 Smith, *Memoirs of the Marquis of Pombal*, II, 332.

10 Ibid, II, 322–323.

11 Stephens to Pombal, 14 February 1778 (PBA 691, 1).

12 Smith, II, 323.

13 Ibid, II, 323–326.

14 Stephens, annual report for 1776 (Marques, 61–62).

15 Junta do Comércio to Stephens, 18 July 1775 (Barros, 256–257).

16 Junta do Comércio, 7 August 1775 (Barros, 257–258).

17 Junta do Comércio to Stephens, 5 May, 13 July 1778 (Barros, 258).

18 Junta do Comércio, 4 June 1778 (Barros, 258–260).

19 Stephens to Pombal, 7 April 1778 (PBA 704, 89).

20 Junta do Comércio, 4 June 1778 (Barros, 258–260).

21 Stephens to Pombal, 17 September 1778 (PBA 704, 29).

22 Wraxall, I, 35.

23 Cormatin, I, 126.

24 Cheke, 267.

25 Ibid, 281.

26 Ibid, 282–283.

27 Ibid, 283.

28 Diary of W J Mickle, January 1780 (West, 10–11).

29 Cheke, 289.

30 Smith, II, 352–354.

8. The Largo dos Stephens (pp. 86–93)

1 Hawkey, 144.

2 Hort to Weymouth, 15 March 1778 (SP 89/85, 154).

3 Consul's office to J J Stephens, 31 October 1777 (89/85, 32).

4 J J Stephens to Hort, 7 November 1777 (89/85, 33).

5 Stephens brothers to Weymouth, December 1777 (89/85, 30–31).

6 J J Stephens to Hort, 1 December 1777 (89/85, 34).

7 Ibid, 2 December 1777 (89/85, 35).

8 Ibid, 3 December 1777 (89/85, 36).

9 Ibid, 4 December 1777 (89/85, 37).

10 Stephens brothers to Weymouth, December 1777 (89/85, 27).

11 Weymouth to Hort, 27 January 1778 (89/85, 25).

12 J J Stephens to Hort, 27 February 1778 (89/92, 256).

13 Hort to J J Stephens, 27 February 1778 (89/92, 256).

14 Hort to W Stephens, 21 February 1778 (89/92, 257).

15 W Stephens to Hort, 6 March 1778 (89/92, 257).

16 Ibid.

17 Walpole to Rochford, 3 November 1773 (89/74, 159).

18 Costigan, I, 374–375.

19 Ibid, II, 264.

20   Hickey, II, 372.

Interlude (pp. 94–96)

1   P N Wenmouth, *The Parish Church of St Ive*, 18.
2   Cardew, 7.
3   Ibid.
4   A de C Glubb, *Cornish Times*, 1 November 1935.
5   Harris, 447–450.
6   This question, verbatim, has come down the generations in several branches of the Lyne family.
7   Hawkey, 146.
8   Beckford, *Italy, with Sketches of Spain and Portugal*, II, 5.
9   Contemporary handwritten notes.

9.   Dona Maria (pp. 97–106)

1   Beckford, *Italy with Sketches of Spain and Portugal*, II, 88.
2   Twiss, 22, 32.
3   Hawkey, 147–148.
4   Marriages, Anglican chaplaincy, 27 November 1779; will of Lewis Stephens, PCC, 22 December 1795.
5   Diary of W J Mickle, December 1779 (West, 6).
6   Ibid, January 1780 (West, 8–10).
7   Croker, 294.
8   Decree dated 11 December 1780 (Barros, 261–263).
9   William had first asked for this privilege in June 1772.
10   Barros, 23.
11   Young, 52.
12   Legal proceedings, April 1782 to March 1783 (Barros, 264–282).
13   Contemporary handwritten notes.
14   Araújo, 19–20.
15   Bombelles, 83–84.
16   Barosa, 27–28.
17   Petition by Stephens brothers (Barros, 264).
18   Decree of October 1786 referred to in royal order, 7 October 1799 (Barros, 287–288).
19   Southey, *Journals of a Residence in Portugal*, 19–20. Reprinted by permission of Oxford University Press.

20   *Gazeta de Lisboa*, no. 43, 24 October 1786.
21   Pinto, I, 216–217.
22   Accounts book, Marinha Grande, May–August 1788.
23   Withering, I, 314–315.
24   Extract from will of William Stephens (Barros, 16).
25   Beckford, *Italy, with Sketches of Spain and Portugal*, II, 73.
26   Southey, *Letters Written during a Short Residence*, 306.
27   Beckford, *Italy, with Sketches of Spain and Portugal*, II, 101.
28   Araújo, 25.
29   Beckford, *Recollections of an Excursion*, 223.

10.   A Time of Change (pp. 107–120)

1   W Stephens to Manuel do Cenáculo Vilas Boas, 11 September 1792 (Biblioteca Pública de Évora, CXXVII, 1–10, 315).
2   *The Lisbon Guide*, 58.
3   Withering, I, 144.
4   Murphy, 128.
5   Southey, *Journals of a Residence in Portugal*, 15, 20. Reprinted by permission of Oxford University Press.
6   Southey, 28 March 1801 (*Selections from Letters of Southey,* I, 143–144).
7   Ratton, 138.
8   Ibid, 137–140; *O Século*, 19 August 1945.
9   W Stephens to British Hospital Committee, 6 June 1789 (BHSP, de Visme's Hospital Committee book, 12–13).
10   Aranha, 159; Barosa, 26.
11   Ratton, 315.
12   Petition by Sousa, 28 April 1821 (Marques, 87).
13   Withering to Banks, 31 October 1797; Watt to Banks, 5 November 1797 (NHM, BL DTC, X(1), 204–208).
14   Banks to Withering, 23 December 1797, 18 May 1798 (NHM, Banks Project).

15 A Gibbs, 10 December 1798 (GL 11021/5, 243–244).
16 Junta do Comércio, 7 May 1789, 28 January, 5 February 1790 (Barros, 283–284).
17 W Stephens, annual report for 1776 (Marques, 61–62).
18 Petition by Stephens brothers (Barros, 284–285).
19 Barros, 61.
20 Junta do Comércio, 19 July 1804 (Barros, 315).
21 Valente, 52–53; Barros, 25.
22 Chance, 11.
23 Hoffmansegg, 256–257.
24 Aranha, 163–165; Barros, 25.
25 Decree dated 7 May 1794 (Barros, 285).
26 A Gibbs, 10 December 1798 (11021/5, 243).
27 Ibid.
28 F Lyne, 128.
29 Deposition by A M Palmer (Cogan vs Stephens, TS 11/681).
30 Will of Lewis Stephens, PCC, 22 December 1795.
31 F Lyne, 131–135.
32 Lisbon directories, 1788–1791, 1794.
33 F Lyne, 136–138.
34 Walford, *The British Factory*, 73.
35 F Lyne, 144.
36 A Gibbs, 10 December 1798 (11021/5, 239).
37 F Lyne, 143–144.
38 Burials, Anglican chaplaincy, 7 September 1795.
39 Will of Lewis Stephens.
40 W and J J Stephens to City of Exeter, 17 October 1795 (ECA, Dr Stephens bequest papers).
41 Ibid, 29 October 1795.
42 Philbrick Collection on the Post Office Packet Service, 1794–1796 (CL).
43 Withering, I, 165.
44 Marriages, Liskeard, 1 October 1796.
45 Lisbon directory, 1802.
46 Marriages, Anglican chaplaincy, 31 August 1797.
47 Baptisms, Anglican chaplaincy, 24 January 1798.

11. The First Hostilities (pp. 123–129)

1 Jervis to Nepean, 28 December 1796 (Tucker, I, 278–279).
2 Jervis to Spencer, 29 December 1796 (Tucker, I, 279–280).
3 Decree dated 7 October 1799 (Barros, 287–288).
4 Southey, 23 June 1800 (*Selections from Letters of Southey*, I, 114).
5 Ibid, 15 June 1800 (*Life and Correspondence*, II, 84).
6 Ibid (*Life and Correspondence*, II, 85).
7 A Gibbs, 22 February 1800 (GL 11021/5, 603).
8 Southey, 22 February 1800 (*Journals of a Residence in Portugal*, 151). Reprinted by permission of Oxford University Press.
9 Jervis to Spencer, 29 December 1796 (Tucker, I, 279–280).
10 Southey, 28 March 1801 (*Life and Correspondence*, II, 137).
11 Junta do Comércio, 13 July 1818 (Barros, 319–321); petition by Sousa, 28 April 1821 (Marques, 87); Gândara, 10, footnote 2.
12 F Lyne, 142.
13 Royal order, 3 November 1801 (Barros, 288–289).
14 H Gibbs, 28 August 1801 (11021/6, 191).
15 A Gibbs, 4 November 1801 (11021/6, 237).
16 F Lyne, 157.

Interlude (pp. 130–134)

1 Southey, *Letters from England*, I, 6–7.
2 *Exeter Flying Post*, 16 June 1785; *Sherborne Mercury*, 27 July 1785.
3 *Sherborne Mercury*, 11 October 1790.
4 Ibid, 28 December 1795.
5 Hawkey, 147.
6 F Lyne, 51.

7 Chudleigh, *Midnight Meditations*, 65.
8 R Lyne, *The Departed Saint* (MS).
9 Ibid.
10 Allen, 359.
11 C Lyne to A Gibbs, 1 January 1801 (GL 11021/6, 1–3).
12 Thackeray, *Letters and Private Papers*, I, 212.
13 Gilbert, III, 230.
14 Baptisms, St Ive, October 1801.
15 D Gibbs, 29 October 1801, 14 April 1802 (11021/6, 234, 374).
16 C Lyne to D Gibbs, 9 May 1802 (11021/6, 391–392).

12. Bereavement (pp. 135–145)

1 Barros, 16.
2 Ibid.
3 Burials, Anglican chaplaincy, 12 May 1803.
4 Aranha, 165–166.
5 *Gentleman's Magazine*, 1803, II, 990; burials, Anglican chaplaincy, 28 September 1803.
6 Gambier to Hawkesbury, 2 October 1803 (FO 63/42).
7 H Gibbs, 7 October 1803 (GL 11021/7, 242).
8 Withering, I, 164–165.
9 Deposition by A M Palmer (Cogan vs Stephens, TS 11/681).
10 H Gibbs, 7 October 1803 (11021/7, 239–240).
11 Vassall, 186–187.
12 Letters of administration, Jedediah Stephens, 4 January 1804.
13 Deposition by A M Palmer (TS 11/681).
14 Trollope, 167.
15 Ibid, 166.
16 Isaac Watts (Williams, 120–121).
17 Trollope, 166.
18 Marinha Grande, annual report for 1803 (Barros, 290–314).
19 Gândara, 5–6.
20 Junta do Comércio, 19 July 1804 (Barros, 315).
21 Affidavit of Samuel Acton (Cogan vs Stephens, C 118/36).
22 Junot, III, 83.

23 Macaulay, *They Went to Portugal*, 364.
24 Brougham, 335–336.
25 St Vincent to Howick, 24 August 1806 (Tucker, II, 292–293).
26 St Vincent to Jervis, 10 October 1806 (Tucker, II, 302–303).
27 Howick to St Vincent, 9 October 1806 (Tucker, II, 299–302).
28 Affidavit of Samuel Acton (C 118/36).
29 Gândara, 6; petition by Sousa, 28 April 1821 (Marques, 86–87).
30 Petition by Sousa, 28 April 1821 (Marques, 86).
31 Junta do Comércio, 19 July 1804, with resolution on 23 November 1804 (Barros, 315).
32 Ibid, 17 November 1807 (Barros, 315–316).
33 Ibid, 19 July 1804 (Barros, 315).
34 Ibid, 17 November 1807 (Barros, 315–316).

13. Invasion (pp. 146–158)

1 Macaulay, *They Went to Portugal*, 369.
2 Gambier to Canning, 28 September 1807 (FO 63/62).
3 Edmund Power & Co, 30 September 1807 (Hipwell, 182–183).
4 Gambier to Canning, 4 October 1807 (63/62).
5 Henry Gallwey, 10 October 1807 (Hipwell, 187–189).
6 Edmund Power & Co, 19 October 1807 (Hipwell, 183–184).
7 Gambier, 5 November 1807 (63/62).
8 Strangford to Canning, 26 September 1807 (Macaulay, *Dom Pedro*, 12).
9 *Le Moniteur Universel*, 13 October 1807 (Bryant, 217).
10 Gambier to Canning, 8 November 1807 (63/62).
11 Hawkey, 148.
12 Ibid.
13 Thiébault, II, 199.
14 Ibid.
15 Gândara, 10–11, footnote 3.

16 *Progresso Industrial*, 10.
17 Ibid.
18 Ibid, 10–11.
19 Petition by Sousa, 28 April 1821 (Marques, 87).
20 *Progresso Industrial*, 11.
21 Barros, 315–316; Valente, 196.
22 *Progresso Industrial*, 11.
23 Walford, *The British Factory*, 83.
24 *Progresso Industrial*, 11.
25 Brown to Wellesley, 21 July 1808 (Neale, 32).
26 *Progresso Industrial*, 11.
27 Wellesley to Castlereagh, 23 August 1808 (Glover, 142–144).
28 Porter, 12.
29 Beresford to Dalrymple, 18 September 1808 (Landmann, I, 492).
30 'G,' A P D, 52.
31 Beresford to Dalrymple, 18 September 1808 (Landmann, I, 490).
32 Trant, 5.
33 *Progresso Industrial*, 11.
34 Neale, 68.
35 Ibid, 69.

Interlude (pp. 159–160)

1 London court guide, 1809.
2 A Gibbs, 27 January 1808 (GL 11021/9, 491).
3 London directory, 1809; Gambier to Canning, 25 January 1808, with enclosure (FO 63/62).
4 London court guides, 1804, 1809.
5 G Gibbs, 11 July 1806 (11021/8, 626).
6 London/Liverpool directories, 1805; Bank of England drawing account, Lyne, Hathorn & Roberts, 1804–1806.
7 Bank of England drawing account, Lyne, Hathorn & Roberts, 1806–1808.
8 London directory, 1809.
9 A Gibbs, 15 February, 15 April, 18 May 1808 (11021/9, 599, 743; 11021/10, 9).

14. Devastation (pp. 161–171)

1 Sherer, 8.

2 Schaumann, 343–344.
3 Minutes were written in de Visme's Hospital Committee book (BHSP).
4 Warre, 38.
5 Vassall, 243–245.
6 Stewart, 247.
7 Sherer, 45–47.
8 Minutes of English Factory, 25 October 1809 (BHSP, de Visme's Hospital Committee book)
9 Petition by Stephens, 28 May 1810 (Barros, 317).
10 Ibid.
11 Simmons, 99–100.
12 Sherer, 158–159.
13 Stewart, 436.
14 Marbot, II, 108.
15 Schaumann, 259–260.
16 Stewart, 434–435.
17 Boutflower, 64.
18 Macaulay, *They Went to Portugal Too*, 167.
19 Berkeley to Jeffery, 5 October 1810 (Walford, *The British Factory*, 99).
20 Broughton, 81–82.
21 Committee minutes, October 1810 (BHSP, de Visme's Hospital Committee book).
22 Broughton, 81.
23 Sherer, 170–171.
24 Petition by Sousa, 28 April 1821 (Marques, 87).
25 Pelet, 246.
26 Ibid, 347–348.
27 Broughton, 113.
28 Robinson, I, 403–404, footnote.
29 Longford, 247.

15. Reconstruction (pp. 172–177)

1 Trant, 8–9.
2 Ibid, 9.
3 Petition by Sousa, 28 April 1821 (Marques, 87).
4 Ibid.
5 Balsemão, chapter 1, paragraphs 2–4; Aranha, 154–156.
6 Ibid.
7 Ibid.
8 Stephens to Sousa, April 1811. Cullet is broken glass re-used in the mixtures (it liquefies at a lower

temperature than the raw materials, speeding up the melting process).

9   Petition by Sousa, 28 April 1821 (Marques, 87).

10 Stephens to Sousa, 24 February, 16 March 1812.

11 Pinto, 297.

12 Petition by Sousa, 28 April 1821 (Marques, 87).

13 Stephens to Sousa, 2 September 1811.

14 Ibid, 14 September 1811, February 1812.

15 Representation by Sousa (Barros, 318); report by intendant of police (Barros, 318–319).

16 Stephens to Sousa, October 1812.

17 Petition by Stephens (Barros, 319–321); Stephens to Sousa, May 1812, February 1813.

18 Stephens to Sousa, 16 September 1811; Junta do Comércio, 13 July 1818 (Barros, 319–321).

19 Stephens to Sousa, 1 June 1811, 12 January 1812, 13 September 1813.

20 Broughton, 51–53.

21 Stephens to Sousa, January 1813.

22 Society of British Merchants & Factors, 26 January 1813 (Lisbon Factory book, FO 173/7).

Interlude (pp. 181–185)

1   Stephens to Sousa, 30 December 1811, July 1812; London court guide, 1814.

2   Burials, Charles (Plymouth), 4 December 1810; marriages, St James Clerkenwell, 7 January 1813.

3   F Lyne, 51, 162; list of students at Castle Hill, 28 January 1805.

4   R Lyne, *The Departed Saint* (MS).

5   Ibid.

6   C Lyne to Castlereagh, 23 February 1813 (BT 1/74, 44–45).

7   C Lyne, *A Letter to the Rt. Hon. Lord Castlereagh*, 6–8, 33–34.

8   Bullion Committee, 47–55.

9   C Lyne, *A Letter to the Rt. Hon. George Rose*, ii, 8, 46–47.

10 Koster, 71–72.

11 Bank of England, 29 August 1811 (court book, GA 4/34).

12 C Lyne to Gill (F Lyne, 215–242).

13 W Gibbs, April 1812 (GL 11021/11, 322–327).

16. *An Uneasy Peace* (pp. 186–196)

1   Stephens to Sousa, January–July 1814.

2   Ibid, October 1813.

3   Ibid, January 1815.

4   Styles, 258–261.

5   Canning to Castlereagh, 20 April 1815 (FO 63/176).

6   Ibid, 20 June 1815 (63/187).

7   Long, 68.

8   Macaulay, *They Went to Portugal Too*, 200.

9   Stephens to Sousa, April 1817.

10 Macaulay, *They Went to Portugal Too*, 205.

11 Ibid, 206.

12 Aitchison, 59.

13 Stephens to Sousa, October 1816, 7 June 1817.

14 Junta do Comércio, 18 November 1817, 13 July 1818 (Barros, 319–321).

15 Ibid, 13 July 1818 (Barros, 319–321).

16 Stephens to Sousa, April 1818.

17 Junta do Comércio, 19 June 1820 (Barros, 321).

18 Stephens to Sousa, 7 June 1817; will of John James Stephens, London, 13 December 1826.

19 Canning to Castlereagh, 20 June 1815 (FO 63/187).

20 Stephens to Sousa, November–December 1817.

21 Ibid, 31 October 1825.

22 Ibid, December 1816.

23 Ibid, November–December 1817, 4 April 1818, 31 December 1825.

24 Anonymous report, 20 January 1827 (Marques, 90–91).

25 Stephens to Sousa, September 1825.

26 Anonymous report, 20 January 1827 (Marques, 90–91).

27 Report by Sousa, 24 April 1821 (Marques, 87); Duarte, *Os Stephens*, 24.

28 Junta do Comércio, 15 August 1821 (Barros, 321); report by Sousa, 24 April 1821 (Marques, 87–88).

Interlude (pp. 197–200)

1 Stephens to Sousa, 19 August, 26 October, 18 November 1816.
2 Ibid, 11 January 1817.
3 Ibid, January–March 1817; London court guide, 1817.
4 Stephens to Sousa, April–August 1817.
5 Ibid, September 1817.
6 Ibid, 6 December 1817; deposition by A M Palmer (Cogan vs Stephens, TS 11/681).
7 Burials, St Marylebone, 7 November 1817.
8 Liverpool directories, 1817–1818; *London Gazette*: 1817, II, 1668; 1818, I, 1179.
9 Indenture, 31 August 1831 (GLA, BRA 686/2/7).
10 C Lyne, *A Letter to the Rt. Hon. the Earl of Liverpool*, 25, 30.
11 F Lyne, 170.
12 C Lyne, *A Letter to the Rt. Hon. Lord Viscount Castlereagh*, 3–4.
13 Burials, St Marylebone, 31 August 1820.
14 *Exeter Flying Post*, 21 May 1818; *London Gazette*: 1818, I, 918; II, 1675; bankruptcy papers (B 3/3011).
15 C Lyne, *A Letter to the Lord High Chancellor*, 6.
16 Burials, St Leonard's Shoreditch, 1 October 1820.

17. A Mild and Placid Spirit (pp. 201–211)

1 Baillie, I, 30–31.
2 Ibid, I, 33.
3 Ibid, II, 76–77.
4 Ibid, II, 3–4.

5 M E Chudleigh, *Royal Cornwall Gazette*, 13 April 1860.
6 F Lyne,152–156.
7 Stephens to Sousa, April 1819.
8 F Lyne, 156.
9 Cheke, *Carlota Joaquina*, 113.
10 Stephens to Sousa, 1 May 1824; Cheke, 133.
11 Thornton, May 1824 (Macaulay, *They Went to Portugal Too*, 301).
12 Deposition by A M Palmer (Cogan vs Stephens, TS 11/681).
13 Stephens to Sousa, 17, 21 April 1824.
14 Letters of administration, Philadelphia Stephens, 3 May 1824.
15 Trollope, 165.
16 Will of John James Stephens, London, 13 December 1826.
17 Deposition by Jeremiah Meagher, attached to the will.
18 Stephens to Sousa, July–September 1826.
19 Ibid, April–May, October–November 1826.
20 Deposition by Jeremiah Meagher.
21 Burials, Anglican chaplaincy, 14 November 1826.
22 'G,' A P D, 113.
23 Will of John James Stephens.

Interlude (pp. 212–215)

1 C Lyne, *A Letter to the Lord High Chancellor*, 5, 10–11, 18–19.
2 F Lyne, 167.
3 *Western Morning News*, 1860; *Royal Cornwall Gazette*, 13 April 1860.
4 Mackenzie to Douglas, 4 March 1830 (Attorney-general & Matthews vs Lyne Stephens, TS 25/18).
5 Royal licence, 16 December 1826; grants of arms, 5, 8 April 1828 (College of Arms).
6 C Lyne Stephens to Hermano, 31 January 1827 (BN Reservados 10,695, F 2852, 16).
7 Report by *provedor* of Leiria, 12 February 1827 (F 2852, 7–8).
8 Anonymous report, 20 January 1827 (Marques, 91); report by

provedor, 12 February 1827 (F 2852, 7).

9 Anonymous report, 20 January 1827 (Marques, 92).

10 C Lyne Stephens to Hermano, 31 January 1827 (F 2852, 16).

11 Report by *provedor*, 12 February 1827 (F 2852, 7); report by Sousa, 29 January 1827 (Marques, 94–95).

12 Christ's Hospital committee minutes, 21 February 1827 (GL 12811/17).

13 *Royal Cornwall Gazette*, 10 March 1827.

18. Transfer to the State (pp. 216–225)

1 Kinsey, 56–58.

2 Aranha, 165–166.

3 Royal order, 23 December 1826 (BN Reservados, 10,695, F 2852, 3).

4 Conselho da Fazenda, 1 March 1827 (Almeida, *Relatorio*, 8–10).

5 Smith, *Memoirs of Field Marshal the Duke de Saldanha*, I, 121–122.

6 Pardoe, II, 204.

7 Ibid, I, 247–248.

8 *The Times*, 27 April 1827.

9 Ibid.

10 Ibid.

11 Stephens to Sousa, September 1823.

12 Pardoe, I, 170.

13 Report by *provedor* of Leiria, 20 November 1826 (F 2852, 6).

14 Report by Sousa, 29 January 1827 (Marques, 95).

15 Almeida, *Relatorio*, 10.

16 *The Times*, 18 May 1827.

17 Almeida, *Relatorio*, 10; Barosa, 40–41.

18 M J de Sousa, 12 May 1827 (*Autonomia*, 24 November 1895).

19 Representation by Stephens brothers, 1790 (Marques, 71); Gândara, 8.

20 Almeida, *Relatorio*, 10; Barosa, 40–41.

21 *Royal Cornwall Gazette*, May 1827.

22 Sousa to M J de Sousa, 26 May 1827 (*Autonomia*, 1 December 1895).

23 Ibid.

24 *The Times*, 25 June 1827.

25 Almeida, *Relatorio*, 11; Barosa, 40–41.

26 Almeida, *Relatorio*, 11–13.

27 *Royal Cornwall Gazette*, May 1827; Philbrick Collection on the Post Office Packet Service, May 1827 (CL).

28 Kinsey, 472–474.

29 Baillie, II, 203–204.

30 Kinsey, 105.

19. Consolidation (pp. 229–237)

1 C Lyne Stephens to R Lyne, 10 November 1828.

2 Ibid.

3 *London Gazette*, 1827, II, 2023.

4 London court guide, 1829.

5 Cheke, *Carlota Joaquina*, 181.

6 Feret, II, 115–116.

7 Lytton, I, 115–116.

8 Venn, *Alumni Cantabrigienses*.

9 *Real Life in London*, II, 519–521.

10 Army lists; Paget, I, 161.

11 Tenth Hussars, muster lists and pay books (WO 12/938); Cannon; Liddell.

12 Liddell, 211–212.

13 Burials, St Marylebone, 7 November 1828.

14 Ibid, 7 November 1817, 31 August 1820, 30 January 1824.

15 C Lyne Stephens to R Lyne, 10 November 1828.

16 Chudleigh, *Midnight Meditations*, 63.

17 Martin, 4–5.

18 R Lyne to his children, 27 July 1831.

19 F Lyne, 174.

20 Garrick Club archives.

21 Gronow, *Anecdotes of Celebrities*, 83.

22 Ibid, 82.

23 Register of electors, 1829, 1830 (Bedfordshire Archives)

24 Marriages, St Mary's Bryanston Square, 1 June 1830; F Lyne, 174–176.

25 Frances Ongley, 10 June 1830 (Bedfordshire Archives, D 119).

26 B H Lyne to R Lyne, 2 August 1830 (North Devon Record Office, B 456/9).

27 Stanbury to Glubb, 10 December 1830 (B 456/10).

20. _Reform and Litigation_ (pp. 238–249)

1 C Lyne Stephens to Matthews, 14 August 1830; Meagher to Hopp-ner, 1 February 1832 (Attorney-general & Matthews vs Lyne Stephens, TS 25/18).

2 Mackenzie to Douglas, 30 March, 9 June 1830 (25/18).

3 C Lyne Stephens to Matthews, 14 August 1830 (25/18).

4 Dickens, preface to _Bleak House_, August 1853.

5 C Lyne Stephens to Matthews, 14 August 1830 (25/18).

6 Ibid.

7 House of Commons, 15 November 1830 (Hansard Parliamentary Debates, Third Series, I).

8 Greville, II, 121.

9 Butler, 194–195.

10 House of Commons, 22 March 1831 (Hansard Parliamentary Debates, Third Series, III).

11 Macaulay (Butler, 207).

12 F Lyne, 170.

13 Creevey, 23 March 1831 (_The Creevey Papers_, II, 225).

14 _Leicester Chronicle_, 9 April 1831.

15 House of Commons, 19 April 1831 (Hansard Parliamentary Debates, Third Series, III).

16 Martineau, VII, 347–348.

17 Ibid, VII, 348.

18 Barnstaple flyer, 2 July 1832 (_A Collection of Addresses, Squibs etc_).

19 Baptisms, St Mary's Bryanston Square, 30 October 1831; burials, St Marylebone, 28 November 1831.

20 _The Satirist_, 22 July 1832.

21 Marriages, Campton (Bedford-shire), 2 December 1833.

22 R Lyne to his children, 26 July 1831.

23 Ibid, September 1834.

24 Chudleigh, _Midnight Meditations_, 62–63.

25 Hawkey, 147.

26 Glubb to Eliot, November 1834.

27 Stephens Lyne Stephens, election address, 25 November 1834.

28 Glubb to Kekewich, 6 December 1834.

29 Baptisms, St Mary's Bryanston Square, 21 October 1835.

30 F Lyne, 176–177.

31 London court guide, January 1836.

32 Bill filed by Cogan, 1828 (Cogan vs Stephens, TS 11/681).

33 Order dated 20 January 1829 (11/681).

34 Report by Master Martin, 25 June 1834 (11/681).

35 Report by Master of the Rolls, 24 November 1835 (11/681).

36 Bill filed by Cogan, 1828 (11/681).

37 Hawkey, 150–151.

38 Register of electors, 1836, 1837 (Bedfordshire Archives).

39 Bankruptcy papers (B 3/3011, 3012); indenture, 9 February 1837 (GLA, BRA 686/2/8).

21. _The Fair Brimstone_ (pp. 250–262)

1 _Journal des Débats_, 14 February 1832.

2 Duvernay to Lubbert, 25 October 1829 (ANF, AJ/13/126, dossier 3).

3 Alberic Sécond (Guest, _The Romantic Ballet in Paris_, 25–26).

4 Nestor Roqueplan (Guest, _The Romantic Ballet in Paris_, 27).

5 Duvernay to Lubbert, 25 October, 2 November 1829 (AJ/13/126, dossier 3).

6 Véron, III, 304.

7 Ibid, III, 302.

8 Ibid, III, 225.

9   Les Cancans de l'Opéra (BO), 206–209.
10   Véron, III, 279.
11   Ibid.
12   L'Entr'acte, 21 June 1832.
13   De Boigne, 25.
14   C-P Séchan (Beaumont, 16).
15   Véron (Beaumont, 18).
16   De Boigne, 26–27.
17   Les Cancans de l'Opéra, 239–241.
18   De Boigne, 27–28.
19   Ibid, 28–29.
20   Marie Taglioni, 1832 (Peacock, 82).
21   Playbill, Theatre Royal Drury Lane, 28 March 1833.
22   Thackeray, Roundabout Papers, 117.
23   Newspaper cutting, no date or source (Duvernay dossier, Theatre Museum).
24   The Satirist, 9 June 1833.
25   The Times, 24 March 1834.
26   Marie Taglioni, 15 March 1834 (Beaumont, 16).
27   Creevey, 3 May 1834 (The Creevey Papers, II, 273).
28   The Satirist, 4 May 1834.
29   Ibid, 11 May 1834.
30   Ibid, 18 May 1834.
31   Ibid, 1 June 1834.
32   Ibid, 15 June 1834.
33   Les Cancans de l'Opéra, 115–120.
34   Véron, III, 261–262.
35   Guest, Fanny Elssler, 68.
36   De Boigne, 29; Mahalin, 117.
37   Guest, Fanny Elssler, 93–94.
38   The New Satirist, 21 November 1841.
39   Guest, The Romantic Ballet in Paris, 140.
40   Les Cancans de l'Opéra, 22–23.
41   Courrier des Théâtres, 23 May 1835.
42   Ibid, 22 May 1835.
43   Ibid, 23 October 1835.
44   Ibid, 1 February 1836.
45   Les Cancans de l'Opéra, 228–229; Vaillat, 316–317.
46   Playbill, Theatre Royal Drury Lane, 1 November 1836.

47   Town Magazine, 25 November 1837.
48   Théophile Gautier (Guest, The Romantic Ballet in Paris, 152), describing a performance by Elssler.
49   De Boigne (Guest, The Romantic Ballet in Paris, 153), also describing a performance by Elssler.
50   Courrier des Théâtres, 6 February 1837.
51   The Satirist, 5 March 1837.
52   Beaumont, 15.
53   The Times, 30 June 1837.

22. Amongst the Dandies (pp. 263–270)

1   Barham, The Ingoldsby Legends, 194–195. Malibran was an opera singer who died in 1836.
2   Nimrod, The Chace (Bovill, 106, 89).
3   Surtees, 57.
4   Liddell, 566.
5   Brownlow, 130.
6   Nimrod, The Chace (Brownlow, 123).
7   Blew, 16, 151.
8   London Examiner (Brownlow, 257).
9   Duncombe, I, 174–175.
10   Gronow, Reminiscences, I, 278.
11   Les Cancans de l'Opéra, (BO) 49–57.
12   Ibid.
13   Ibid.
14   The Satirist, 11 June 1837.
15   Ibid, 27 August 1837.
16   Courrier des Théâtres, 20 September 1837, 11 May 1838.
17   L'Entr'acte, 15 March 1857.
18   De Boigne, 29–30.
19   Brownlow, 239.
20   Cecil, 429–431.
21   The New Satirist, 21 November 1841.
22   The Satirist, 19 December 1841.
23   Gerhold, 16, 38; assignment, Grove House estate, 20 June 1843 (GLA, BRA 686/2/15).

24 Véron, III, 278.
25 Ibid, III, 278–279; Mahalin, 117–118.
26 De Boigne, 29; F Lyne, 178; marriage settlement, 5 July 1845.
27 *Morning Herald*, 18 July 1845.

23. **The Richest Commoner**
     (pp. 271–281)

1   Mrs Smith (Froebel archives).
2   London court directories, January, September 1846.
3   F Lyne, 182.
4   Bontemps, 100–101.
5   Death certificate, Charles Lyne Stephens, 10 May 1851.
6   Burials, St Marylebone, 15 May 1851.
7   Will of Charles Lyne Stephens, PCC, 11 June 1851.
8   M E Chudleigh, *Royal Cornwall Gazette*, 13 April 1860.
9   Crimean Army Fund to Lubbock & Robarts, 31 January 1855.
10 Newspaper cutting (unidentified), September 1894.
11 Davidson, Part IV, 20.
12 Christie, Manson & Woods, May 1895.
13 Lubbock & Robarts, statement of income, 1851–1858.
14 Obituary of William Burn (*RIBA Transactions*, 28 March 1870, 126).
15 S Lyne Stephens to Wardell, 1858 (Wandsworth Local History Library).
16 *L'Entr'acte*, 15 March 1857.
17 Ibid, 9 June 1857.
18 Sale particulars, Lynford Hall estate, July 1856 (Norfolk Record Office, WLS XVIII/13).
19 Note on back of sale particulars.
20 *Country Life*, 28 November 1903, 758–768.
21 Ibid; preliminary notice of sale, Lynford Hall estate, 26 January 1895.
22 Death certificate, Stephens Lyne Stephens, 3 March 1860.
23 F Lyne, 197.

24 Will of Stephens Lyne Stephens, London, 29 March 1860.
25 Burials, Kensal Green cemetery, 6 March 1860; F Lyne, 197.
26 Bill of complaint (Bulkeley vs Stephens), July 1860, paragraph 5.
27 Ibid, paragraphs 6–7.
28 Ibid, paragraphs 9, 11.
29 Ibid, paragraphs 5–7.
30 Will of Stephens Lyne Stephens.
31 Bill of complaint, paragraph 8.
32 Mrs Smith (Froebel archives).
33 Royal Archives (Hepworth, 13).
34 *Country Life*, 28 November 1903, 758–768.
35 Newspaper cutting (unidentified), 23 November 1863.
36 Guest, *The Romantic Ballet in England*, 74.
37 Architectural plans, November 1862, April 1863 (Surrey Record Office).
38 Kensal Green cemetery records, 29 August 1864.

Interlude (pp. 285–286)

1   Will of Philadelphia Lyne, Bodmin, 8 May 1860; R B Lyne to Mayne, 17 October 1861.
2   Mayne to R B Lyne, 23 July 1861.
3   Ibid.
4   R B Lyne to Mayne, 17 October 1861.

24. **A Lawyer's Will (pp. 287–295)**

1   *The Times*, 22 March 1860.
2   *Norfolk Chronicle & Norwich Gazette*, 24 March 1860; *Royal Cornwall Gazette*, 30 March 1860.
3   M E Chudleigh, *Royal Cornwall Gazette*, 13 April 1860.
4   Ibid.
5   Will of Stephens Lyne Stephens, London, 29 March 1860.
6   Tatham to R B Lyne, 16 February 1861. Meaburn Tatham Snr drafted the will; his son (and namesake) handled matters for the beneficiaries.
7   F Lyne, 189–192.

8   V S Lyne to R B Lyne, 28 December 1863.
9   Death duty register, Yolande Lyne Stephens (IR 26/6332, 7201–08, 7210, 7231–33).
10 F Lyne, 190–191.
11 Notice of auction, 3 January 1861.
12 Tatham to R B Lyne, 27 May 1865.
13 House of Commons, 22 August 1887 (Extracts of Statements, 1396–1398).
14 W Philp, 23 January 1862.
15 Ibid, 3 February 1862.
16 Ibid (undated), with enclosures.
17 Ibid, 1 April 1862.
18 Ibid, 10 April 1862.
19 M Dymond, 8 February 1887.
20 W Philp, 7 March 1887.

25. Dolls' Eyes for Idols
(pp. 296–308)

1   John Pym (Pym, 220–221).
2   Census, Roehampton, 2 April 1871.
3   Guest, The Romantic Ballet in England, 74.
4   Will of Yolande Lyne Stephens, London, 5 October 1894; Christie, Manson & Woods, May 1895.
5   Claremont to Lyons, 30 December 1870 (FO 146/1514, 157–158).
6   Ibid, 26 September 1870 (146/1484).
7   Lyons to Granville, 12 January 1871 (146/1530); Claremont to Hammond, 3 February 1871 (146/1510).
8   Claremont to Hammond, 3 February 1871 (146/1510).
9   McCrea, 39–40; Legh, I, 194.
10 Horne, 211–212.
11 Blount, 265–266; Wallace to Claremont, November 1871, January 1872.
12 Claremont to West, 6 March 1871 (146/1532).
13 Claremont to Lyons, 15 March 1871 (146/1532), 16 March 1871 (146/1533).
14 Conolly to Lyons, 4 May 1871 (146/1535).
15 Lyons to Granville, 26 May 1871 (Legh, I, 386).
16 Mrs Smith (Froebel archives).
17 Summons, Bulkeley vs Stephens, 21 May 1906.
18 E R Chudleigh, 336.
19 Katharine Claremont to her mother, 11 June 1882.
20 Davidson, Part IV, 20.
21 Wandsworth Board of Works, report for year ended March 1883, 44.
22 Guest, The Romantic Ballet in England, 74; F Lyne, 178.
23 The Church of Our Lady of Consolation and St Stephen (undated leaflet).
24 Scott, A Sermon, 13–14; Bishop of Northampton, pastoral letter, Advent 1894.
25 Catholic directory, 1867.
26 Wilkins, 42.
27 Scott, The Story of the Church.
28 Scott, A Sermon, 18.
29 E Conybeare, Cambridge Chronicle, 22 February 1922.
30 See E M Forster, The Longest Journey, chapter 6.
31 Scott, The Story of the Church.
32 Scott, A Sermon, 16; notes by Katharine Claremont.
33 Croucher, 57–60.
34 Harry Claremont to Katharine Claremont, 28 April 1889.
35 Ibid, 25, 28, 29 April 1889.
36 Yolande to Katharine, 13 May 1890.
37 Frances Claremont to Katherine, 30 May 1890.
38 Harry to Katharine, 6 July 1890.
39 Ibid, 10, 11, 13 July 1890.
40 The Times, 17 July 1890; Harry to Katherine, 18 July 1890.
41 Yolande to Harry, 20 July 1890.
42 Croucher, 57–60.
43 Ibid.
44 Cambridge Chronicle, 17 October 1890.

26. The Bitter End (pp. 309–318)

1   Mrs Smith (Froebel archives).
2   Dwane to Harry, 3 March 1892.

3 Yolande to Harry, undated.
4 Pym to Harry, 16 January 1891.
5 Yolande to Harry, 23 February 1891.
6 Mrs Smith (Froebel archives).
7 Yolande to Harry, 28 August, 28 September 1891.
8 Dwane to Harry, 6 February 1892.
9 Ibid, 24 February 1892.
10 Frances Claremont to Harry, February, March 1892.
11 Yolande to Harry, 8 November 1891.
12 Ibid, 18 January 1892.
13 Frances Claremont to Harry, 21 March 1892.
14 Will of Edward Claremont, London, 11 September 1890.
15 Dwane to Harry, 3 March 1892.
16 Yolande to Harry, 8 March 1892.
17 Ibid, 20, 21 June 1892.
18 Dwane to Harry, 22, 27 June 1892.
19 Yolande to Harry, 8 November 1891.
20 Will of Yolande Lyne Stephens, codicils dated 6 October 1892, 22 July 1893.
21 Ibid, codicil dated 1 May 1893.
22 Pym to his daughter, 23 September 1893.
23 Yolande to Harry, 5 July 1894.
24 Harry to Katharine, 19 August 1894.
25 Ibid, 22 August 1894.
26 Scott, *A Sermon*, 19–20.
27 *Cambridge Chronicle*, 7 September 1894; *Cambridge Daily News*, 7 September 1894.
28 Scott, *A Sermon*, 11–13.
29 *The Times*, 10 September 1894. Richard Wallace was created baronet in 1871.
30 *The Tablet*, 15 September 1894.
31 Mrs Smith (Froebel archives).

27. Distribution (pp. 319–328)

1 *The Universe* (Rayner, 196).
2 *Pall Mall Gazette*, 5 September 1894.
3 Will of Yolande Lyne Stephens, London, 5 October 1894.
4 *The Times*, 7 November 1894.
5 Mrs Smith (Froebel archives).
6 Newspaper cutting, no date or source.
7 *Pall Mall Gazette*, 5 September 1894.
8 £141,000. *The Times*, 22 May 1895.
9 Christie, Manson & Woods, May 1895.
10 Weston, 17–19.
11 Officers' services, First World War (WO 339/92736).
12 Will of Stephen Lyne Stephens, London, 10 November 1923; information provided by the family.
13 *Cornish Times*, 15 September 1894.
14 Cutting from *The Times*, 1895; sale particulars of Lynford Hall, 23 July 1895.
15 F J Varcoe, 23 October 1905.
16 Ibid, October 1905.
17 Philp to Varcoe, 7 September 1906.
18 Tathams & Pym to R S Lyne, 21 December 1894.
19 Certificate from London & River Plate Bank, Buenos Aires, 6 March 1900.
20 Will of R B Lyne, London, 13 July 1899.
21 MacLean to Ewens, 14 July 1899.
22 Ibid, 27 August 1899.
23 Ewens to Carolina Lyne, 16 July 1900.
24 Private investigator's report, Buenos Aires, January 1901.
25 Watts to Ewens, 17 January 1903.
26 Ibid, 16 June 1903.
27 Ibid, with enclosure, 16 June 1903.
28 Ewens to Watts, 12 August 1903.
29 Watts to Ewens, 16 June 1905.
30 Deed of family arrangement, 21 February 1908.
31 Summons, Bulkeley vs Stephens, 21 May 1906.
32 Carr, Scott, Smith & Gorringe to Ewens, 7 April 1908.
33 Tathams & Pym to Ewens, 25 May 1908.
34 Son of William Lyne of Liverpool, first cousin to Stephens Lyne Stephens.
35 R Lyne to his children, 26 July 1831.

Select Bibliography

Manuscript Sources

England

Bank of England

Court book, 1811
Drawing account ledgers: Lyne, Hathorn &
Roberts, 1804–1819

Banks Project, National
History Museum

Correspondence of Sir Joseph Banks,
Carter transcription, 1797–1798

Bedingfeld MSS
Oxburgh Hall, Norfolk

Claremont/Lyne Stephens papers

Courtney Library, Royal
Institution of Cornwall

Philbrick Collection on the Post Office
Packet Service

Exeter City Archives
Devon Record Office

Dr Stephens bequest papers

Froebel Archives
Froebel College

Extract from autobiography of Mrs Smith
of Mount Clare (c.1912)

Greater London
Archives

Lyne Stephens deeds and papers

Guildhall Library
Corporation of London

Christ's Hospital: children's registers and
presentation papers, committee and court
minute books
Anglican chaplaincy registers, Lisbon
Archives of Antony Gibbs & Sons

North Devon Record
Office

General election papers, Barnstaple, 1830

Public Record Office

Foreign Office papers: Portugal, France
Bankruptcy papers, 1820
Board of Trade papers, 1813
Chancery papers: Cogan vs Stephens
Lisbon Factory book, 1811–1824
State papers: Portugal, Spain

Public Record Office (cont'd)	Treasury solicitor's papers: Cogan vs Stephens; Attorney-general & Matthews vs Lyne Stephens War Office papers: Muster books and pay lists, Tenth Royal Hussars; Officers' services, First World War
Theatre Museum London	Theatre Royal (Drury Lane) and King's Theatre (Haymarket): Playbills and press cuttings

Letters and papers in private collections

Portugal

Arquivos Nacionais Torre de Tombo, Lisbon	João Christiano de Faria e Sousa de Vasconcellos e Sá, *Diário da Jornada do Marquês de Pombal para Coimbra neste anno de 1770*
Biblioteca Nacional Lisbon	Transfer of glassworks to the state, transcription of documents, 1826–1827 William Stephens, letters to Marquês de Pombal
British Historical Society of Portugal, Lisbon branch	Gerald de Visme, Hospital Committee book, 1789
Câmara Municipal da Marinha Grande	Accounts book, Marinha Grande, 1786–1802 John James Stephens, letters to José de Sousa e Oliveira, 1811–1826

Papers in private collections

France

Archives Nationales Paris	Archives of the Paris Opéra
Bibliotèque de l'Opéra Paris	M. Gentil, *Les Cancans de l'Opéra en 1836, 1837 et 1838* (MS notebooks)

Published Sources

An Account by an Eye-Witness of the Lisbon Earthquake of November 1, 1755 (British Historical Society of Portugal, Lisbon, 1985)

Aitchison, John, *An Ensign in the Peninsular War: The Letters of John Aitchison*, ed. W F K Thompson (London, 1981)

Allen, John, *History of the Borough of Liskeard* (London and Liskeard, 1856)

Almeida, Luís Ferrand de, 'A Fábrica de Vidros da Marinha Grande em 1774,' in *Revista Portuguesa de História*, XVIII (Coimbra, 1980)

Almeida, Sebastião Bettamio de, *Relatorio sobre a Fábrica Nacional de Vidros da Marinha Grande* (Lisbon, 1860)

Aranha, P W de Brito, *Memórias Histórico-Estatísticas de Algumas, Villas e Povoações de Portugal* (Lisbon, 1871)

Araújo, Agostinho, *The British Assembly in Lisbon*, trans. Margaret Kelting (British Historical Society of Portugal, Lisbon, 1988)

Baillie, Marianne, *Lisbon in the Years 1821, 1822 and 1823*, 2 vols (London, 1824)

Balsemão, Visconde de, 'Memória sobre a Descripção Física e Económica do Lugar da Marinha Grande e suas Visinhanças,' in *Memórias Económicas da Academia Real das Sciências de Lisboa*, V (Lisbon, 1815)

Baretti, Joseph, *A Journey from London to Genoa, through England, Portugal, Spain and France*, 2 vols (London, 1770)

Barham, R H, *The Ingoldsby Legends*, 2nd edition (London and New York, 1843)

Barosa, Joaquim, *Memórias da Marinha Grande 1911–1912* (Leiria, 1913)

Barros, Carlos Vitorino da Silva, *Real Fábrica de Vidros da Marinha Grande, II Centenário 1769–1969* (Lisbon, 1969)

Beaumont, Cyril W, *Three French Dancers of the Nineteenth Century: Duvernay, Livry, Beaugrand* (London, 1935)

Beckford, William, *Italy, with Sketches of Spain and Portugal*, 2 vols (London, 1834)

——*The Journal of William Beckford in Portugal and Spain 1787–1788*, ed. Boyd Alexander (London, 1954)

——*Recollections of an Excursion to the Monasteries of Alcobaça and Batalha*, ed. Boyd Alexander (Arundel, 1972)

Blew, William C A, *The Quorn Hunt and its Masters* (London, 1899)

Blount, Edward, *Memoirs of Sir Edward Blount*, ed. Stuart J Reid (London, 1902)

Boigne, Charles de, *Petits Mémoires de l'Opéra* (Paris, 1857)

Bombelles, Marquis de, *Journal d'un Ambassadeur de France au Portugal, 1786–1788*, ed. Roger Kann (Paris, 1979)

Bontemps, Georges, *Examen Historique et Critique des Verres, Vitraux et Cristaux composant la Classe XXIV de l'Exposition Universelle de 1851* (London and Paris, 1851)

Boutflower, Charles, *The Journal of an Army Surgeon during the Peninsular War* (Staplehurst, 1997)

Bovill, E W, *The England of Nimrod and Surtees 1815–1854* (London, 1959)

Boxer, C R, 'Pombal's Dictatorship and the Great Lisbon Earthquake 1755,' in *History Today*, V, no. 11 (November 1955)

Bradbeer, Doris M, *Joyful Schooldays, a Digest of the History of the Exeter Grammar Schools* (Exeter, 1973)

Brougham, Henry, *The Life and Times of Henry, Lord Brougham*, 3 vols (London, 1871)

Broughton, S D, *Letters from Portugal, Spain and France during the Campaigns of 1812, 1813 and 1814* (London, 1815)

Brownlow, Jack, *Melton Mowbray, Queen of the Shires* (Wymondham, 1980)

Bryant, Arthur, *Years of Victory, 1802–1812* (London, 1944)

Bullion Committee, *Report from the Select Committee Appointed to Inquire into the Cause of the High Price of Bullion* (London, 1810)

Bunn, Alfred, *The Stage: Both Before and Behind the Curtain*, 3 vols (London, 1840)

Bush, R J E, *Exeter Free Grammar School* (Exeter, 1962)

Butler, J R M, *The Passing of the Great Reform Bill* (London, 1914)

Cannon, Richard, *Historical Record of the Tenth, the Prince of Wales Own Royal Regiment of Hussars* (London, 1843)

Cardew, Sir Alexander, *A Memoir of the Rev'd Cornelius Cardew DD* (Truro, 1926)

Cecil (Cornelius Tongue), *Records of the Chase* (London, 1854)

Chance, James Frederick, *A History of the Firm of Chance Brothers & Co, Glass and Alkali Manufacturers* (London, 1919)

Cheke, Marcus, *Dictator of Portugal: A Life of the Marquis of Pombal* (London, 1938)

——*Carlota Joaquina: Queen of Portugal* (London, 1947)

Christie, Manson & Woods, *Catalogue of the Celebrated Collection of Pictures, Porcelain, Objects of Art, and Decorative Furniture of Mrs Lyne Stephens* (London, May 1895)

——*Catalogue of the Collection of Fine Old English and Foreign Silver Plate and Casket of Beautiful Jewels of Mrs Lyne Stephens* (London, May 1895)

Chudleigh, E R, *Diary of E R Chudleigh, 1862–1921*, ed. E C Richards (Christchurch, 1950)

Chudleigh, M E, *Midnight Meditations* (London, 1854)

A Collection of Addresses, Squibs etc which were circulated in reference to the Election of Members to serve in Parliament for the Borough of Barnstaple in the year 1832 (Barnstaple, 1833)

Cormatin, P M F D, Duc du Châtelet, *Travels of the Duke du Châtelet in Portugal*, ed. J-F Bourgoing, trans. J J Stockdale, 2 vols (London, 1809)

Correia, Joaquim, *A Fábrica dos Vidros de João Beare na Marinha Grande* (Marinha Grande, 1999)

Costigan, Arthur William, *Sketches of Society and Manners in Portugal*, 2 vols (London, 1787)

Creevey, Thomas, *The Creevey Papers, a Selection from the Correspondence and Diaries of the Late Thomas Creevey MP*, ed. Sir Herbert Maxwell, 2 vols (London, 1903)

Croker, Richard, *Travels through Several Provinces of Spain and Portugal* (London, 1799)

Croucher, Maurice, 'The Opening of the New Catholic Church in Cambridge,' in *Cambridge Catholic Magazine* (August 1933)

Custódio, Jorge, 'Reflexos da Industrialização na Fisionomia e Vida da Cidade,' in *O Livro de Lisboa*, ed. I Moita (Lisbon, 1994)

Dalrymple, William, *Travels through Spain and Portugal in 1774* (London, 1777)

Davidson, Hilary, 'The History of Elm Grove,' in *The Chronicle*, Digby Stuart College (Roehampton, 1958–1961)

Dickens, Charles, *Bleak House* (London, 1853)

Duarte, Acácio de Calazans, *Os Stephens na Indústria Vidreira Nacional* (Figueira da Foz, 1937)

——*A Indústria Vidreira na Marinha Grande* (Lisbon, 1942)

Duncombe, T H, *The Life and Correspondence of Thomas Slingsby Duncombe*, 2 vols (London, 1868)

Feret, C J, *Fulham Old and New*, 3 vols (London, 1900)

Ferrão, Antonio, *A Reforma Pombalina da Universidade de Coimbra* (Coimbra, 1926)

Ferro, Maria Inês, *Queluz: The Palace and Gardens* (London, 1997)

Forster, E M, *The Longest Journey* (London, 1907)

Francis, A D, *Portugal 1715–1808* (London, 1985)

'G,' A P D, *Sketches of Portuguese Life, Manners, Costume and Character* (London, 1826)

Gândara, Alfredo, *As Bases Históricas e Morais do Desenvolvimento da Indústria do Vidro na Marinha Grande* (Lisbon, 1967)

Gerhold, Dorian, *Villas and Mansions of Roehampton and Putney Heath* (Wandsworth Historical Society, 1997)

Gilbert, Davies, *Parochial History of Cornwall*, 4 vols (London, 1838)

Glover, Michael, *Britannia Sickens: Sir Arthur Wellesley and the Convention of Cintra* (London, 1970)

Greville, C C, *The Greville Memoirs: A Journal of the Reigns of King George IV and King William IV*, ed. Henry Reeve, 3 vols (London, 1874)

Gronow, R H, *Anecdotes of Celebrities of London and Paris* (London, 1873)

——*Reminiscences and Recollections*, 2 vols (London, 1889)

Guest, Ivor, *The Romantic Ballet in England* (London, 1954)

——*The Romantic Ballet in Paris* (London, 2nd edition, 1980)

——*Fanny Elssler* (London, 1970)

Harris, R W, *England in the Eighteenth Century* (London, 1963)

Hawkey, Charlotte, *Neota* (Taunton, 1871)

Hepworth, Philip, *Royal Sandringham* (Norwich, 1978)

Hervey, Christopher, *Letters from Portugal, Spain, Italy and Germany in the years 1759, 1760 and 1761*, 3 vols (London, 1785)

Hickey, William, *Memoirs*, ed. Alfred Spencer, 4 vols (London, 1913)

Hipwell, H Hallam, 'Lisbon on the Eve of Invasion, as Seen in Unpublished Letters of a Local Merchant-Banker of 1807,' in report of British Historical Society of Portugal (Lisbon, 1939)

Hoffmansegg, J C, *Voyage en Portugal par M. le Comte de Hoffmansegg* (Paris, 1805)

Horne, Alistair, *The Fall of Paris: The Siege and the Commune 1870–1871* (London, 1965)

Huskisson, William, *The Question concerning the Depreciation of our Currency Stated and Examined* (London, 1810)

Johnson, R B (ed.), *Christ's Hospital: Recollections of Lamb, Coleridge and Leigh Hunt* (London, 1896)

Junot, Laure, *Memoirs of the Duchess d'Abrantes*, 8 vols (London, 1831–1835)

Keene, Sir Benjamin, *The Private Correspondence of Sir Benjamin Keene, KB*, ed. Richard Lodge (Cambridge, 1933)

Kendrick, T D, *The Lisbon Earthquake* (London, 1956)

Kinsey, W M, *Portugal Illustrated in a Series of Letters* (London, 1829)

Koster, John Theodore, *A Short Statement of the Trade in Gold Bullion* (Liverpool, 1811)

Landmann, George, *Historical, Military and Picturesque Observations on Portugal*, 2 vols (London, 1818)

Legh, T W (Lord Newton), *Lord Lyons: A Record of British Diplomacy*, 2 vols (London, 1913)

Letters from Portugal on the Late and Present State of that Kingdom, anon. but attributed to John Blankett (London, 1777)

Liddell, R S, *The Memoirs of the Tenth Royal Hussars* (London, 1891)

The Lisbon Earthquake of 1755: Some British Eye-Witness Accounts, British Historical Society of Portugal (Lisbon, 1987)

The Lisbon Guide, containing Directions to Invalids who visit Lisbon, anon. (London, 1800)

Lodge, Sir Richard, 'The English Factory in Lisbon,' in *Royal Historical Society Transactions* (1933)

Long, R B, *Peninsular Cavalry General 1811–1813: The Correspondence of Lt. Gen. Robert Ballard Long*, ed. T H McGuffie (London, 1851)

Longford, Elizabeth, *Wellington: The Years of the Sword* (London, 1969)

Lyne, Charles, *A Letter to the Rt. Hon. George Rose, MP, Vice-President of the Board of Trade, in which the Real Causes of the Scarcity and Consequent High Price of Gold and Silver are Stated and Exemplified* (London, 22 November 1810)

——*A Letter to the Rt. Hon. Lord Castlereagh... on the North American Export Trade during the War* (London, 2 March 1813)

——*A Letter to the Rt. Hon. the Earl of Liverpool... on the Impossibility of a Speedy Return to a Gold Currency* (London, 30 January 1819)

——*A Letter to the Rt. Hon. Lord Viscount Castlereagh on the Conflicting and Otherwise Evil Consequences of the Corn and Cash Payment Bills* (London, 10 January 1820)

——*A Letter to the Lord High Chancellor on the Nature and Causes of the Late and Present Distress in Commercial, Manufacturing, and Banking Concerns; with Proposed Partial Remedies* (London, 15 March 1826)

Lyne, Edward, *Letters passed by Benjamin Tucker of Trematon Castle and Mr E Lyne of Plymouth to Messrs Woollcombe & Jago, Solicitors*, 2nd edition (London, 1816)

Lyne, Francis, *A Letter to Father Ignatius on the Death of his Mother* (London, 1878)

Lytton, Lord Edward Bulmer, *The Life, Letters and Literary Remains of Edward Bulmer, Lord Lytton, by his son*, 2 vols (London, 1883)

Macaulay, Neill, *Dom Pedro, the Struggle for Liberty in Brazil and Portugal 1798–1834* (Durham, 1986)

Macaulay, Rose, *They went to Portugal* (London, 1946)

——*They went to Portugal Too* (Manchester, 1990)

Mahalin, Paul (un vieil abonné), *Ces Demoiselles de l'Opéra* (Paris, 1887)

Marbot, Jean Baptiste Antoine de Marcellin, Baron de, *Memoirs of Baron de Marbot, late Lieutenant-General in the French Army*, trans. A J Butler, 2 vols (London and New York, 1892)

Marques, Emilia Margarida, *O Período Stephens: Na Real Fábrica de Vidros da Marinha Grande* (Marinha Grande, 1999)

Martin, Fanny, *Gunilda, or Sketches of Life in a Country Town* (London, 1875)

Martineau, Harriet, *History of the Peace: Pictorial History of England during the Thirty Years' Peace, 1816–1846*, revised edition, 7 vols, London, 1858

Matthews, Henry, *The Diary of an Invalid, being the Journal of a Tour in Pursuit of Health, in Portugal, Italy, Switzerland and France in the years 1817, 1818 and 1819* (London, 1820)

Maxwell, Kenneth, *Pombal, Paradox of the Enlightenment* (Cambridge, 1995)

McCrea, Frederick Bradford, *Tree and Services of the Wetherall Family* (1912)

Murphy, James C, *Travels in Portugal in the years 1789 and 1790* (London, 1795)

Neale, Adam, *Letters from Portugal and Spain* (London, 1809)

Nimrod (C J Apperley), 'The Chace,' in *Quarterly Review*, XLVII (1832)

Paget, G C H V, *A History of the British Cavalry*, Vol. I (London, 1973)

Pardoe, Julia H S, *Traits and Traditions of Portugal collected during a Residence*, 2 vols (London, 1833)

Peacock, Bernard, 'Paris, London, Lynford,' in *East Anglian Magazine* (December 1958)

Pelet, Jean-Jacques, *The French Campaign in Portugal 1810–1811*, trans. and ed. Donald D Horward (Minneapolis, 1973)

Penn, James, *A St Matthew's Day Sermon, with an account of Christ's Hospital* (London, 1761)

Pinto, A Arala, *O Pinhal do Rei*, 2 vols (Alcobaça, 1938–1939)

Polsue, Joseph, *Lake's Parochial History of the County of Cornwall*, 4 vols (Truro, 1867–1873)

Porter, Robert Ker, *Letters from Portugal and Spain written during the march of the British troops under Sir John Moore*, anon. but attributed to Porter (London, 1809)

'Publicus,' *A Letter to the Merchants of the Portugal Committee from a Lisbon Trader* (London, 1754)

Pym, Francis, *Sentimental Journey* (1998)

Ramecourt, M Fourcroy de, *Art du Chaufournier* (Paris, 1766)

Ratton, Jacome, *Recordações: sobre occurrências do seu tempo em Portugal* (London, 1813)

Rayner, Eric, 'The Lovely Lady Bountiful,' in *Catholic Fireside*, CLXXI, no. 4151 (19 September 1969)

Real Life in London, or the rambles and adventures of Bob Tallyho Esq and his cousin, the Hon Tom Dashall, through the Metropolis, anon., 2 vols (London, 1822)

Robinson, H B, *Memoirs of Sir Thomas Picton*, 2 vols (London, 1836)

Scargill, W P, *Recollections of a Blue-coat Boy, or a View of Christ's Hospital* (Swaffham, 1829)

Schaumann, A L F, *On the Road with Wellington: the Diary of a War Commissary in the Peninsular Campaign*, trans. and ed. A M Ludovici (London, 1924)

Scott, Christopher, *A Sermon preached in the Church of Our Lady and the English Martyrs* (September 1894)

——'The Story of the Church of Our Lady and the English Martyrs,' in *Cambridge Chronicle* (27 October, 3 November 1915)

Shaw, L M E, *The Anglo-Portuguese Alliance and the English Merchants in Portugal, 1645–1810* (Aldershot, 1998)

Sherer, Joseph Moyle, *Recollections of the Peninsula* (London, 1825)

Simmons, George, *A British Rifle Man during the Peninsular War*, ed. W Verner (London, 1899)

Smith J A, Conde da Carnota, *Memoirs of the Marquis of Pombal*, 2 vols (London, 1843)

——*Memoirs of the Duke de Saldanha*, 2 vols (London, 1880)

Southey, C C, *Life and Correspondence of Robert Southey*, 6 vols (London, 1849–1850)

Southey, Robert, *Journals of a Residence in Portugal 1800–1801*, ed. Adolfo Cabral (Oxford, 1960)

——*Letters written during a Short Residence in Spain and Portugal*, 2nd edition (London, 1799)

——*Selections from Letters of Southey*, ed. J W Warter, 4 vols (London, 1856)

——(alias Espriella), *Letters from England*, 3 vols (London, 1807)

Stewart, Charles, Marquis of Londonderry, *Narrative of the Peninsular War from 1808 to 1813* (London, 1828)

Styles, J, *Memoirs of the Life of the Right Honourable George Canning*, anon. but attributed to Styles, 2 vols (London, 1828)

Surtees, R S, *Town and Country Papers*, ed. E D Cuming (Edinburgh, 1929)

Thackeray, William Makepiece, *The Letters and Private Papers of William Makepiece Thackeray*, ed. Gordon N Ray, 4 vols (Oxford, 1945)

——*Roundabout Papers* (London, 1863)

Thiébault, Baron de, *The Memoirs of Baron Thiébault, late Lieutenant-General in the French Army*, trans. and ed. J A Butler, 2 vols (London, 1896)

Trant, Clarissa, *The Journal of Clarissa Trant*, ed. C G Luard (London, 1925)

Trend, J B, *Portugal* (London, 1957)

Trollope, William, *A History of the Royal Foundation of Christ's Hospital* (London, 1834)

Tucker, Jedediah Stephens, *Memoirs of Admiral the Right Hon. the Earl of St Vincent*, 2 vols (London, 1844)

Twiss, Richard, *Travels through Portugal and Spain in 1772 and 1773* (London, 1775)

Vaillat, Léandre, *La Taglioni ou la Vie d'une Danseuse* (Paris, 1942)

Valente, Vasco, *O Vidro em Portugal* (Oporto, 1950)

Vassall, Elizabeth, *The Spanish Journal of Elizabeth, Lady Holland*, ed. Lord Ilchester (London, 1910)

Véron, Louis, *Mémoires d'un Bourgeois de Paris*, 6 vols (Paris, 1853–1855)

Walford, A R, 'The British Community in Lisbon, 1755,' in report of British Historical Society of Portugal (Lisbon, 1946–1950)

——*The British Factory in Lisbon* (Lisbon, 1940)

Warre, William, *Letters from the Peninsula 1808–1812*, ed. Edmond Warre (London, 1909)

West, S George, *The Visit to Portugal in 1779–80 of William Julius Mickle* (Lisbon, 1972)

Weston, Peter, *From Roehampton Great House to Grove House* (London, 1998)

Wilkins, Philip, *Our Lady and the English Martyrs, Cambridge*, 4th edition (Cambridge, 1995)

Williams, E N, *Life in Georgian England* (London, 1962)

Withering, William, *The Miscellaneous Tracts of the Late William Withering MD FRS, written by his son*, 2 vols (London, 1822)

Wraxall, Sir William, *Historical Memoirs of my Own Time*, 2 vols (London, 1815)

Young, William, *Portugal in 1828: The Kingdom under Don Miguel* (London, 1828)

Periodicals

Autonomia, October–December 1895: 'Elementos para História da Marinha' by António Maria de Freitas (alias Nicolau Florentino)

Country Life, 28 November 1903: 'Lynford Hall, Norfolk, the seat of Mr H A Campbell'

O Século, 19 August 1945: 'A Fábrica de Vidros da Marinha Grande'

Progresso Industrial, Issue 1, 15 February 1896: 'A Real Fábrica da Marinha Grande e a Invasão Franceza'

Index

This story of five people who possessed a fortune is intended for the general reader. The events of their lives (and the main places where those events took place) form the subject of the book and are not itemised in detail in the index.